# The Low Road

*Also by Valerie Miner*

NOVELS

*Range of Light*

*A Walking Fire*

*All Good Women*

*Winter's Edge*

*Murder in the English Department*

*Movement*

*Blood Sisters*

SHORT FICTION

*Trespassing and Other Stories*

NONFICTION

*Rumors from the Cauldron: Selected Essays, Reviews and Reportage*

# The Low Road

A SCOTTISH FAMILY MEMOIR

*Valerie Miner*

Michigan State University Press

*East Lansing*

♾ The paper used in this publication meets the minimum requirements
of ANSI/NISO Z39.48–1992 (R 1997) (Permanence of Paper).

Michigan State University Press
East Lansing, Michigan 48823-5202

Printed and bound in the United States of America.

07  06  05  04  03  02  01    1  2  3  4  5  6  7  8  9  10

LIBRARY OF CONGRESS CATALOGING-IN-PUBLICATION DATA
Miner, Valerie.
The low road : a Scottish family memoir / Valerie Miner.
p. cm.
ISBN 0-87013-592-9 (alk. paper)
1. Miner, Valerie—Family. 2. Authors, American—20th century—Family
relationships. 3. Scotland—Emigration and immigration—History.
4. Authors, American—20th century—Biography. 5. English teachers—
United States—Biography. 6. Women immigrants—United States—Biography.
7. Mothers and daughters—United States. 8. Mothers and daughters—
Scotland. 9. Scottish Americans—Biography. I. Title.
PS3563.I4647 Z465 2001
813'.54—dc21
2001003694

Book and cover design by Sharp Des!gns, Lansing, MI

Cover painting is *Waitresses* © 1930 estate of
Raphael Soyer, courtesy of Forum Gallery, New York

Visit Michigan State University Press on the World Wide Web at:
www.msupress.msu.edu

*To the memory of*
*Mary Gill McKenzie-Campbell Miner*

*and to the future of her great-grandchildren*
*Hailey Isobel, Kristin Anne, Morgan Elisabeth,*
*and Taylor Elise*

*Ye tak the High Road*
*And I'll tak the Low Road*
*And I'll be in Scotland*
*Afore ye*

*For me and my true love*
*Will never meet again*
*On the bonnie, bonnie banks*
*O'Loch Lomand.*

ONE INTERPRETATION OF THIS SCOTS FOLK SONG TELLS THE STORY OF two eighteenth-century Scottish prisoners held in England—one of whom, who was to be released, would take the High Road to Scotland, while the other, who was to be executed, would be taking the Low Road home. This is in accordance with the old belief that when Celts meet death in a foreign land, their spirits return to their birthplace by an underground, fairy way, the Low Road.*

My mother and most of her brothers and sisters were emigrants from Scotland who returned on the Low Road.

*Ronald Macdonald Douglas, *Scottish Lore and Folklore* (London: Beekman House, 1982).

# Legend

*Daniel Campbell marries Maggie Thompson* (1884)

CHILDREN
Bella
Alex
Donald
Chrissie
Matt
Nan
Mae

*Mary Jane Gill (Mae) marries John McKenzie* (1897)

CHILDREN
Johnny
Danny
Chrissie
Jack

*Mary Jane Gill McKenzie in love with Daniel Campbell* (1895–1917)

CHILDREN
Mary (Mae)
Peggy
Colin

Daniel Campbell is my grandfather.
Mary Jane Gill McKenzie (Mae) is my grandmother.
Mary McKenzie-Campbell (Mae) is my mother.

# Contents

Acknowledgments / *xv*
Preface / *xvii*
Introduction / *xxi*

I.

1. Daniel, 1865–1897 / *3*
2. Mae, 1895 / *9*
3. Mary, "Tomorrow" / *13*
4. Valerie, "From Tenement to Castle" / *19*

II.

5. Daniel, 1896 / *25*
6. Mary, "Sketchbook of Edinburgh" / *27*
7. Valerie, "Legacy" / *33*

III.

8. Mae, 1896 / *39*
9. Chorus, "Family Conversation" / *43*
10. Mary, "Ship's Manifest" / *45*

IV.

11. Mae, 1897-1904 / *51*
12. Mary, "On Her Way" / *55*
13. Valerie, "Red Shoes Mama" / *65*

## V.

14. Daniel, 1906–1907 / *71*
15. Mary, "New World Diary" / *73*
16. Valerie, "My Life with the Windsors" / *77*

## VI.

17. Daniel, 1907–1908 / *87*
18. Mary, "Night Lights at Earth Central" / *89*
19. Valerie, "View from the Escalator" / *97*

## VII.

20. Mae, 1909–1914 / *103*
21. Mary, "New Jersey/New Jersey" / *109*
22. Valerie, "Slut with a Vacuum" / *119*

## VIII.

23. Mae, 1916 / *125*
24. Valerie, "A Habit of Vanishing" / *129*
25. Mary, "Learning To Swim" / *133*

## IX.

26. Mae, 1917 / *143*
27. Valerie, "Ghostwriter" / *147*
28. Mary, "The Light Should Last Forever" / *151*

## X.

29. Daniel, 1917 / *167*
30. Valerie, "A Scottish Opera" / *173*
31. Mary, "Yesterday" / *183*

## XI.

32. Daniel, 1920 / *193*
33. Valerie, "Ritual Meals" / *201*
34. Valerie, "Slipped Lives" / *207*

## XII.

35. Daniel, 1925 / *215*
36. Mary and M.Q. S., "The Last Page" / *223*
37. Valerie, "White Lunch" / *225*

## XIII.

38. Family Reunion, 1860s–1990s / *237*
39. Valerie, "Thistles in California" / *243*
40. Valerie, "A Spare Umbrella" / *253*

# Acknowledgments

THE AUTHOR IS GRATEFUL FOR RECENT RESIDENCIES AT THE ROCKE-feller Foundation's Bellagio Study Center, the Heinz Foundation's Hawthornden Castle, the Virginia Center for the Creative Arts, and the Master Artists Program of the Atlantic Center for the Arts. I also acknowledge the financial support this book has received from the Jerome Foundation, the Bush Foundation, the McKnight Foundation, the University of Minnesota, and the University of Edinburgh.

Most of all, I want to acknowledge the individual people who have provoked me to write *The Low Road* and who have encouraged me during the research, composition, and revision. First, I thank family members for sharing their stories over the years. Throughout this project, Helen Longino has been an acute critic, stalwart supporter, and patient partner. In Edinburgh, I am especially grateful to Rose Pipes and Kath Davies, whose interest in and help with the book have been invaluable. Other friends in Britain to whom I am greatly indebted are Susan Innes, Zoë Fairbairns, Richard Rodger, and Fran Wasoff.

A number of people have read sections from or entire drafts of the book, providing generous feedback. These people include Kath Davies, Maria Damon, Janice Eidus, Heid Erdrich, Zoë Fairbairns, Pamela Fletcher, Tess Gallagher, Myra Goldberg, Helen Hoy, Ruth-Ellen Joeres, Deborah Johnson, Amy Kaminsky, Helen Longino, Toni McNaron, Leslie Adrienne Miller, Mary Jane Moffat, Rose Pipes, Madelon Sprengnether, Mary Rockcastle, Martha Roth, and Susan Welch. I am grateful to Deborah Schneider, Martha Bates, and Leslie Gardner for assistance on the publishing front.

My research was facilitated by Edinburgh librarians and archivists at Register House, the National Library, the Edinburgh Public Library, and the National Map Library, as well as by informative people I met through friends and on the streets of Edinburgh. In the United States, during the last six years I was aided by splendid research assistants: Kristin Bolton, Julie Gard, Scott Muskin, Rebecca Pierre, and Andrea Weiss.

The inspiration for and heart of *The Low Road* is my mother, the incomparable Mary Miner. My debt to and my love for her are larger than any book can express.

*R*

The following chapters have appeared in literary journals (sometimes in slightly different incarnations). Many thanks to the editors of these journals.

Chapter 40 in *Ploughshares* (fall 1994); chapter 39 in *The American Voice* (summer 1995); chapter 16 in *The Michigan Quarterly Review* (spring 1996), and also chapter 13 (spring 2000); chapter 37 in *The Alaska Quarterly* (fall 1997); chapter 30 in *The Gettysburg Review* (winter 1998); chapters 13, 19, and 33 in *Prairie Schooner* (fall 1998), also in *Best of Prairie Schooner: Personal Essays,* ed. Hilda Raz and Kate Flaherty (Lincoln: University of Nebraska Press, 2000); chapter 34 in *The Colorado Review* (spring 1999); chapter 31 in *The Red Rock Review* (spring 1999); chapter 28 in *The Green Mountains Review* (fall 1999); and chapters 10 and 12 in *Thirteenth Moon* (fall 2000); chapter 3 in *Witness* (2001).

## *Valerie, Edinburgh, 1990s*

I LIE IN BED, ON THE TOP FLOOR OF A FRIEND'S GEORGIAN HOUSE IN Central Edinburgh. It's 11 P.M., mid-July, and I watch pink fade from the sky, remembering how one of the best parts of those long ago years I lived in Britain was the endless summer night. Outside the bedroom, I see roofs and chimneys across the alley, a few aerials and the branches from those rare Edinburgh trees that have managed to struggle three stories high. I wonder what Mom saw from her room at night. If she had a window. If she had a room.

During the day, Edinburgh's smells are so evocative—a combination of brewery and old soot. Although this soot is what destroyed my family's lungs, I always find it a tantalizing scent. My body relaxes with it; I feel at home. I've also been noticing the familiar music of Scottish accents. (Last year a Bulgarian friend said she enjoyed the thickness of Scots Talk because it was the only language that seemed as hardy as hers.) I love the Edinburgh accent's heavy body, its wet sensuality.

It is a warm Sunday evening as I wander down Leith Walk, through my mother's old neighborhoods. Strange how these hills and this wind and water make me think of Mom in San Francisco. No, not so strange that the city where she was born resembles the city where she chose to live in her last decades. The colors are different, of course, (people, buildings, sky, flowers) but the contours and climate are quite similar.

The Union Place tenement where Mom lived most of her childhood was torn down to make room for a traffic roundabout now named Picardy Place. I take a few desolate photos and continue my stroll down Leith

Walk, a straight city street (past tenements and Pakistani grocers and fish and chips shops and pubs) that leads to Leith Docks. As I approach Springfield Street, where she was born, I pray that this more remote part of the Leith district has survived better than Union Place. Yes, a pub, the Volunteer Arms, is still on the corner. But the rest of the landmarks on the still-cobbled street have been leveled. The main building now is a motorcycle repair firm, "Silencer Distributors," a bloody good metaphor for Scots historiography.

I turn back to Leith Walk and take photos of the general neighborhood. Then I almost trip on two tipsy old men emerging from the pub. Eventually, I wind up walking beside one of them. He's friendly, well-lubricated, this early evening. So I ask if he knows Fairley's Cafe.

"Oh, aye." He points up the hill. "It was quite a lively dance hall."

"My mother worked there," I smile.

"Are you sure about that now?" He regards me curiously.

"Yes," I reassure him. "Mom said it wasn't so nice."

"Och, some people said so, but I thought it was a fine place." He had been a Leither all his life, but didn't recall the McKenzies of Springfield Street. He would have been twelve years younger than Mom. By the time he'd been born, she'd long been a Campbell.

We continue strolling toward the docks. Out of my way, but I am lonely.

He points to the Palace Ballroom at the bottom of Leith Walk. "Another nice place for a good time. We had the best dance halls in Leith."

After we part, I turn and head back uphill toward Broughton Street. I stop for chips across from Mom's corner of Springfield and Leith Walk, at a dilapidated shop called Michael's. The chips are wrapped in newspaper the way Mom liked, but there's not enough vinegar. Hard to enjoy, because of that and the exorbitant 80P charge. Perhaps they cost so much because I look like a tourist, like I don't belong. Is that what I am, a tourist in my mother's life? Before it gets dark, I set off in search of Milton House School. (Mom and I visited there on our first trip to Edinburgh in 1968. After classes one day, I cajoled her to walk down the empty corridors with me. She peeked into classrooms, exclaimed at the wee desks, and said in happy wonderment, "Even the smell, exactly the same smell."

All my life I had heard about Milton House School, a place filled with her fondest memories of Edinburgh, and here we were together.)

No luck this first evening. For two days I look—maybe it wasn't on the High Street?—finally checking the phone book. Milton House School is not listed. Another casualty. It makes me grateful that Mom showed me the two-storey, dark stone building almost thirty years ago. Then, on Tuesday evening, I'm in Mom's neighborhood again, walking down the side of Calton Hill to have supper with my old friend Susie. Beautiful views of the choppy, grey Forth, of the green velvet mountain they call Arthur's Seat. I am almost at the bottom when I see a familiar sight— Milton House School.

I think.

Yes, Susie later confirms. She is surprised that I know the old name. It's now Royal Mile Primary School, she tells me. Her daughter was a student there.

I'm delighted to have recognized it after all these years. Delighted that it still stands, this sturdy building that could outwit both memory and imagination.

# Introduction

THIS IS THE STORY I HAVE BEEN WRITING FOR MY WHOLE LIFE. WITH MY
life. This is the story I will never know well enough to write. *The Low
Road* is about location and dislocation in a large, poor Scottish family. My
family. Over the years I discovered thirteen of my mother's siblings while
collecting memories and secrets from Aunt Bella in British Columbia,
Aunt Chrissie in Toronto, Uncle Johnny in Fife, Uncle Colin on the
south coast of Australia. During the last thirty years, at first unconsciously
and then intentionally, I pieced together a story.

For too long, Mom told me nothing, ashamed of being "illegitimate."
Her parents—Mrs. McKenzie and Mr. Campbell—were married to other
people when Mom was born in Edinburgh in 1910. My grandparents conceived a second child together. I eventually learned that they were
divorced and married to each other in time for the birth of their third
baby. This new life meant that Grandmother relinquished her first four
children to Mr. McKenzie. Grandfather left his seven kids behind with
Mrs. Campbell. A terrible rift. A Scottish Opera. Then, when Mom was
seven, Grandmother got pregnant once again and decided to have an
abortion. She died on the kitchen table of their tenement flat. Seven years
later, Grandfather died of tuberculosis. Mom was fourteen. She quit
school, rented lodgings, and got a job in a dance hall. Eventually, the fourteen children scattered, as many poor Scots did—to Canada, the United
States, India, England, New Zealand, and Australia. In 1930 my mother
immigrated alone to the States, traveling in steerage at age twenty. At the
age of seventy-seven she was laid off her job at an all-night coffee house
in San Francisco's Tenderloin.

People went literally to the ends of the earth to escape this history.
What right do I have to dig it up? Is this my story, too? Is curiosity a form
of loyalty? These questions nag me throughout six years of writing,

answers emerging and submerging, sharpening and blurring. Ultimately I have come to understand that the reasons to hide or tell the story have less to do with morality and more to do with survival.

*The Low Road* slowly metamorphoses from personal puzzle to literary novel to reluctant memoir. For my first twenty years of going back and forth to Scotland, this isn't a coherent story, just snippets of news about my ever-expanding cast of uncles and aunts. Then people begin to die. One day, they are no longer Aunt Bella or Uncle Johnny, who, strangely, are not related to each other, they are characters. The pain or contradiction I cannot bear in a relative become endurable, even fascinating, when that person is a character. My friends insist this is the novel I was meant to write. Now it does seem safe to call together a story, to face the poverty and loss and early death and estrangement and exile, because this is as ordinary as any novel.

Thus, in the mid-1990s, I start the novel. It will come more easily than the others I think, because the narrative is already written, in my blood. Yet fiction requires imaginative distance from characters, who emerge with their own living integrity from a land the writer has yet to travel. And this new book isn't driven by my subconscious or my sixth sense or my guardian angel, but by bond with and an increasingly passionate interest in real people.

I confess that I have never wanted to write a memoir. My resistance is both ethical and temperamental. Yes, I have enjoyed and been enlarged by some splendid, transcendent memoirs. However, I'm suspicious of the current literary trendiness of autobiography, embarrassed by the frequent solipsism and grandiosity of such projects. As literature by people of color becomes more prominent in the academy, I wonder if some contemporary memoir and autobiographical criticism are covert or unconscious ways to reposition the middle-class white writer at the center of public consciousness. On a more psychological level, I am a reticent narrator, who inherited a reserve and an excessive politeness from my mother. I am timid about going deeper, worried about self-indulgence, afraid of letting go. Yet, I cannot honestly tell the fascinating, valuable stories about my grandparents and mother and her siblings without revealing fragments of my own life, for every book reflects the author's prejudices and dreams. I am implicated in their sentences. Trapped in expression or silence.

So this is *my* story of the story. Each family member hears different legends, senses different absences. No doubt my Mom and brothers as well as aunts and uncles and cousins understand the story of this family differently. If there are fourteen siblings, there are fourteen times fourteen versions. It is the way we understand life, what we do with the story of the story, that makes us the individuals we are.

What interests me most are the connections and disconnections among three generations of McKenzie-Campbell women. Another author might write more extensively about my brothers and my father. Yet my brothers are still living their stories, and I cannot, in any case, represent their experiences. My now departed father does have a part here, the ghostly, peripheral role that he played as the merchant seaman who sailed in and out of Mom's life. In contrast, I believe her father, as she remembered and imagined him, was the important man in her world, hence his story unfolds here in relation to his daughter and his wife. *The Low Road* begins in the nineteenth century and reaches to the tip of the twenty-first century as a chronicle of the lives of my grandmother, my mother, and myself.

As a little girl, I learned to read conversations closely because Mom was so reticent. I would peer between the lines (to question, weigh, pursue deeper meaning), for I intuited that she *couldn't* tell the whole story. As her middle child, the only girl, a classic first-generation American, I became mediator, messenger, translator. I knew my job. I learned that secrets were good for the imagination.

In composing this book, will I finally separate from my mother? Is this the reason I couldn't write it while she was alive, and why it's taken so damn long to finish? The book feels at once too intimate a communion and too cruel an abandonment. In telling the story, in revealing the truth as far as I know it, I am no longer just her daughter; I am claiming my own part in the family that also shaped me.

The child is a product of her mother's imagination as well as of her genes and experience. What does "know" mean in a family story? If I have always pictured Mom's childhood in a cosy city apartment and then discover that her whole family was stuffed in one room of a red-light tenement building that was shared by a non-temperance hotel, am I shaped by fact or fiction? If I locate aunts and uncles my mother never mentioned to me as a child, are they related to me? Are they truly relatives? Ultimately I understand the fable marks us as much as the fact.

Not until I begin this book do I realize there is so much I haven't ever *imagined.* From Mom's stories, I have such a clear image of her living with her brother Colin and their parents on Union Place, but haven't logically considered how they got there. It never occurs to me until I start to place the nostalgic fragments into a coherent narrative (in which present is related to past and actions have consequences) that when my grandparents exit their first marriages, they leave eleven children behind. I have never considered how the children from those earlier unions might resent my mother, the first love child. Nor have I consciously questioned why Mom remembered so little about her mother. Thus I move from believing that *The Low Road* is already written to learning day by silent day how little I do know.

ᕯᑋ

So many questions I wish I had asked Mom before she died.

Was she skinny as a girl? Pretty? Lively? How did she and Grandpa talk to each other? With what degree of formality? I wonder about her accent then, wonder how it changed in the United States.

I want to phone her for the answers.

Once I asked her if I could interview her with a tape recorder, to get down the details (but also, secretly, to preserve her voice after I had lost the rest of her). No, she said, she didn't care to. That's how she talked. Succinctly. Waste not, want not. And that was the end of that.

I do keep a note from her in my top desk drawer, a photo on the refrigerator. Yet her voice is gone.

Once I had an inspiration: Maybe, I thought, she's on the other side of my answering machine tape, the side I haven't used for years. Anxiously I listened to the whole tape. Nothing. Just orders arrived at the stationery shop; friends ringing about the movies, those calls that always seemed more urgent than hers.

ᕯᑋ

Mary Gill McKenzie-Campbell Miner gave me many gifts, allowed me privileges of education and income she never acquired. Maybe she gauged her life against that of her mother, who had more children, fewer material comforts. This I know from Edinburgh's Register House: My grand-mother was an eleven-year-old live-in servant in a one-room tenement. At eighteen, she was an illiterate hospital ward maid. At age thirty-seven, my pregnant grandmother died of a botched abortion. At age thirty-seven, my mother gave birth to me. Do we grow up beneath our mothers' skirts or on their shoulders? In trying to answer this, *The Low Road* has become a passage through questions about poverty, immigration, national and sexual identity among the women in our family.

I have been going back and forth to Edinburgh for thirty years, but after making a commitment to write this book ("To write *this* book?" No, I had no idea how it would turn out. "To write *a* book."), the research takes me on three long trips to Scotland. I travel there in summer 1995, fall 1996, and spring 1997. Three different seasons, three different years, watching the shifts in light, listening to the complicated music of Scots' speech. I spend days swimming in microfiche of census records as well as birth and death and marriage certificates at Register House. I dig up voter rolls in the National Library and post office directories in the Edinburgh Public Library. After several rewarding forays to the National Map Library, I obtain blueprints of various Edinburgh neighborhoods as they looked during the decades my family lived there or there or there.

I haunt Mom's beloved Milton House School and the Royal Infirmary, where Grandpa died. Archives and museums and shops offer books about Edinburgh, Leith, nineteenth- and early-twentieth-century Scotland. Also oral histories and sheet music from traditional songs. I consult an ancient encyclopedia to learn the contemporary wisdom about tuberculosis. My fieldwork takes me to the City Chambers, India House, the Adoption Advisory Group. I talk with shopkeepers, cab drivers, and people on the streets about Mom's neighborhoods. On the pretext of wanting to rent office space, I call a realtor and inspect the inside of a tenement constructed in the same year and the same neighborhood by the same architect who built my mother's now demolished building. I interview a ninety-three-year-old piano teacher who used to play popular tunes in the dance hall where Mom worked as a teenager.

Back in the States, I find the original manifest as well as newspaper photos of the S.S. *Transylvannia,* the ship on which Mom immigrated. The manifest is from the extensive Mormon archives in Salt Lake City. The photos appear in a book from the University of Minnesota library.

*The Low Road*, then, comes alive in layers, of narrative speculation followed by research followed by revision followed by another draft narrative, more research, and so on. New material shines from a wedding registration I've been staring at for three years. Other documents turn me into an abyss. Will I ever know enough?

*The Low Road* is a cross-genre book, made from shards of fact, lie, intuition. Some shards—particularly about my grandparents, now dead for over seventy years—are unavailable, and thus daily lives must be imagined. Some shards—like those from my own mute childhood—I remember too well, or think I do, and these pass as memoir. Some shards are tales from Mom and her siblings. Often I picture these fragments as pieces of a pot, which I'm re-membering in an archeological way. At other times, I imagine them as slivers of colored glass, out of which I'm constructing a larger narrative from archetypal stories. Regardless of which image is more apt, I know that the *seams* between the shards are significant.

Since Mae and Daniel, my grandparents, were poor people, they left behind few records: just two photos, and no letters or wills or deeds. Knowledge of them comes from family stories and from government records. These are the lives that come closest to fiction in *The Low Road*. Yet if I find something that contradicts my evolving narrative, I alter the story, to embrace the fact. For instance, in the first drafts, the love-smitten Mae was reading books recommended by Daniel. Then I learned she was illiterate until she was eighteen. Likewise, my mother and aunts always said Daniel came from Ayr, but documents show "Airdrie," a less bucolic address, and so I have named Ayr as the place of Daniel's dreams rather than his growing up.

Premonition is an important part of any author's journey. Like other storytellers, I have found that my novels are "autobiographical" not from the practice of recording memory, but because of premonition. Things I write about later happen, or things I have imagined turn out to have a historical base. So, too, in this non-novel. I "knew" that Maggie Thompson was pregnant with her first child when she wed Daniel Campbell, a fact confirmed by marriage and census records. And while my mother never told me that she immigrated in September, I had the sense that that must have been the month she traveled in in 1930, so it was relatively easy to find the ship's manifest. I don't hold séances, but I do question the conventional boundaries of autobiographical research.

The chapters about my mother and myself come closer to familiar connotations of memoir. Mom's chapters are drawn from forty years of our conversations, from stories other relatives told me, and from documents. The diary chapters, here, about leaving Edinburgh, and about arriving in Connecticut, are based on historical and geographical fact, but are not actual journals (Mom was a talker, not a writer). Do the chapters about my own childhood and growing up come closest to the "truth?" I don't know. I have tried to reveal my quiet, bumbling daughterhood and self-righteous youth for what it was, but perhaps ego has made those grievances larger or smaller than they were. Each Valerie chapter is a hesitant addition—and I have said little of my professional life—because the daughter's role is important, but not central. I see my mother as the *heart* of *The Low Road*.

If my mother is the heart, then my grandparents are the *spine*. Hence every section is introduced by a chapter about Mae and or Daniel. Their dramatic romance is the opera that frames all our lives. After each grandparent section are the vertebrae of the generations who followed them. The book's fragmented form is a metaphor for disruption within the home. I ask a lot of the reader—to accompany this family narrative with the patience of friendship—to share my own jigsaw journey of understanding.

*The Low Road* is a concert of voices. My mother may not have been a singer, but she taught me everything I know about the rhythm of language. This book had to be written for a chorus, a sometimes dissonant one. Mom's voice is the first-person past; mine is the first-person present. Mae's voice is third-person past, and Daniel is revealed in the second-person poetic. I began my grandfather's story full of accusation, but the conversational voice evoked a surprising compassion, which is evident in his portrait by the end. This is how the voices came to me; that's all the analysis I can offer. The formality and politeness of my family may seem odd to many American readers, yet that's the way we are. As Mom sometimes said of her adopted compatriots, "I just don't understand how *rude* people can be." Other readers may be struck by Mom's vocabulary, unusual, perhaps, for an American who didn't finish grade eight, but Scottish schools are rigorous and my mother always loved reading. I often found her spending an afternoon hour with a cup of coffee and the dictionary.

It's natural, at the finishing line, to see what the book is *not*. I could have spent years and years in Register House (growing a tweed skirt from waist to mid-calf and a white cotton blouse from waist to neck), gathering more details about details. Maybe it's because I'm not a historian that I fear I haven't done sufficient digging. The point, of course, is to get enough material, not to tunnel all the way to China. I worry that the structure isn't clear enough. Most of all, I wonder what Mom would think of *The Low Road*. She was modest about her extraordinary, ordinary life and no doubt would feel rueful about the pain exposed here. Yet this is the woman who taught me to be honest and to laugh at human foibles. I think she would be astonished by what some records revealed about her parents' lives, touched by several of my childhood memories of the two of us together, and thrilled that her son's daughters now have daughters of their own. Did she want me to write this book? I'm not sure. I do think she expected it, at times encouraged it. How would she feel about the final book? I will always wonder.

Despite all the traveling and interviewing and sifting through microfiche and crumbling papers, I still weigh everything against memory, against family photos and greeting cards. Then I read the old letters—hers to me as well as mine to her.

One afternoon, three years before she died, Mom handed me a box in which she had saved all my letters for the past thirty years. When I protested, she said, "No, no. Take these. You'll need them some day."

Yes, this is the story I have been writing for my whole life. This is the story I will never know well enough to write.

# I

---

*Daniel, 1865–1897*

*Mae, 1895*

# CHAPTER ONE

*Daniel, Edinburgh, Airdrie, 1865–1897*

LONG AGO I LEARNED THAT THE CURSE OF GOOD STORYTELLING IS THE surrender of that simple ballad, blessed and evil. The genuine writer relinquishes blame, cultivates understanding. Does this leave room for fury, or even anger? Yes, yes. Writing is a record of the practice of life, of history experienced. A record written through windows of choice—however narrow—where we remain culpable and permeable and alive. Hence, my "conversations" with Daniel, which began as accusatory, shifted as the story and the teller progressed.

Grandfather, I have to say that once I recovered from the blind adoration of you I inherited from Mom, I knew you were an emotional con artist.

You really sucked in that earnest daughter of yours. Told her she "would always be a Campbell." You would always be with her. You were the myth around which she organized her life. This was a clever way of insuring your survival without having to cope with the painful vigil of it. I understand that you were a man of great intelligence, talent, ambition, pride, and passion, who simply had *bad luck*. Your capacity for ill fortune was fuelled by willfulness. I know that you were not cross-circuited by reason. And that when you left, you left more than you imagined behind.

You were born in Edinburgh, within a mile of where your parents met, you raised your children and you died. You were handsome, black-haired, the second son of four in a sisterless family that migrated to

Airdrie. Yours was a lucky family until your older brother died. This tragedy made you all the more attractive to the girls, who didn't exactly swarm, but some did rather flutter. You had your pick, and you picked several. Maggie wasn't the prettiest, yet there was something about her. You promised a house on the hill after you completed your accountancy course, and she believed you all the way to the stable and back several times. When she got pregnant, you couldn't restrain your romantic, ethical enthusiasm, and you wed in enough time to show yourselves prudent if not exactly chaste. When Bella was born, you celebrated with a resolution to quit the iron works, take that accountancy course, and hold down a truly promising job. This resolve was strengthened when Alex was born. Your own son, such a celebration, Alex Campbell, you were in love with life and your family and you could do anything. You were surprised the next year when Chrissie arrived.

Yet you didn't start to fret until after Matt, a sweet wee boy, far more like you in coloring and temperament than Alex would ever be. Your brothers teased you about such virility, and you felt as pleased as worried. What I want to know is why you didn't do something to stem the flood of children. Perhaps this seemed a female responsibility. As much as you loved Maggie—and you did, even I see that, even if it didn't approach the way in which you later loved Mae—you couldn't broach the topic with her. It was now, after Matt, that you decided to return to your native Edinburgh to work for Mr. Menzies and take the accountancy course.

ℛℯ

You saw Mae the minute you entered the bakery, a blond beauty in her succulent later teens and very much a woman. What did you feel? Did you know right away or was there just a small glow that caught hold and burned up your spine? Unexpected, the spark between you (apparently you wore early thirties and fatherhood lightly), and all the more seductive for the surprise of it. There was something fragile in her sturdy responsibility. Something heartbreakingly tender. I'm as sentimental as the next person, perhaps more so, and I've had my share of lovers, perhaps more so, male and female. So I comprehend your attraction to this young, supple wisp of iron. And the hunger she felt for your solid, fey angularity.

Yet I don't appreciate the lies you told Mae at the beginning—that first year—about being a confirmed bachelor who'd had only the slightest matrimonial temptations. How much of your seduction was vanity? Lust? The pleasure of storymaking? I suppose I could ask the same of myself, question my own lies, again and again. Yet I didn't conceive five and seven and ten children (I gave up at minus one). In comparison to you, Grandpa, I'm a tedious Girl Scout, a driver never ticketed for a moving violation. Still I am weighted by inherited venality, afraid to look over my shoulder into the shadow you cast, and maybe this fear of peering backward was a fear of Mom's inexpressible anger at you. I've never really liked older men. (Of course there was my father, but he was too immature ever to be an older man.) You have become a genetic memory.

You've never told your story. Of course your immortality is more ironic than mine (after all, I'm part of yours). You left so many children in different families that you felt sure your life would stay under wraps due to their embarrassment or grief or rage. Now, I'm going to *out* you after seventy years.

℞

So you brought the family to Edinburgh and settled near Milton House School and got yourself a new job and had a few more children. They all loved you madly and were happy to be with you, with each other, eating watery mince and potatoes and chipped fruit. You were lucky and unlucky that none of them died. As the older ones grew, they were willing enough to work.

You were just as happy to be away from Airdrie, in truth, because your mother could imagine you to be living a more comfortable life, especially since every month you sent (unknown to Maggie) a quid or two to put something special on Mam's table. You had so many games running, Danny, that it's hard to find a straight story. No linear narrative here. Should we dismiss prevarication as confusion? Let's not and say we did.

1895: You met Mae this year. Maybe you compared Mae's fresh, unlined face to the good-humored, care-worn wife you looked at every day. Something came over you, a whole new persona, by the time you stopped by Macmillan's for a second drink, I mean scone.

You liked the dark ones with currants. They were sold out, and she looked distressed at not being able to please you. Was she first to feel the attraction? Something in the bright way she looked at you, admiring that high forehead. Then you saw him, Jock McKenzie, looking at her looking at you. That sweet, self-defeating man said,

"I'll see in the kitchen. They baked double this morning."

You two stood there, warmed by each other's shy smiles. Not too long after Jock volunteered to enter the inferno, you heard yourself telling Mae you had just arrived from Ayr for an accounting course. You were a hot-air balloon released of your wife and children and dead-end job, a man ten years younger in your blessedly busy hair, and all the leaner for looking at her.

"Ta," you said to Jock, as he stepped between the two of you to deliver the scone.

He nodded, holding his ground, blocking her view, your glance, my future.

Cheers, you tipped your hat, which was politely in your hand, and you don't remember leaving the sweet aromas behind as you walked out, jingling the bell, to the milky cold fog of a February morning. By the next turning, you found yourself sniffing the scone, as if it were her linen handkerchief, and realizing she had made you a new person. You knew nothing about her—none of the census details—but you felt young, free, a real man. Large with the impossibility of love.

Now I see you fear I'll judge you harshly because I'm a raving feminist bent on retribution for my women. The truth is, I know what it's like to be trapped in someone else's life.

I know a few things. I know she was with you for the rest of the day at your large, solid desk at the back of the shop. That shadowed, stuffy corner was bright and airy, and you managed to accomplish Mr. Menzie's monotonous copying faster than usual. The old squirrel actually commented—although not exactly complimented you—on the felicity of the day's transcription. She was with you all afternoon, her light, her voice, her scent (which you must have imagined) over all those sweet and savory smells from the back kitchen. Yet what I don't know is whether Maggie and the children sensed her presence when you returned that night. Did they notice your cockeyed smile, wondering if you had stopped off at the pub on the way home?

Time passed. Things happened. Not much between the two of you, as far as you were concerned—just small exchanges of sentiment. You stopped by the bakery—once a week, well, twice a week at most. You were grateful for the texture and shine she gave your days.

I remember (as one does in the marrow of one's bones—there's nothing witchy about it, we all have these powers but tend to waste them) when Maggie and Bella were hit by the trolley. (Well, yes, Aunt Bella told me something about it, but that's not nearly as much as I remember), how Alex came running to get you at work, annoying Mr. Menzies with his boyish physical intrusion until the urgency was registered. How you and the lad raced to the hospital together, only to have the door shut against ineffectual relations.

Sitting at the Royal Infirmary, you prayed for her safe return, took stock of your life—what more could a man want than a good wife, healthy children, and an indoor job? One could want a lot more, which is why the fourteen children spread around the world. (This was an inheritance you hadn't intended and that would have left you both pleased and sad.) Hours passed. You sent Alex home to tell Chrissie to fix a meal. At age ten, you thought, she could do this. He returned, having forgotten to eat, himself, but sustained by leaning against you, sleeping softly. You reckoned, on and off between bouts of confidence, what it would be like to raise these children alone. You shivered, imagining the long loneliness of a half-empty bed in a flat busy with the coughing and teasing and crying of six children. Then you bargained with God, waging the only capital a poor man has, his dreams. You promised to give up all thoughts of Mae if Maggie and your favorite child, Bella, recovered.

❧

Why do I find it easier to write about you than about the others, even Mom? Is it because I'm writing *to* you and this seems more mutual? Is it because I'm angriest at you? Unfairly so? Is it because Grandmother died first, because *she* was much younger than you, because I assume the man is the operative party? Or is it because Mom idolized you and remembered nothing about her mother except her dead body at the end of the bed and once seeing her pubic hair?

When I was growing up, I had a hard enough time believing that my mother came from a foreign country—let alone that *you* did too and that *you* never left the place. You weren't quite real. And then she would speak about you in that hallowed voice, as if you had made great sacrifices for your children, rather than vice versa. You were reputed to be good, kind, authoritative, gentle, generous, intellectually brilliant, compassionate. So I grew up imagining grandfathers as biblical heroes. I wouldn't mind a grandfather who was brave or full of integrity or just some poor schlump run over by the Industrial Revolution. But a charmer? A lover? A gambler?

You seem to have made Mom happy, to have been a bright spot in her life. Yet you were also responsible (culpable in all its urgent weight) for her heavy melancholy. I tried to take care of her, this gift you bequeathed me, my mother. As she kept saying to me, "you're the girl," so I got the secrets and the terrors and the gossip. I held her hand after Dad left. I took her back to Scotland twice. I discovered Aunt Chrissie in Canada and Uncle Colin in Australia. I slept with her longer than anyone.

# CHAPTER TWO

## Mae, Edinburgh, 1895

BEFORE WALKING HOME ONE EVENING, MAE STOPPED BY PRINCES' STREET gardens and sat in the soft, early evening sun, dreaming that she was far from the noise of trolleys and the stench of city streets and rude, indifferent, argumentative strangers. Superstitiously, appreciatively, Mae touched the pin at her collar. She closed her eyes, soaked in the warm, thinking on her life and especially on the progress of her summer.

Mary Jane Gill was already eleven in 1891 when she became a live-in servant, and thirteen when she took work at Macmillan's Bakery to help support her family. Mae's poor father was ill on and off. She didn't mind the bakery job, the leaving of childhood. All her friends did it. Mae wasn't a girl to dwell on her responsibilities; they didn't really bear thinking about.

And when she met Daniel Campbell—well, maybe the second time she met him—she knew her life would turn out fine. On the first date, he took her to tea. He explained how he was newly arrived from Ayr, here for an accounting class, then to seek his fortune. When he looked at her, she knew she was part of that fortune.

Meanwhile, at home, Dad was drinking. Mam was more and more unhappy. Mae couldn't stand the pressure, and she couldn't name it, either. Apparently nerves were showing on her face because Jock McKenzie had been quite solicitous, asking after her health, kindly bringing glasses of water.

She knew she was responding to the eager, unfailingly nice Jock only until Daniel was ready to be serious. She daydreamed, night dreamed, that she would go back to Ayr with him and they would start a wee business together. Emphasis on the word "wee." She imagined no grand life. Just a degree of comfort and a certain station. She wasn't born to serve behind a counter all her days. Life with Daniel would rescue her from this tedious job, the cuffing and bruising at home. They would have a nice little family.

Mae admired her mother, but she planned a different life. For one thing, she wouldn't marry into a family containing anyone remotely like Uncle Davy. Davy could speak more quickly and deeply and loudly than Father, especially after they went together on a drinking trail to end all binges. Davy drove Mam out of her mind. Her sister, Jessie, had tipped completely into the well of panic. Big-boned Jessie had a reticent streak, owned more volume than forthrightness, and told Mae she simply had to *do* something. So Mae did step in to sort things out. And for that Davy had belted her in the face.

The next day when Jock observed her blackened eye, Mae witnessed a new side to him. Rage swelled his shoulders, straightened his back.

"Oh, it's nothing," she said, halfway meaning it, because she'd seen a lot of eyes repair themselves.

"I don't want any stories about doorknobs this time, Mae." He dropped a tray, bent to retrieve it, and said, "Was it that bullying uncle of yours? Tell me the truth and I'll put an end to this for good."

She shuddered at the thought of sweet Jock confronting burly Uncle Davy. "Simmer down," she whispered, not wanting the MacMillans to think she was bringing her troubles to work.

"But, but . . ." his face grew redder. "This behavior is barbaric. This is . . ."

Now she was close enough to him to smell a different kind of sweat, and she found herself unaccountably attracted to this fellow she had always seen as a decent, but ineffectual, bloke, and who often reminded her of her younger brother in his stuttering and fumbling.

Just then, a strange woman walked into the shop and asked for a ginger cake.

Mae was glad for the interruption, blushed, and dismissed her temporary attraction to the overly nice Jock. She thought about how when she had first worked here, as a junior helper in the back, she had known the patrons by name and family history. But the shop was getting more and more custom straight off the Waverley trains. People down from Perth or Stirling for a day's shopping. Or over from Glasgow, looking for work. Or even up from London in search of God-knew-what because they never seemed to be happy here as they ordered scones and asked directions (confused, petulant, as if they had suddenly slipped into Purgatory) in their beeping, high-pitched English accents.

Mae relaxed back on the bench and breathed in the scents of Edinburgh in August. The perfect month altogether, even with *haar*— warm days, long nights. Not as long as June or July, but long enough and hemmed with an awareness of diminishing light. August, a month when the numbing disappointment of summer had risen and receded (every season has its limits, even summer). A month when one was simply grateful for the lingering warmth.

August was not a month of surprises. Except this year. It happened so fast, in the mid-morning crush. One minute she was wrapping a cake for Mrs. Anderson and the next minute *he* was standing there, ushering her out to the pavement.

Mr. MacMillan wouldn't mind, she told herself. You needed to take a breath of fresh air occasionally. "Just for a moment, then," she acquiesced.

He laughed at her dutifulness and handed her a small box.

She stared at the red ribbon, at the dark hairs on his meticulous, long fingers.

"You're meant to open it," he grinned.

"Oh," she said stupidly, her heart pounding with a huge, unnamable terror. He pulled one leg of the ribbon to urge her on.

When she lifted the lid, she found a small silver pin in the shape of a thistle with a tiny amethyst flower, the perfect purple for August.

Her cheeks drew blood.

He was still grinning.

"Oh, you shouldn't have." Her brimming-over gratitude felt awkward, clownish.

Suddenly she was distracted by a girl about her own age, dark hair pouring down her shoulders. The alarmed lass was waving, warning. Mae looked around; no one else was paying any attention.

The girl's expression was urgent.

"Look, just there," Mae drew Daniel's attention to her.

But when they turned together, the girl had disappeared.

The pin gleamed brilliantly, elegantly, and Mae was as much delighted by his thought as by the gift itself. For the rest of the day she bubbled, barely containing her raw joy.

That evening Mae inhaled the fuzzy August scent of flowers in the Gardens and fingered the brooch near her collarbone. Life would be different out of the city, in Ayr, a town big enough to plant a business and small enough for neighborliness, for the modest courtesies that colored and shaped a day. They would have a wee cottage with a garden at the back—a place to grow cabbages and parsnips for table, for their own small family. She wouldn't make the mistake Mother had made. She wouldn't have a brood so large and noisy that thinking was impossible.

Mam often said that for a practical girl, Mae possessed a startlingly wistful side. For someone who had dutifully taken up her responsibilities, she had a strange taste for the possible over the actual. More of a Papist temperament, really. Mae tried not to be annoyed when her mother mused like this. It was nice enough to see her attention on something besides clothes washing and food cooking.

Mae wasn't used to being the center of anyone's attention. The thing she didn't understand, and what she could never say to her mother, was that she needed this sentimental nonsense, as Mam called it, to pull her through a day. How did Mam manage to manage without some hope? How could she dream, so surrounded by tasks and worries? No, that kind of marriage was not for Mae. And just as she acknowledged this, she also understood that people reproduced to see their blood flowing forward to a better life.

Any day, Mam would have preferred Jock McKenzie to Daniel Campbell. Jock was conscientious, hardworking, kind. Just as well Mam rarely stopped by the bakery. The few times she did appear, Jock was back in the kitchen. Meanwhile, Mae thought, even when Jock noticed the two of them together, he didn't pick up a thing. He was that innocent. Still, he kept a watch on her. He did observe the progress of her blackened eye repairing itself, and stopped asking daily questions about her welfare once he was satisfied that Uncle Davy had returned to Belfast. All this good-willed attention, from Mother at home and Jock at work, would drive her raving mad.

Often as she could now, once a week, twice a week if she were lucky, she would stop here in Princes' Street Gardens and close her eyes for fifteen minutes, imagining she were off somewhere exotic—camping in the middle of the Canadian Rockies, maybe. Or tending a hearth in Ayr.

# CHAPTER THREE

# "Tomorrow"

## *Mary, Edinburgh, 1925*

TUESDAY LUNCH WAS UNUSUALLY QUIET. JOANIE SAID I COULD HAVE THE window tables. Everyone wanted that station and Joanie tried to be fair by giving us each a turn. More customers sat there, of course, which meant better tips. But I liked it mostly because of the light and life streaming in from the street. The back of Fairley's restaurant and dance hall could get dark, gloomy, setting you to useless thoughts. Some older customers complained that it was too dim for reading the menu. The smells of lard and vinegar certainly hung heavier back there, as if they stuck to the walls. My imagination, most probably. I had learned to doubt my imagination.

For weeks after I moved into Mrs. Millar's, I thought someone was tapping—like a ghost working the teletype or something—in my closet. When I finally drummed up the courage to inquire about the noise, she shook her head sadly.

"You just need more rest, hen. You've had a big shock, your father dying, your wee brother off at the orphan home."

I supposed she was right, but people exaggerated my circumstances.

"Only fourteen and out on your own."

Well, I was hardly the only one in that position.

"No family to take you in?"

That wasn't exactly right. But what would the McKenzies or the Campbells want with me? I was the source of the trouble—the first child of my parents, the first undeniable fissure in their own parents' marriages.

"Poor lass."

Truth was, I was just as happy on my own.

The way I viewed it, I was lucky. Lucky Mrs. Millar had agreed to take me in at the rooming house in exchange for kitchen work and cleaning. Lucky that Mrs. Millar had a roomer who was leaving Fairley's kitchen to go to England. Soon I had a job, a room in a good, clean house, and every Sunday off to read and visit Colin. I did miss my brother and father and school. But the days were too busy for loneliness. And in the evenings, there were books. Sometimes Mr. Stewart, who was studying to be a university lecturer, would lend me one of his texts or journals. Father would have liked Mr. Stewart, would have approved of the cleanliness and good order and nourishment of Mrs. Millar's house. When I felt too confused, I thought of Father and that set me straight. He would always be with me.

Mr. Stewart encouraged the reading, said there were ways I could still get schooling, and told me about night courses. He reminded me of my teacher, Miss Geddes. Some days I mourned Miss Geddes almost as much as I did my father. A shameful admission. I'll never forget the day she brought me here to Fairley's for lunch—I was eleven, so that would have been four years ago now. This was always a special restaurant.

❧

*We sit by the windows because she has booked a seat there. I will always remember the perfect details. Miss Geddes wears an olive green felt hat with a pheasant's feather and a woolen suit to match the hat. I wear my almost-blue-as-navy Sunday dress, and she praises my lace collar. Since this delicate collar has been saved from my mother's wardrobe, the compliment pleases and saddens me. I don't remember much about Mother—rarely called her that, rather, "my mother," as if discussing a historical fact rather than a close relation. After all, I was seven when she died in childbirth. It's odd. Yet every time I try to think about it, she disappears. Whereas I can describe Father perfectly—his dark eyes and greying hair, the dapper moustache, his deep, mellow voice, breathless laugh, straight posture.*

*Miss Geddes sits right there in the window with me. New sun washes in across our table. Miss Geddes orders beef stew. I do the same, but eat slowly, I am so caught up in our conversation about her holiday to Skye, her sister in Perth, and the school scholarship for which she is going to nominate me. She says that if I like the school and do well there, I might even think of going to university. Father will be pleased. I can hardly wait to tell him, and find it difficult to concentrate on the rest of our conversation.*

❧

Tuesdays moved slowly at Fairley's, but tables were filling up now. Business increased as we neared the weekend. Maybe people grew more relaxed with the week passing, said Mr. Stewart, who was from Glasgow, which he described as a raucous, individualistic place, compared to "Edinburgh, The Good." When he finished his university studies, Mr. Stewart wanted to go back to the West and teach at Glasgow University. I wondered what it would feel like to be married to a university lecturer in that other city.

Approaching the far table, I knew there was no need for my order pad because Mr. Mintner would ask for haddock and chips and Mr. Cowan would have his usual liver and bacon. I liked this predictability. I enjoyed the easy, regular way a waitress could fit into other people's lives. It was a wee ceremony, really, the greeting, ordering, serving, even the tipping. I knew that Mr. Mintner would leave threepence and Mr. Cowan sixpence. It was nice that way, the security of knowing ahead of time.

The not knowing was also fun on occasion. I still kept that nickel the American left me for my "trip to Miami." He was truly a gentleman, although Mrs. Millar thought he took too much interest in a young girl. In Edinburgh for a week on business and every day he sat at my table and ordered mince pie. He told me about his family in Florida, how you had to watch for alligators. Alligators were American crocodiles, only uglier and meaner. A great joker. I knew Mrs. Millar shouldn't worry, that his teasing was just another way of shaking away loneliness. When he invited me to visit the family in Miami, he didn't expect me to come. Occasionally, particularly on cold, grey days like this, I thought I might surprise him.

Just then, as I was daydreaming—almost as if *because* I was daydreaming, I saw them come in the side door. Miss Geddes in a dark brown dress and cape. And a little girl, an ugly, pin-faced, blond child. They were chatting eagerly, so I was able to retreat, unseen, to the kitchen. Some sort of instinct sent me there, something deep, illogical, and scared.

"Are you well?" Sara asked. "You've gone all pale."

I hadn't noticed Sara waiting to collect her order. Hadn't registered anyone. I was back at that lunch so long ago when Miss Geddes was telling me about public school and the jobs a young lady could get with a good diploma. Accounting, business, foreign service. Miss Fiona Geddes had worked in Paris for three years, just out of school. She had returned to marry an Edinburgh man, who got killed on his way home from the Front. Every family seemed to lose someone. Miss Geddes grieved the love of her life and she knew she would never find anyone to give her sons and daughters, so she went into teaching. That way, she would always have young folk around her. When people who didn't know she was a "Miss" asked if she had any children, she would say, "Yes, thirty this year." Her cheerfulness was noble. I planned to have four children some day, two boys and two girls. One of them would be named Fiona.

As conscientiously fair as Miss Geddes always was, as kind as she was to *every* student, she always had a favorite girl. Like winning the sweeps, it was, to be her girl. I knew I had been chosen the day she invited me to Fairley's Cafe.

Afterward, once I was settled from Father's death, I should have stayed in touch. She had invited me to. I remembered the expression in her eyes that last day, sympathy with a touch of betrayal as if I were choosing not to remain at school. Her desk was piled with writing exercises. "Come and visit me," she had said disappointedly. "Don't vanish on us."

I had failed. Failed to answer her kind Easter card. Failed because, at first, I was so caught up in the details of Father's burial and Colin's placement in the orphan home and getting established at Mrs. Millar's and, several months later, taking the job at Fairley's in the kitchen. I thought about Miss Geddes every time I went to the library, every time I had to pass Milton House School.

I was waiting until I could take one of those night courses Mr. Stewart talked about. Waiting to achieve Miss Geddes' expectations.

"Sara," I said finally, "would you change with me today?"

She regarded me cockeyed. "Your window tables? Your precious light?"

"Aye, just for today?"

Her puzzled face relaxed. "Oh, Mr. Mintner! Has he been fussing at you again?"

I shrugged, knowing it was unfair to lay blame on Mr. Mintner, but since his behavior was legendary, I wasn't exactly originating a rumor.

"Sure, love, he always leaves me alone. I don't know whether to be grateful or insulted." she winked.

I liked Sara, but harbored a dread of turning into her: twenty-eight or twenty-nine, still unmarried, although she had had her share of boyfriends, at Fairley's ten years and coasting into middle age. Yet, she seemed happy enough.

Monty, the cook—or "chef" as he archly insisted—laughed. "The old guy must go for these dark, sincere types. Nothing against your Viking beauty, Sara. I'd happily marry you."

"Well, I'm not shopping, thanks, Monty," she grinned, "and I don't owe your wife any favors."

"Haddock and chips?" He ignored the insult.

"Mr. M." Sara nodded to me.

"How did you guess?"

For the next hour I stayed to the rear of the restaurant, ducking into the kitchen when I felt Miss Geddes glancing away from the girl.

I found myself fingering that dull, grey nickel, thinking about Colin and me traveling around America to see buffaloes and cowboys and alligators. They had restaurants in America and accountancy courses. There was lots of work. Bella had written from Canada, inviting me to stay with young Winnie and her until I got settled in British Columbia, but I preferred the idea of America. Canada sounded like a second-hand Britain. They even put the king on their stamps. When I left this place, I wasn't settling in any colony; I planned to step off into the universe. I couldn't keep my eyes from the corner table. The little girl chatted and chatted, not touching her nice meal. How could Miss Geddes bear her rudeness? She was leaning forward, elbows by her plate, talking, laughing, pointing. Miss Geddes sat back, posture perfect, as she listened intently. (Beef stew was on the menu today. I wondered if Miss Geddes came here for the beef stew. It was a complicated dish to cook and store if you lived alone. Did Miss Geddes know I worked at Fairley's? Had she passed once and noticed me though the window?) How could a little girl—she couldn't have been much more than eleven—think of so much to say? Miss Geddes attended to her patiently. When Sara swung open the kitchen doors, carrying their desserts, I looked the other way.

Mr. Mintner and Mr. Cowan collected their coats. Before he went out, Mr. Mintner came over, squeezed my chin, and laughed, "We missed our dolly."

I told myself I was lucky to work in a warm restaurant with table-cloths and a high-class clientele and friendly staff who treated me like a kid sister, and strangers, who came all the way from America, inviting me to visit.

# CHAPTER FOUR

# "From Tenement to Castle"

## *Valerie, Edinburgh, 1990s*

TIRED FROM A LONG DAY OF RESEARCH AT REGISTER HOUSE, I SLUMP IN my bus seat next to a post-mod lad listening to metallic music on leaking earphones. In front of me two compact little ladies gossip, talking so fast their language is as foreign to me as Navajo or Norwegian. Each keeps a tight grip on her plastic bags of Christmas presents and groceries.

The thirty-five-minute bus journey from Edinburgh through Dalkieth and Bonnyrigg and Poltonhall is sheer time travel, because if Mom had stayed in Edinburgh, chances are it would have been progress for her daughter to live in one of these quieter villages on the edge of town. And when I look closely at the little ladies, I see that they're no older than I. Indeed, one is younger. I am a forty-nine-year-old Scot/American riding through my other life. Most of the passengers disembark before my stop. This is a relief, because I'm always embarrassed to tell the driver that I need to get off at the Castle.

During this darkening November–December, I am living at Hawthornden Castle. The fifteenth-century castle, opened as a writers' retreat by the Heinz Foundation, is about a quarter mile from the bus stop on the main road. I find it romantic to walk from the stop up the icy drive with my miniature flashlight (which offers more solace than illumination). Amazing to know I can walk straight up to the wood and iron door and enter without knocking. Home in the castle. Not in my mother's wildest dreams.

Yet every morning I write about my mother's life as I sit at the castle desk. This grand building is filled with winding stairwells and deep-set windows and surrounded by tree-covered hills. My third-floor room looks out onto the ancient walls and turrets. The bed is firm, covered with pounds of blankets and duvet and warmed every night by a blue hot-water bottle. On the second floor there is an aristocratic sitting room with attached conservatory. On the first floor, I work in the castle's keep-turned-library. Before dinner, I assemble with the other fellows for sherry in a cocktail room with murals that almost persuade you it is a sunny day in Tuscany. Margaret and Jean and Marjorie and Lorraine cook our meals on an elaborate Aga in a venerable wooden-countered, copper-potted kitchen.

When I take a writing break, I love walking in the nearby glen down to the River Esk. The only company are pheasant and magpie and, when I'm lucky, the fox. It's strange, though, to be writing about my family while living amid these private, manicured trails and quiet vistas. Sometimes this setting makes me feel sad. Or guilty. Sometimes just lucky.

Each day in Scotland I am struck by the posture or profile of someone I am sure is Aunt Bella or Aunt Chrissie or Uncle Johnny. This fall, as during many trips to Edinburgh these last thirty years, the city feels happily familiar. I'll hear Mom's voice in a shop. See her handwriting on the receipt. The gestures and phrases that made my mother odd when I was growing up in the States are unremarkable in Edinburgh. I feel at home. Then a friendly stranger inquires if I'm "here on holiday for a few days," I am at once embarrassed, irritated, and confused. "No," I say, "I'm working." If pressed, I will say that I am doing historical research or writing a novel. Never do I admit I am writing about my family, mortified by the idea of being confused with those American tourists searching for great-grandfather's coat of arms. Perhaps this is a frivolous and vain distinction: I am not on an ancestor search; I'm just trying to meet my family. Hello, are you here? I know you're here. I just don't know who you are.

To learn about Grandfather, I need to locate the birth certificates of Uncle Colin and Aunt Bella. So I use the castle telephone (and my ATT calling card) to dial my cousin Anita in Australia for Colin's birthdate and my cousin John in British Columbia for Aunt Bella's birthdate. Eventually, at Register House, I discover Grandfather's marriage certificate to Maggie Thompson, and from there, his birth certificate and details about his parents.

Perhaps the strangest news is where Grandfather's parents lived before they were married—13 High School Yards and 15 High School Yards. High School Yards, where the buildings date back to 1627, is now part of the University of Edinburgh. When I return in the spring, as a university research associate, I am scheduled to have an office in High School Yards.

In December, just before I leave the Castle, I return some books I have borrowed from the Heinz Collection. I find Margaret and Jean, the cook-housekeepers, sneaking a smoke in the freezing conservatory. They ask me what I was doing with the Scottish books, and I render the potted version of our family saga. They sit there smoking, looking more intrigued and more uncomfortable by the minute. They know all about the dancehall where Mom worked—had been told not to go there by their parents. Margaret nods when I say that Grandfather died of TB. "Aye," there would have been a lot of it in that part of town."

They are impressed, if not astounded, by Mom's decision to emigrate. Jean declares, "She must have had a big heart, your mother." (An empty purse is more like it, but I take her point.)

Then, as I'm leaving, Margaret says something I don't quite register until I am back in my room before the roaring fire. "It sounds like something out of a Catherine Cookson novel. You've got more than one book there." I have always hated the fact that Mom read those silly historical romances. But of course, that was her life. If you grew up like that, you learned to expect a good story.

Just before I leave Hawthornden in December, I assemble the relevant birth and marriage certificates for John and Anita. Then I walk through the chilly afternoon down to the tiny post office-cum-newsagent in Rosewell. This feels like a metaphor for the whole project, a small ceremony—American cousin sending the news to Australian and Canadian cousins. I feel relieved and exhilarated as I walk. Yet the aged, taciturn postal clerk doesn't seem to notice any import. He weighs the envelopes, accepts my money. Then he stamps each envelope with a different colored image of Queen Elizabeth II.

# II

---

*Daniel, 1896*

# CHAPTER FIVE

## Daniel, Edinburgh, 1896

YOU DIDN'T DO MORE THAN LOOK IN THE SHOP WINDOW, I KNOW THAT. You were just taking a quick glance, walking by. And there she was, wrapping a pie, the thistle pin attached jauntily to the collar of that startlingly white blouse. Pristine, she was, one of the qualities that had appealed to you from the start. How could she keep clothes so clean while working in a bakery? You admired her unwrinkled apron, white nails, scrubbed face. I suppose if you hadn't noticed the pin, you might have moved faster, before she felt you cherishing her, before she presented the pie to her customer and looked out curiously, as if scratching an itch, and saw her misery and redemption beating there, like a mad bird thumping against a glass pane.

With rapid grace, she removed her apron, wiped her hands, and dashed out to the pavement. You two didn't touch, but the embrace of her smile was almost more intimacy than you could bear. (Is it *you* I have to thank for my own stiff reserve? Maybe not just you. *Loosen up* is advice coined for Scots.) And when you dared look deeply into her eyes, you found none of the shaming or blaming you might have expected, had you allowed yourself to anticipate *anything*. She wore only shy amazement and fragile gratitude.

You explained that you had been called out of town by family troubles, and, pained by the fear in her eyes, immediately added that all had been resolved happily. You had intended to write, but didn't know what her family would think and . . .

So easily the deception formed. More lies stacked up inside your head.

Not to worry then, she said, grateful to have you back, her amethyst fairly winking at you.

And because you could not bear her ravishing sincerity, you looked away, over her shoulder. Jock McKenzie watched carefully. In that moment you saw something in him that was also in you—a timidity, an acceptance of the finite—and you decided to cede to him a bit of what you shared, although not Mae, not what he wanted you to cede. You bequeathed him your ration of common sense. You took her hand and made a date for the following evening after work.

That was the day where you and I touched lives, the point at which I became possible. The first flirtation or romance or engagement was fate. Now, however, you were making a choice. This was related to will. A sense, for all your modesty, that you had a right to the best, a strange confidence that pulsed beneath the unremarkable skin of your discreet social camouflage.

# CHAPTER SIX

# "Sketchbook of Edinburgh"

## *Mary, Edinburgh, 1930*

A MONTH BEFORE THE VOYAGE TO AMERICA, I VISITED PLACES I WANTED to remember. I could never draw, so I took the small notebook Mr. Stewart gave me. I suppose it was silly—a twenty-year-old woman drawing—but I tried a few word sketches, a different place each day. Who knew when or if I would get back to Scotland, and I wanted to remember. Father said memories were a treasure only time could take, and this notebook would protect me against time. Of course, America had libraries. I had read that Mr. Carnegie had endowed them. There I could get all the books about Scotland I might crave. But I had no camera, and this was my way of making personal pictures. A kind of keepsake journal. Here is something of what I wrote:

### THE GRASSMARKET

It's a cold day, bitter, Father would say. Strange for summer. Wet wind slices through the Grassmarket, turning it even more lonely than my room. The skin on my cheekbones hurts; you can get burned by chill. I've come to watch people cheerily greeting one another, but I find no light in anyone's eyes. A bloke who looks like my neighbor Keith Petrie leans flat and tense toward his wheelbarrow. An old woman hugs a basket close to her belly and I imagine her a kangaroo, with baby Joey swaddled inside the wicker packet. Does Alex see many kangaroos in New Zealand? Imagine having a brother at the end of the earth like that. I mourn Peggy, who has only gone over to Cupar, for heaven's sake. I think she's still there. The Antipodes make disappearing relative, in more ways than one.

Even on this bitter day the Grassmarket vibrates: tapping, clomping horses. Friends shouting to friends. Light lasts long enough. Our greyed castle up there hovers over the younger buildings.

## THE SCOTT MONUMENT

Trees near the Scott Monument are still bright green. I think of the leaves breeze dancing, but ever since Sara talked about leaves as dead men swinging from the gallows, I've felt a shiver. One sudden wind, dozens detach and fly at once, swirling above the branches like tropical birds, and those same leaves, on the way down, turn to snow, a reminder of the irrevocable colding and darkening of my home.

Sara thinks the Scott Monument looks like a spire, like something Cromwell might have lopped off an English church. It is kind of peculiar—the top of a wedding cake without the base—ungrounded sentiment. Here on Princes Street the feeling is so different from the Grassmarket, where people walk for commerce and gossip. On Princes Street, everyone's eyes fix not on the street, only on one another, simply to avoid collision. The world is coming or going. A man in a top hat with a brass-tipped cane. A mother and lad lugging parcels from Binns. What a peculiar place for a writer to sit, in the middle of a congested street. Perhaps Scott likes it that way. After all, as a novelist, Scott was meant to notice, not to be noticed.

## CHARLOTTE SQUARE

Who was Charlotte? Who is Charlotte? An English queen, most certainly. Father said we shouldn't name streets and monuments after the English. I'm always drawn here because of the odd, forbidden, mood. The name—so *un*-English—a painful, passionate, blood-red comes to mind. A loose woman. A live woman. Charlotte, scarlet, harlot, charlatan, charade, shady, sarcophagus.

Charlotte Square. Surname hollowed out of the life of the gorgeous given name. Square: those formal, grey, Robert Adam buildings. Sometimes, on errands, I make brief detours here. I like intruding in this silent domain of business and government, everything hardened and contained, the life carved away.

At the square's heart, within the fenced park, trees blaze with the character of Charlotte. I stand in a corner, ready to escape down the road, yet lingering over the seductive garden plot, wondering how many spirits Charlotte has gathered to keep her company, confined within this spikey fence.

### ST. GILES

St. Giles is the High Kirk. That's what I think whenever I look at it. Grey, ornate, but ugly in its ornateness. Father brought me here once, when I was very wee, maybe after my mother died. We sat in the back pew, quietly, for a long time.

On a chill day it would only be colder inside the church. Despite its authoritative air, St. Giles's history is anything but straight or clear or rigid. Once a medieval Roman Catholic church, it was named after an Athenian saint who moved to France and spent his last days in isolation with a Hind. (Does that mean a deer or a farmworker? I've always wondered. Which companion would be more humbling for a classy Greek?) St. Giles Church became a martyr in Richard II's fire in 1365. After its Catholic period, the place turned Anglican and was finally rescued to its present—and no doubt real—identity by John Knox.

They say the arm bone relic of St. Giles was sold with other plunder from the church's palmy days to pay for serious restoration—of one kind or another. Whenever I pass on the kirk side of the street, a deep unhappiness reaches out toward me. A finger pointing, beckoning, scolding.

### ROYAL MILE

One walk I'll miss almost as much as that along Princes Street is my Saturday stroll from the Lawnmarket to the High Street to Canongate. I like to imagine the processions of Scottish kings and queens from the Castle down to Holyrood House. I'm lucky to have been born in a historical city.

Here I take in the old, gabled roof. There's surprising vitality within the covert closes. This old town is ancient and delicate, yet in places thick with the same ruddy life I love down Leith Walk. Sometimes when sunshine pours over the buildings, the veteran stones reveal hidden glints of yellow.

Edinburgh is a city gold as well as silver. Everyone, it seems, has lived on one end of this high street or the other—Malcolm in the castle, Mary in Holyrood House. In between, Robert Burns in the Lawnmarket. John Knox, David Hume, Daniel DeFoe. Father used to love to walk along here with me, touring Scottish history. Today I came for history, but also to say good-bye to Milton House School. As I take in the solid grey and red-brown stone building, I feel grateful for my time here. Grateful for Miss Geddes. Grateful for the sight from the back classrooms of Arthur's Seat and the Salisbury Crags. How many other cities have a mountain in the middle? I think on my long walks over Calton Hill, through Campbell's Close, to this place where I was happier than I had ever been. I take one last look, and because I know it will not be long enough, I walk downhill past the next-door house with the stone inscribed: "1612. Blissit Be God in all His Giftis."

Some day, Father said often enough, you'll make *your* own mark. And now I am leaving, deserting, betraying the promises he made for me. Maybe I can make some modest claim in America. Or maybe I'll save enough to return here. What does one owe a parent? What dues? How much obedience? I know he'll always be with me. Yet as I walk along this street in the late summer of my twenty-first year, I know how time has changed my life. I'm no longer Father's lassie or Miss Geddes's pupil or—God forgive me—Colin's big sister. Moving into the polished air of Canongate, I feel sad because I can't forget Queen Mary's trials there at the base of Arthur's Seat and because I cannot remember all the Marys I, myself, have been.

## CALTON HILL

There's something stark about Calton Hill. A sad promise smiling thinly down on our busy pattern of black and grey. Perhaps since Father died I've needed some trace of authority. Yet, the weight of power here is fleeting. Monuments to Dugald Stuart, Admiral Nelson, the Nation. To our Greek heritage in Edinburgh, Athens of the North. They make a funny-looking set of chess pieces, not particularly graceful or well matched. Still, if they weren't here, I'd miss their sober presence.

This old hill is as good a place as any from which to look down on and say farewell to Milton House School.

## ROYAL INFIRMARY

It looks as if a baron should live here, as if he holds sumptuous dinners every night and fancy dress balls on holidays. I used to love this swooping, peaked building with the clock in the middle of its forehead. When I was small, I gawked at the skinny pairs of windows and the flutes on either side of the spire. I used to dream of living here, crocheting by a window under northern light.

Now, when I glance up at that second-floor window, I think "how sad, this was his ward." And I know that another person is living and dying there because Father made space for him. It's hard to remember—or even to imagine—that terrible day. Father is no more. This is where he left me, us, Colin and me.

This afternoon, I see a woman in an elaborate hat, carrying an armful of flowers. A daring bicyclist cuts his path across the pavement. Carriages, drawn by clomping, sweating horses, roll past the imposing front steps. A stream of inviting, warm blue smoke rises from the chimney.

Do they cremate the bodies right there, for efficiency's sake, to save space and to heat the buildings for those fancy midnight balls?

# CHAPTER SEVEN

# "Legacy"

## *Valerie, New Jersey, 1949*

MY MOTHER IS TALKING WITH A GREY, OLD WOMAN. A FAT PERSON. FACE lumpy like cold mashed potatoes. Mommy is skinny and eager, praising the rose garden. I am way down, near the sidewalk.

The flowers are boring. Bright smelling, but quickly boring. I look up at the fat woman's blue cotton skirt, at her legs descending, shapeless as pudding, to thick, black-laced shoes.

Still, they are chatting.

Mommy is tall today. So far away. Up there talking, forgetting me.

Nearby, children play under our front porch. Someday I will be big enough to do that.

Finally, we continue down the street, Mommy and I. She tells me not to pout, explains that the grey lady is our neighbor. I understand you have to be friendly with neighbors. It's part of being grown up. I'm more interested in playing under the house than in smiling at fat people.

*R*

### 1950

Falling, Mommy and I are falling.

Scared, I scream.

But her arms are around me.

The scream again, louder, a wail.

We are tumbling, heels over head, like a bumper car at Ashbury Park. Down the basement stairs. Down into the earth.

Am I pulling her or is she pulling me? Down, down, over the rubber-lined steps.

It's happening too fast. She can't stop us.

Bump. Bang.

Down, down.

Until we hit hard, on the cold, cement basement floor, after that special bottom step, the one that opens to store winter gloves and hats.

Mommy checks me first (Doesn't stop apologizing for thirty years.) She seems strangely happy (maybe just relieved she hasn't killed another baby).

Gradually, over the next week, she reckons she has broken her toe. But her daughter, her wee lassie, is all right, thank god. She never gets the toe fixed.

℞

### 1952

The aquarium has white angelfish and sparkling gold and black-striped ones. I can't remember all the names. Teddy has seen real ones, swimming in the wild ocean. It's funny to imagine an adult swimming. But Teddy lives in this basement Greenwich Village apartment and has a different life. Exotic, Mom tells me, laughing. I like words with x's.

Mom is talking to Teddy, my godmother, her best friend, leaving me to watch the fish.

They are drinking gin with little onions. Sipping something clear as aquarium water. Mom and Teddy are giggling, the two of them, together.

I sit there, prettily, as expected. I know there is something between them, a separate world. Outside, people walk by. All kinds of shoes. Exxxxxxciting to live underground like this, surrounded by tapping feet.

Teddy says *Our Gang* is on TV. I know I'm like that gawky Alfalfa and wish I had more of Spanky in me. The kids in *Our Gang* live a real life, in the back alleys of a big city.

Mommy and Teddy are laughing on the couch. Not at the television. How can adults talk this much? So boring. I will play more games when

I am adult. Their faces shine in the white fluorescent aquarium light and the yellow midafternoon sun flooding in from the street.

Nice to see Her happy like this.

꩜

## 1953

My brother Larry and I sleep with Mommy in our parents' bedroom. I love the friendly telephone and the sweet, dark scent of old mahogany bureaux. We never speak about periodic bloodstains on the big sheet. After all, we are used to Grandma's daily bandages, dark with pus as well as blood.

When Daddy is gone and the house is quiet, one of us snuggles up on each of Mommy's sides. In the morning, later than most mothers, she fumbles into the kitchen to make toast. Larry and I stay in bed and play house under the top white sheet.

Once or twice we talk about Mommy's death. We always know it is coming. We know she will leave us.

So we squabble, as siblings often do—over the inheritance. Who will get her arm bones? Who will get the legs?

# III

---

*Mae, 1896*

# CHAPTER EIGHT

## Mae, Edinburgh, 1896

MAE SHIFTED GENTLY IN THE BED, SO AS NOT TO WAKE JESSIE. WHEN SHE had seen Daniel today, it was as if someone had peeled away the bakery roof and let the sun pour in. She felt it by the shine on her skin, the easiness in the muscles of her back, the spirit with which she rearranged the cakes, the smile she bestowed on crotchety Mrs. Hamilton. Of course her worrying about his absence had been silly. Tomorrow night, twenty-two more hours, and she'd be meeting Daniel in the tearoom.

She had known he would return, had known that if she wore the pin and hoped, kept her eye on tasks, he would reappear, their dreams intact. Who was to say what *his* dreams were, where they diverged from hers? No one, not yet. Nothing had been promised. Still, she knew how often the feeling was truer than the saying—even when they contradicted one another. It wasn't until she lay in bed that night, Jessie snoring beside her, that Mae felt the fear. A deep shivering terror she had resisted these past months. What had she done to make him leave her? Done to him? Done before God? Did she deserve this intelligent, debonair—yes, that was the word—dashing man?

Nonsense. Her guilt was nonsense. He had explained the very good reasons for his absence. Modesty would have kept him from writing, from making assumptions. Would that she had the same humility. Her father had told her more than once that pride courted trouble. "Your independence!" he would exclaim, as if doubting her virtue. Of course, for a woman, virtue and independence were incompatible. He worried about her, he really did. Mae worried about Mam and the children, under Father's erratic reins when he had shore leave from the Merchant Marines. Yet things were easier now, with Uncle Davy back in Belfast. Mae was beginning to think worries had more to do with the character of the person worrying than with the person being worried about.

Despite her sister's ample warmth, Mae shivered in the bed. A big woman, Jessie was usually an ideal companion on cold nights. Mae shivered from fear, but that was odd, now that he had returned, now that she knew they would meet the next evening. In less than a full day. Her mind swung between despair and ecstasy. She needed this sleep, to be fresh for him tomorrow, but an invisible net held her back, held her up, away, apart. Now was the time to feel safe, she told herself; now was the time to close her eyes in relief, to rest and repair for future days.

Wind sliced through the casement, and the girl appeared, the one she had dreamed about. Was she dreaming now? Long dark hair streaming, the girl paced the shore of a grey ocean, in a faraway land, where the sun set over the water. She seemed unhappy, concentrating very hard. How odd. Yes, she must be sleeping now, if she were seeing the girl again. Yet when Jessie shook her in the morning, Mae felt stiff and too bright-eyed for having had a deep, dream-filled rest.

ℛℯ

A late summer afternoon at the bakery, and Mae stretched in the yawning expansiveness of it. She loved how the summer light invigorated Edinburgh, as if the world were on fire from the inside. She had muffed a few orders at work today, but hoped her general sunniness made up for it. Everyone left smiling. Everyone but Jock, who seemed oddly cautious, solicitous. He offered to walk her home and was more than disappointed when she politely declined. In fact, if she hadn't known better, she might have thought him angry.

On her way to the tearoom, she saw the dream girl again. She wore a proper skirt and blouse on this luscious warm night. There was something foreign but eerily familiar about her. The lass stood by Jenners' entrance, beckoning her. Yet she was sure this girl was no one she'd ever met, and she swiveled to discover the object of her agitation. A fat old man with a worn-down black cocker spaniel. The ancient man nodded to Mae respectfully, as one might to an *older* woman. Rudely, she looked away toward Jenners' entrance, but the long-haired girl was gone. Mae shook herself, resolving to sleep well tonight and hoping she would be alert enough to maintain intelligent conversation with Daniel.

It was just as she had wished. No time seemed to have passed. They sat across from one another, alone in the tearoom. Daniel talked avidly about the accountancy course. The war in South Africa. The turn of the century. His hopes to one day marry and have a family. In four years, it would be the 1900s and she would be twenty-one. Now *that* made her feel old.

"So what will you have?" he asked.

"Oh, China tea would be lovely, thanks."

"And a cake, which cake? The chocolate? The fruited one?"

"Och, no," she protested, because of the expense.

"Och, yes," he grinned. "You can't just order tea. That will make me look parsimonious."

Parsimonious. She liked the word. Persimmon, strangely she remembered a picture of that red-orange fruit, an image so contrary to the tightness of parsimony.

"No thank you," she demurred.

"Well, you look like a chocolate lass to me." He winked.

Bothered by the extravagance, she let him buy her a cake with tea, for the food would make her more alert. Daniel *was* a very lively talker. She thought of someone she knew, she couldn't remember who, who had married a dull man for safety and then tried to make him into an interesting man. She knew in this moment, knew as much as she knew anything in the world, that the only safety was *love*. And there would be no deeper love, admiration, passion than what she now felt for Daniel.

❧

Their romance flourished in the late summer, each day a confirmation of enlarging promise. When she found herself with him in the small, blue room in Crammond, her doubts were inconsequential currents to their magic glider, high, high in the winds.

He stroked her temple with his long, freckled fingers, felt round the back to her hair clasp to release the wheatened curls over her shoulders. Her hands roved his clean-shaven face; his lips sweetly brushed hers. Again. And again. The tongue licked her almost sealed mouth and entered slowly, surprising and confirming at the same time.

Rocking down to the bed with him, she felt his hand lightly cupped over her breast, and when he finally—finally, oh, who knew such desire existed—began to unhook her dress, she moaned with pleasure. Looking down at her, his eyes moved from concern to delight, and laughter roared up inside them.

That summer was so merry—much more a July and August word than a December word—that she hardly noticed the season passing. She wondered at her lovely, guiltless lust. And at their laughter that was, itself, a kind of marrying.

Mae kept a shell in her right pocket. Small, whitish-pink, translucent, a sweet memento, but also like a tiny knife. Sometimes she pressed her thumb against the sharp rim, aroused by the slight pain. Then she would skim her fingers over the delicately fanned ribbing. What would Daniel think if he knew that she treasured his gift from Crammond? Would he find it silly and sentimental? The touch of it brought back the cold smell of the North Sea, the slipping, foamy waves, the whole joyful memory of their stolen night.

She and Daniel talked about another trip to Crammond in October, and this carried her through the long, light nights.

# CHAPTER NINE

# "Family Conversation"

## *Chorus, 1865–1999*

THERE'S NEVER A BAD THAT COULDN'T BE A WORSE.
Well, you're a cheerful earful.
Enter the duke farting furiously.
She comes out of it without water.
He broke his arm and can't walk.
Remember to keep your pecker up.
She really knows how to roll her r's.
Round and round the radical road, the radical rascal ran, how many
    r's are in that?
She comes by it honestly.
That's j-u-n-k.
He looks like death warmed over.
There's no point dwelling on it.
Every country has its problems.
You do what you have to do.
This happens in the best of families.
I've brought a bonnie wee nothing with a tassel on the end.
Let's not and say we did.
He's worth the price of admission.
If you do that, you'll have to marry me.
Righto.
Ificky Iicky Hadicky Gunicky Iicky Wouldicky Shooticky Yonicky
    Manicky Onicky Yonicky Hillicky.
It doesn't bear thinking about.

There's no accounting for taste.
Some hae meat and canna eat.
"Common sense is the genius of the workingman," Rabbie Burns.
I'm shy but willing.
I have a cold in my eye.
Now where have you put the doings?
Don't be a dizzy Lizzie.
No one is a harder worker.
I feel like Stiffie the Goalpost.
You look like Skinny Millinky Long Legs.
If I were as shitty as I am witty, I'd be in a hell of a mess.
Toss those pants in the hamper before they walk there by themselves.
You sound like a common fishwife.
You can't take her anywhere.
I'll always be with you.

# CHAPTER TEN

# "Ship's Manifest"

## *Mary, Atlantic Ocean, 1930*

MANIFEST OF ALIEN PASSENGERS FOR THE
U.S. IMMIGRATION OFFICER AT PORT OF ARRIVAL

S.S. *Translyvania.*
Passengers sailing from Glasgow, 6 September 1930
Arriving Port of New York, 14 September 1930

ᖇᵒ

STEERAGE PASSENGERS

| | | |
|---|---|---|
| 1. | Number on list: | 30 |
| 2. | Head Tax Status | — |
| 3. | Family name: | McKenzie |
| | Given name: | Mary Gill |
| 4. | Age | 20 |
| 5. | Sex: | F |
| 6. | Married or single: | S |
| 7. | Calling or occupation | Waitress |
| 8. | Able to read: | Yes |
| | Read what language: | English |
| | Write: | Yes |
| 9. | Nationality (country of which citizen or subject) | Britain |
| 10. | Race or people: | Scottish |

11. Place of birth:
    Country:                          Scotland
    City or town:               Leith
12. Immigration Visa number:    12138
13. Issued at:                     Glasgow
14. Date:                           1/8/30
15. Last permanent residence
    Country:                          Scotland
    City or town:               Edinburgh
16. No. on list                  30
17. The name and complete
    address of nearest relative
    or friend in country whence
    alien came:                Sister:—Mrs. Bella Mathieson
                                        5 Hillview Terrace, Edinburgh
18. Final destination
    (*intended future permanent
    residence) State:         Ct.
    City or town:               New Haven
19. Whether having a ticket to
    such final destination:    N.Y.
20. By whom passage paid:    Self
21. Whether in possession of $50,
    and if less, how much?    $50.00 only
22. Whether ever before in United
    States and if so, where?
    Yes or no:                   No
23. Whether going to join a
    relative or friend; and if so,
    what relative or friend, and
    his name and complete address:  Brother-in-Law: Eric Alden
                                        420 Huntingdon Street, New
                                        Haven, Ct.
24. Purpose of coming to U.S.
    Whether Alien intends to
    return to country whence he

came after engaging temporarily
in laboring position in U.S.:    No
Length of time Alien intends
to remain in United States:    Perm.
Whether Alien intends to
become a citizen of U.S.:    Yes

25. Ever in prison:    No
26. Whether a polygamist:    No
27. Whether an anarchist:    No
28. Whether a person who believes
    in or advances the overthrow by
    force or violence of the govern-
    ment of the United States:    No
29. Whether coming by reason of
    any offer, solicitation, promise, or
    agreement, expressed or implied,
    to labor in the United States:    No
30. Whether Alien had been previously
    deported within one year:    No
31. Condition of health, mental
    and physical:    Good
32. Deformed or crippled. Nature,
    length of time, and cause:    No
33. Height
    Feet:    5
    Inches:    5
34. Complexion:    Fair
35. Color of Hair:    Brown
    Eyes:    Hzl.
36. Marks of identification:    None.

---

*Ship's Master:*    David W. Boul
*Ship's Flag:*    British
*Movement of ship:*    Londonderry to Glasgow to N.Y.

| | |
|---|---|
| *Ship's doctor:* | J. H. McDowell, performed "personal examination of each of the aliens named herein" |
| *Total passengers:* | |
| Aliens: | 1073 |
| U.S. Citizens: | 598 |
| First class: | 154 |
| Second class: | 229 |
| Third class: | 690 |
| *Crew at arrival:* | 425 |
| *Discharged:* | None |
| *Deserted* | 1, Lindsay Taylor, 46, British |
| *Left in hospital (or died)* | 2 |
| *Seamen signed at this port* | 11 |
| *Total crew this date* | 425 |

"Vessel is consigned to Cunard-Anchor Lines, New York; is now lying at Pier 56 N.R., and is expected to sail 20th September, 1930 for Glasgow, Scotland."

# IV

*Mae, 1897–1904*

# CHAPTER ELEVEN

# Mae, Edinburgh, 1897–1904

SHE WASN'T SURE UNTIL JANUARY. HER MONTHLY HAD NEVER BEEN monthly, but this was the first time she had skipped nine weeks. Besides, the morning illness seemed too regular. A curse to work amid the early bakery scents of butter and sugar and flour. A curse and a penance. She hated Jock's sober face every time she appeared looking a bit peely wally.

Resolution came gradually. Their next Crammond trip was at month's end. She would tell him then. As much as she might wish for a wedding six comfortable months after he set up his accountancy desk, he would be secretly pleased that she was carrying his son. There's never a bad that couldn't be a worse.

Meanwhile, when she could, Mae recouped her strength at the end of the day by visiting the Gardens before going home. Even in the winter chill it was a restful place if you got out of the wind. She would watch people, or just close her eyes and daydream. One late afternoon, midmonth, she was surprised by the sight of Daniel strolling on the other side of the walkway, holding the hand of a round-faced little girl. He had never mentioned relations in the city. Her stomach dipped and she began to perspire.

Automatically, she averted her glance, as if from a private moment, and concentrated on what Daniel had been saying last week about *The Heart of Midlothian*. He made the book come alive just in the telling. She was too shy to ask if he would teach her to read, but she knew one day she would. He also liked to recite poetry by Rabbie Burns. This she preferred to the Scott.

They were resting in their room, enjoying a cup of tea after the long journey from Edinburgh, longer in imagination than reality, an exhausting
trip.

Mae had two secrets: the baby and the memory of him in the
Gardens. She'd start with that, with how she relished seeing him without
him noticing her. For the reverse was often true, he had told her. Daniel
liked to watch through the bakery window while she was busy serving
customers.

She reckoned that sweet child as his niece, visiting from Ayr. Each of
his brothers had two girls, she knew that much about this man who was
at the center of her life.

Lightly, she began, mentioning the surprising warmth of that afternoon, the unusual busyness of the Gardens, and the odd coincidence of
seeing him—too far away for calling distance—with a pretty (she wasn't
pretty, more pleasantly plain, and as she made this distinction, her own
petulance shamed her) girl of twelve or thirteen.

Incredulity rounded his eyes.

Cheerily inquiring which brother was visiting and for how long, she
saw his face fall.

She waited. Then witnessed the life before them evaporating.

Momentarily, he returned, offering a hurtful fact, the only true expression of love.

Mae was with him and with herself, watching coolly as the cards fell.

"Not a niece. No, love. My daughter, Bella."

"But you've never mentioned . . . does she live with your parents in
Ayr? When were you married? How did your wife die?" she demanded,
gently, but firmly, her questions creating a story that left room for her.

Fatigue and defeat invaded their little room.

Not a widower, not a disaffected spouse with a long-ago wife back in
Ayr. But a husband. Father to a growing family.

She was weighted to the chair, nausea rising up. She smelled her own
dark perspiration and knew that while some men could dwell in their
imaginations, all women had to live in their bodies.

She didn't mention the baby, perhaps to protect him, perhaps to keep
something for herself. Mae looked around the room—the same one as the

last time, and the paper on the north wall had faded badly. She hadn't noticed the cheapness in this place before.

"Oh, no, oh, no," he railed, staring out the window as if he were addressing God and Fate and the Universe as much as Mae. "I should have stayed away. I tried. Tried to disappear. But everything got out of control."

Mae felt unaccountable anger when he spoke this way—as if she had nothing to say in the matter, as if everything had been *his* doing. Maybe the end of it was his, for surely there was no option other than ending. But the middle was theirs. They had made their love together. The memory would remain hers, and she would have to own this now if she were going to remember it later.

He paced back and forth by the window, conversing as if in a play.

"If only we hadn't met so late," he moaned.

He didn't know what late meant, she thought.

He stared out toward the river. "I could never love anyone as much as I cherish you."

"Still, still," he struggled, "I can't help but hope that our love isn't an impossible dream."

She bit her lip to keep from crying.

He asked forgiveness, a man starving for the full life he might share with her.

Mae stared numbly at the hideous wallpaper.

"*Now* was all there was," he declared, finally facing her. "Who were we hurting?"

Surely he must have known that by claiming his happiness in the present, he might rob Mae of her future.

"I'll never finish atoning for my sin," he said. "My sin. Not yours. At least I can be grateful you still have your youth, your whole life ahead of you."

Still, at that moment, she ached for him, knowing she must be a mad or a wild woman.

☙

1904

Jock was a good husband, a fine father, and she should be on her toes soon to fix him something special for tea.

She supposed she might have felt cheated years ago that there had been no baby (miscarriage was a word with many meanings), that the point of marrying Jock McKenzie had passed with a dramatic, painful swiftness, a punitive trick of Providence.

Jock was a good man. She knew she was fortunate. Fortunate that after she quit the bakery in shame, he tracked her down. That he made her leave that terrible job as a hospital ward maid and said he would support her and the bairn, who would be his own bairn if she married him. He would love him that much.

A trick made all the worse when Jock plaintively asked if, now that her reason for the wedding was gone, she would leave him. Strange and maddening to have this unwanted power. No, she knew then, seven long years ago, that she had had her brush with recklessness: She would make Jock a good wife and she would gladly bear his children. Now that they didn't have to spend each morning looking into the face of another man's child, they might have a happy family, indeed.

Again, Mae told herself to get up and fix the evening meal. She counted their blessings. Johnny was a sickly, but sweet, wee baby. And Danny (*He* had wanted to name him Danny after his own dad, no memory of their recent nightmare, and how could she deny him this? Mae just cursed the Scots' habit of family names and agreed to Danny)—Danny was a bright one, destined, she thought, to be some kind of teacher, with that patient intelligence. Chrissie brought light into the house, a bountiful laugh, and a knowing prettiness.

Mae was blessed, lucky to be absolved of her youthful mistakes. The youth, to which some women cling, she left willingly for matronhood. Eagerly, Mae headed toward middle age, putting on weight, allowing too much sun on her face. She was bound to be a mature woman and lead a competent, useful life for her husband and children.

# CHAPTER TWELVE

# "On Her Way"

## *Mary, Atlantic Ocean, 1930*

LYING IN MY NARROW BERTH, FRESH, WHITE SHEETS PULLED BENEATH my chin, I meditated about Mary Queen of Scots. Twenty-five when she was forced to abdicate, to leave her ten-month-old son behind. So much to forget, such faith she had in Elizabeth. Of course, my small, private story bore none of her nobility or suffering. Yet, I identified, despite her Catholicism and royalty. An odd preoccupation, some would say. Maybe I just admired her, aspired to that dignified courage. Light seeped into our cabin from the corridor. Two, perhaps three A.M. I was wide awake.

Turning in the gently swaying berth, I imagined pulsing in Mother's womb, surrounded in that tiny space by water—like this—warm and safe. I was lucky to get the bottom bunk. Yesterday the train journey from Edinburgh to Glasgow. Tonight, the Atlantic Ocean.

Ahead were days at sea to contemplate waves and think on America. I would step ashore in New York, the earth's most glamorous city—busy, loud, competitive, a place where everyone came from somewhere else and no one was a stranger long. Tonight I left my island, a truly tiny island, for a new, large world. Too thrilled for fear, my only difficulty was sadness, guilt at abandoning Colin. He was yet a wee boy—at fourteen—to be left so alone, but in recent years I didn't know how much use I was to him, us living so far apart. Besides, I was twenty, not getting any younger, a crucial time for women.

Berth. Romantically, I wanted to spell it "birth" because it seemed like that to me. I was lucky to have this chance. Lucky to have a job waiting for me in America at Mr. Cockburn's hotel—his "lodge in lovely

Connecticut." He had daughters my age who would introduce me to boyfriends. I would be part of the family. How well I was suited to family after all these years alone, I wasn't sure. But I did know how to get along with people.

American English was so different from Scots talk. Rougher. Hard to comprehend. You could have fooled me that it was English the Americans spoke, drawling their words. And I puzzled them, in the opposite way, I guess. They teased that we Scots spit our sentences. People said I had a burr, which sounded to me like a growth on the foot, but I understood what they meant. My words vibrated in the air long after theirs had vanished.

Here on the S.S. *Transylvania*, I was also lucky in my five cabin mates. The other girls were cheerful, friendly types; we had already learned so much about one another. Louise, a tall Manchester girl, was going to Ohio to marry her beau. Rosaline, the funny girl from Ireland, would live in Florida with her sister. Let's see, the others: Polly, Jenny, and my favorite, Teresa. This quiet nurse slept in the bunk above me, so confident, yet unobtrusive, in the way she scaled the ladder. Physical courage was not my strong point. I could throw myself into new worlds—the lodgings, Fairley's, a train to Glasgow, a boat to America—but climbing to the top bunk was beyond my daring. The other choices didn't feel so voluntary. I mean, you just moved ahead with life. You got up. You walked through the day. You went to bed. It didn't bear thinking about, really. Otherwise you couldn't sleep at night. And then it would be harder to get up the next morning.

Over breakfast, they teased me about a man, one of the ship's officers, as it turned out. They said he had been flirting with me last night. Now, in the light of day—well, not much light to this day—I could see what they meant. His dark eyes smiling for my attention. As if he had to try. This tall, beautiful Italian had all the girls drooling. Why wouldn't he go for gorgeous blond Jenny or buxom Rosaline? The truth was, I could be considered rather plain: a medium-sized girl with medium brown hair, slightly protruding teeth. On the positive side, I did have lucky skin—or people always told me so—and interesting enough, if small, hazel eyes.

*ℛℯ*

"You are a lively one," he laughed.

"Giovanni Moretti, Purser," the badge revealed.

His long, blunted fingertips touched my palm as he handed back the passport.

"Thank you, Giovanni."

"Gianni," he said

"Pardon?" I blushed

"Gianni," he repeated, leaving moist nests of air between the syllables. "It is how my friends and family call me."

"Pat," I said because I had always dreamed of being called Pat. "At home they call *me* Pat." Home where I was going. In Connecticut, they would call me Pat. Such an American name: short, no-nonsense, to the point. My new self.

He looked puzzled, scanning my documents for signs of this name. "Pat."

When he repeated the name after me, I was disappointed that it sounded a little silly. Not the name, really, but the way he said it.

"I shall, if you like, call you 'Pat.'"

"I would like that very much." Already I felt a strange new power in the naming.

ℛℯ

"So instruct us," coaxed Louise. We were both tucked in our bunks again after the first full day at sea. "What did you do to turn on the light in Leonardo's eyes?"

"Giovanni," I said, unwilling to reveal my new intimacy with "Gianni."

"He likes her liveliness," laughed Teresa, and I wondered if she had somehow overheard our conversation.

"It's true, Pat," said Rosaline. "Mediterranean types go for a quick wit."

Did I have a quick wit? I felt happy. Lively. At the crest of life. Here I was: young, free, healthy, setting off on the Big Adventure. I remembered Bella telling me to take my fears and turn them into excitement, that all nervousness was made of the same stuff, you had to view it as a natural resource. I could sense this working. I was lighter. Taller.

"Well, Giovanni is stunning, but I have my eyes on that Glasgow waiter," said Jenny.

"The bloke with red hair?" asked Rosaline.

"I've made my claim," Jenny pulled a stern face.

"Enough said," nodded Rosaline compliantly.

That evening, back in our cosy cabin, we all laughed, and my pleasure in this wacky gaggle was mixed with an odd sadness at how much I had missed by not living with the sisters from Mother's and Father's other families. Imagine a whole life of companionship. Well, I did have a whole life ahead of me.

A shrill whoop from Jenny at something Teresa said. The others joined in, laughing.

We heard a loud thudding on the ceiling from the room above.

"Cranks," whispered Jenny, about the two old maids who lived in that cabin. One, apparently, was a published author and the other a professor. They looked to be in their forties or fifties, a dull, puddling age.

Still, after two more naughty jokes, we did turn out the lights, and I fell into a luxurious, exhausted sleep, as if I had accomplished something that day—aside from sailing twenty-four hours closer to the rest of my life.

℞

Days swam by and back again, some fleeting and others impossibly slow. I came to revise my taste for togetherness and for the girls individually.

Louise was a lovely looking woman, but what a chatterer. She had been everywhere, done everything. If you spoke about waitressing, she had waited on tables; if you talked about having crushes on older men, she revealed her three-year affair with a former schoolteacher. She had lived in cities and towns and villages. It was sad; because she was saying it all to make you like her, make you think she was OK because you had had this or that in common. She used a loud, cheerful voice, as if trying mightily to lift everyone's spirits.

Polly revealed herself to be someone who took all the air out of a room. First with her cigarettes and then with her words. Poverty, we had no idea of poverty if we hadn't lived in London. The East End was a mess, especially during the War, especially after the War. People didn't understand how badly they had suffered—water supply, transport, rations. Regardless of the subject, she turned all the light in our little cabin back on herself with another story about her large, Cockney family. When we played word games, she complained that they excluded her—that we were talking in unintelligible accents or using references she couldn't possibly know—as if we'd all attended the same posh public school in Oxfordshire. What bothered me most was the way she had other people do things for her—pour her water, buy a sweet—because she felt lost on this strange ship. Perhaps something was missing deep inside me for I couldn't bring myself to be a helpful fairy, but well, she'd suck the life from you.

*◈*

Of course, my mind was on other things. He called at our cabin to return a form he had mistakenly kept.

He grinned, delivering my document, bowing as he exited, in playful courtliness.

"Mistakenly, sure," smirked Jenny, whose lightheartedness was weathering the test of time. I could imagine having a seaside holiday with Jenny when I was seventy.

Clipped to my immigration form was a note, which I took to the lavatory to read: an invitation to meet on the deck for a stroll at 9 P.M.

This was a bad idea.

After all, he probably plucked a new shipboard romance with every voyage. Maybe his first three choices had rejected him and that's why he was only now inviting me for a promenade. Even if I were fool enough to believe he could be serious, what future was there with a sailor? No, when I married, it would be a solid businessman or a teacher—someone intelligent, stable, kind, in a safe, reliable job. Lord Byron had never appealed. I was seeking Jon Anderson, my jo, Jon. Still too young for marriage, I was at the perfect age for romance. Finally, I allowed myself to go because I hadn't had any exercise in two days and because the man might teach me something useful to know about ships.

"In Napoli," he walked close to me, "we call this the *passeggiata*."

"*Passeggiata*," I strained after the musical syllables.

Softly, he corrected my pronunciation, "*Passeggiata*."

I nodded, stupidly not knowing what I had said wrong, but knowing that his lips transformed the word.

"Napoli is like Edinburg, no, with the hills and the water."

"Edinburgh," I said, "we pronounce the end somewhat mysteriously."

"I like mysterious."

If he was looking for mysterious, I was the wrong girl. But I laughed, playfully; because I didn't want Gianni to think I was mocking him.

"Well, the *differences* between Scotland and Italy come more readily to mind. But we do have a beach." I thought back on that day long ago with Father and Colin, a sunny, rock-pink Saturday. "Portobello," I said, to keep my mind from going too far back—and because I was pleased at the Latin syllables, so much more graceful, for instance, than a name like "Crammond."

"Is Italian, no?"

"Aye," I laughed. "Maybe you're right. Maybe they are the same, Edinburgh and Napoli."

We stopped now, near the stern, and peered out at the roiling blackness, up at the brilliant sky.

"Bella," he said.

"Yes," I nodded at the Milky Way.

I had never known so many stars. The city lights, Father always said, it's a pity how little you can see at night because of the street lamps' reflection. Father was always promising to take us to Ayr, to show us a world rich with textures and colors, with green velvet hills and glittering stars. I imagined Connecticut to be like Ayr, a place where you could make an ordinary, good life.

"I have something for you, Pat." He held out a small, beautifully wrapped sweet.

"Thank you." I opened it slowly and found a note inside folded around a jewel-like chocolate.

"It's called 'Baci,'" he said, taking the message. Then, striking a match for light, he read, "You will find joy."

"Oh." I was flustered. Joy. And to switch to a safer subject, I said, "*Baci.* A pretty word. Does it mean something?"

"*Baci,*" he said slowly, "*baci* is kisses."

Abruptly, I pointed to the sky. "The North Star. I always have trouble locating the North Star."

He kept his eyes on my face. "You know what I first noticed about you, Pat?"

I shrugged, honestly baffled that he had noticed me at all with the likes of Rosaline and Louise and Jenny about.

"Your hands. I notice the soft, long fingers of your hands."

I studied these hands I had never thought about in one way or the other. Functional, not small, not large, average hands. Staring out at the sea, I saw the silver moonline unfurled alongside our ship.

He reached over with his strong right hand and squeezed mine, moving waves from the ocean into my body, a sensation so strong it was almost painful. With my other fist, I gripped the cold, steel safety railing.

&

Next day, the girls all wanted my story. At least Rosaline and Jenny did. Louise was happy to entertain us all with elaborate fantasies of my Neopolitan wedding, each of them bridesmaids standing atop Mt. Vesuvius, throwing camellias into the volcano. It did sound ridiculously wonderful.

Polly, on the other hand, was worried. What did I know about this man? Who would discover if he took me somewhere strange on the ship and had his way with me?

"Pat would discover it!" laughed Jenny.

Polly ignored her, telling us about an East End friend who went off with a Russian sailor and was never seen again. She knew yet another girl who got syphilis—and worse. The places these sailors had been, you didn't want to know.

They took the life out of our cabin, those two, the perfect mirror images. Louise was lifting us high, high on her false cheer, while Polly was frantically pulling us down, reminding us of life's dangers in her dull, fat sadness.

Jenny winked at me, and it was her face I remembered when I agreed to meet Gianni again.

&

Polly *was* right; Gianni did know secret parts of the ship, or at least places unimaginable to me. The fourth night, he took me to First Class. When I protested, because there were signs everywhere warning us not to leave our deck, he patted my arm. "Don't worry, just pretend you belong there. That is the secret of being a traveler. Always act as if you belong."

I was beginning to understand this.

So I tried not to look astonished at the enormous differences on this deck, two worlds above mine. The chairs were padded, attended by footstools and little glass side tables. The women wore mink and marten necklets. Old men walked with engraved canes. We paused by the dining room, where uniformed waiters scurried around clearing off the tables, each of which was graced with balloons and silver chafing dishes and giant floral displays.

"The blossoms! Where do they get the flowers? They're fresh!" I sounded like a country cousin, a peasant cousin.

"*Si*," he smiled. "Every day, new ones."

I refused to ask another stupid question. But he saw the incredulity in my face.

"The ice boxes. They have two ice boxes just for the bouquets."

This made me both amazed and angry. The waste, the wonderful extravagance of ice boxes just for flowers. Well that was what people said about Americans: They made themselves at home in the world and put too much meat on their plates.

He showed me the turquoise swimming pool. Took me past the lounge where a group of four Negro musicians was playing jazz. In the corridor, I noticed how far apart the cabin doors were.

Still, when he turned his key and opened the light on a room, I was astonished by the hugeness of it. And by the clever, versatile world of bookcases and closets, the wall opening out into a private lavatory with a sweet, wee sink. The couch that turned into a bed.

*Re*

The last three days of our voyage were more spacious for Louise and Polly and Teresa. Rosaline and Jenny also found blokes. We would use the cabin to change our clothes, but the others had it to themselves at night. Strangely, Teresa kept the top bunk, although it was clear enough I wouldn't be needing the lower.

"Three bad girls," we called ourselves, and (while it's true I wouldn't want my daughter behaving like this, that I would never tell her about my reckless youth) our merry affairs were rather tender and innocent. And they kept us busy enough. Too busy to fret about departures and arrivals, to miss people and places, or to fear our fragile futures. The year 1930 was a bad time to immigrate to America, people told us, people with choices. On that ship I found an odd security, an immunity from harm in the real world, because, after all, I had left the real world behind and was casting out toward possibility.

I also learned these things: Once you have slept in a first-class compartment, you know you belong there. In the new world, you imagine a new past as well as a new future. I learned to steer around the talkers, to keep a joke at the ready, to savor the Italian language, and to look for a message in each kiss. It was on this whale of a ship that I would drop all unhappy memories into the fathoms. I was now Pat McKenzie, waking into my dreams.

# CHAPTER THIRTEEN

# "Red Shoes Mama"

*Valerie, New Jersey, 1950s*

SHE IS GONE. OFF WITH LILY OR GERRY OR SOMEONE WHO HAS A CAR. Grandma is taking care of us, or we are taking care of her. It's fine. I am eight years old already and I understand.

My brothers watch cartoons. Grandma, Daddy's mother, is cooking. I am playing dress-up in Mom's bedroom. It's really my parents' bedroom, but when Daddy is at sea, it becomes her bedroom. A big, light, airy place at the back of the house, separated by a floor from the upstairs bedrooms. It's not a very private room, and I feel easy about entering while she's gone. I do close the door because I'll be changing clothes.

First I try on the hats, those close-fitting, feathered hats. Mom has two—yellow and green. The green looks better with my eyes and skin. Then I put on one of her fancy slips and suddenly I am draped in a luxurious ballgown. These satin and lace slips are so pretty, I wish my mother would wear them out—to the theatre or a night club—but Mom doesn't go out. And in the bottom drawer, that fabric Dad sent from Argentina, as if he forgot she couldn't sew. The bright blue and red and green—same color as the hat—material is a little scratchy, but it will work handsomely as a shawl. Now a pair of red shoes from the closet.

There, I stand admiring myself in her mirror and seeing—as I look closely—myself reflected a hundred times (although I stop counting after five) in my father's mirror on the taller bureau across the room. This double reflection is disconcerting, so I try to ignore it, concentrating on the angle of my hat and a detail in the lace bodice. Closer, I lean into he mirror.

Minutes pass. I must wait for the right moment. Finally, the cameras start rolling. Local stations from across the country have tuned in and I modestly introduce myself. Valerie Miner, child star, here to testify to the beauty aid of Ivory Soap. It really is 99.44% pure. So pure it floats.

On Tuesdays I endorse Ponds' Cold Cream.

≈

## 1956

We are driving home in the dark from cousin Ginny's. I am thinking about poor, plain cousin Jane, who never married. My brothers are fighting in the back seat. I feel cold in the front, seated between my parents. Dad's at the wheel, smelling of that last Scotch.

He swerves and Mom grabs my arm.

Dad winks at her, in safe control of the wheel, of his family.

"Let's sing," she says, gently releasing her grip.

He groans good-naturedly.

"She wheeled a wheel barrow / through streets wide and narrow . . ."

He joins us. "She was a fishmonger / And small was the wonder / Her mother and father were fishmongers too."

He quickly tires, falls silent, stares at the road ahead.

She turns to "A roamin' in the gloamin' / On the bonny banks o'Clyde . . ."

I am puzzled about fishmongers and gloamins, but this is not the time to ask. She's just got started.

Now the car is warming up. My father lights a cigarette, spicing the whiskey smell. We are a family, I tell myself, safe from the cold, singing our way home. Together.

"'Abdul a Bull Bull,' Mommy, sing that one," I plead.

My brothers, still tussling in the back seat, could care less.

Again, I have no idea who Abdul a Bull Bull is, but I love his name and I understand my friends' families don't sing these ancient songs. I know this is something special from my mother.

"The sons of the prophet are brave men and bold / And quite unaccustomed to fear /—But the bravest of these in the ranks of the Shah / Was Abdul Abulbul Amir."

Daddy laughs at her squeaky voice. I am frightened she will fall silent.

Instead, she joins him, laughing. "My father scoffed too." She likes to talk about her father. He was a wonderful man. "Vile Infidel, know, you have trod on the toe / Of Abdul Abulbul Amir."

He is laughing louder.

Mom pauses. "Father would look at me and say, 'Mae, your voice! How is it earthly possible?'"

She is laughing, singing again.

My brothers have grown quiet.

We all listen to the final verse.

"They fought all that night 'neath the pale yellow moon / The din, it was heard from afar, / And huge multitudes came, so great was the fame, / Of Abdul and Ivan Skavar."

Too soon, Daddy pulls into the garage and we are home.

᯽

### 1957

Her feet carry an interesting, sour—almost decaying—smell. She doesn't sweat anywhere else, she tells me and it isn't until much later that I see this dryness is a point of pride. The family accepts her foot sweat as a fact of life. Another distinction, like being a Protestant, only not as worrisome.

Truly, it isn't a bad odor. Still, when she takes off her shoes, we all say, "P——hew" and giggle. I watch to make sure she is smiling with us.

Tight shoes, she warns.

Since I was five, I've been advised never, never to wear tight shoes. She believes my double-A foot with its quad-A heel is one of the miracles of reproduction. Ours is not to reason why, she says, nodding fondly and a little enviously, at my dainty feet.

Vanity, she confesses, squeezed her tender toes into narrow vessels. Red shoes. Too many red shoes. Small feet were gifts of God; they could not be cultivated. Examining Mom's poor, barnacled toes, I make a silent vow to avoid tight pumps.

Grandma and the boys are watching TV. Mom pretends to enjoy *Sergeant Bilko,* but she is observing me as I kneel before her with a plastic basin of warm water carefully placed on old newspaper. Unraveling a roll of white toilet paper, I play nurse, call this "doing Mom's feet."

First, I wash her toes over the basin, Ivory soap and warm water on the face cloth.

"Oh, that feels good," she sighs.

Then the serious bandaging. Concentration. A little water, a lot of tissue (I keep waiting for her to complain about the waste of paper, but she never does).

"Oh, that feels good."

Soon, she has mummified feet, bandaged in TP, her yeasty odor dispelled for another day. The boys and Grandma dutifully admire my treatment, during the commercial.

These days, I wish I had asked her, "Where were you going in those tight, red shoes anyway?"

# V

---

*Daniel, 1906–1907*

# CHAPTER FOURTEEN

## Daniel, Edinburgh, 1906–1907

YOU COULD HAVE LET IT GO, AS YOU HAD THE OTHER TIMES YOU SAW HER.

By now you were accustomed to following your feet, one step in front of the other, back and forth between home and work, work and home. Now that you were spending more time with family, the children seemed less colicky. Maggie was wonderful: after your mother died, helping you grieve, sorting the household things. Your brothers pointed out that you were a lucky man to have this generous woman who wore time and children and god knew what trials you gave her, with charming grace. Yet, their teasing was deferential, since you were the oldest. This elder station left you no one in whom to confide.

When wee Mae was born, your brothers smirked. Maggie grinned. And the name? One last hold on memory, a memory that would be the only freedom you could ever know. Of itself, a beautiful name, after May, you suggested, the month she was born. Maggie liked it too, she was liking everything nowadays. You knew you were a lucky man who had been spared disaster.

It was the year after this birth that you saw her, walking along Broughton Street with Jock McKenzie. She was listening intently and you heard his low, whiney voice. You hoped she would—and wouldn't—look up at you across the road. As you battled with yourself—believing your own will could determine her glance—she kept her eyes on Jock, nodding attentively.

Then, a July afternoon down by the Lawnmarket. Of course you didn't go near that place anymore. In fact, your children knew you had a superstition about the neighborhood. Being there that afternoon was accidental, of course; it happened like this:

You had just taken your brother Colin to Waverley Station. He had come to Edinburgh for a short visit before he took his family on assisted passage to Australia. (No sense staying around this pokey country, and with only two children, immigration was possible). It was all so disorienting, your baby brother, the adventurer, that you must have wandered distractedly down to the forbidden Lawnmarket. Sure enough, just what you had avoided all these years was dropped in front of you.

She held the hands of two wee boys outside the bakery window, waving at that painful man in the white hat. She was there, just five yards away, looking even more womanly than you remembered, with a fuller figure, her golden hair wrapped high against a blue-ribboned clasp.

You slipped away unnoticed.

The next sighting was completely unpredictable, unavoidable. Everyone used the GPO once in a while, and you had gone, innocently, obediently enough, with Christmas scarves Maggie had knitted for Colin's children. No matter that they were living in a desert, as Alex and Matt tried to instruct her. A nice piece of knitting was always a welcome present (and light enough to post without paying a fortune). This conviction of how things should be—in the face of drastically opposite evidence—was one of the things that was so magnificently tedious about Maggie.

It was a lively September afternoon and, shifting from one foot to another, you noticed a blond woman juggling a baby while stamping several envelopes and keeping two small lads in tow. I don't know if you understood this, but if you had lifted away your eyes a flicker earlier, she wouldn't have felt your glance pulsing up her neck. She wouldn't have turned, wouldn't have focused on your familiar face.

You registered her alarm as she stared down at her children, recovering equanimity. How she smiled, actually smiled, gave you a completely undeserved smile of pleasure.

"Mammy, who is that man?"

Alarm recaptured her face, a fainter nervousness, but still enough to make her collect the letters. Mae ushered the children outside without looking back.

# CHAPTER FIFTEEN

# "New World Diary"

## *Mary, U. S. A., 1931*

### 26 JANUARY 1931 / CONNECTICUT

Father always said I should be a writer. I don't think he had in mind a green cardboard diary. Well, I may not be Robert Burns, but recording the day is a way of passing time.

The sun is bath-warm, flooding this cold, solid road which links farm to farm as sheets are pinned on a clothesline. Neighbors, buffeting the winds, work beside—yet separate from—one another. From a freshly mown January land rises the smell of wild onions, a green and sour pang. The bleaching light of matins (it's very Anglican here; Episcopal, they say) strips the trees of color, makes them sing from within themselves. Harsh, brilliant whiteness cloaks their trunks. Roots reach out, fingers from the coffin too quickly shut, grasping, pointing toward something distant. Dogs guard the tiny houses when it suits them, barking as if you were the tax collector or a burglar. Yesterday two retrievers snuggled together for warmth, sleeping in a sweep of dead leaves at the roadside. This last light is clear, almost expectant. Something about the frozen nakedness of winter makes me feel secure because at least the weather can get no harder.

### 29 JANUARY 1931

Stubbed blades of yellow straw persist through the snow. In fact last week's lush, white carpet is almost a memory, so thin, pocked by water holes. Sad, yet I wonder why I root for the snow, which is, after all, just dead water. Inhospitably brittle, frozen water. Does Scottish melancholy attract me to this blanket of ice? Bright sun, with its quick melting, makes me blasphemously imagine my parents, tucked tightly beneath solid Edinburgh, waking up to find me gone.

As I walk, carts trundle past. The drivers often pause and ask if I need a ride, ask if I am OK. Americans are friendly that way, in the moment, but there's a separateness to the lives here.

Something about this light today—the reflection of deep blue sky against glaring white earth under butter yellow sun—has turned the beech limbs and trunks a spectral green. Faint promise of spring in the long dead winter still ahead. Above I am surprised by two grey birds—doves?— with coral crowns. They are almost as striking against the blue sky as the red cardinals are against the snowy hill behind Mr. Thompson's barn.

### 31 JANUARY 1931

Not much point in recording my life. There's nothing to it, really: waking, eating, dressing, serving lunch and dinner at the cafe. On Saturday, getting a new book from the library. The life that counts right now is outside me. I know I'll find it in this strange landscape of my future. Otherwise, all I have is memory, and I want a rest from that.

### 1 FEBRUARY 1931

Just a day, and three-quarters of the snow has melted, the plough ruts now visible again in this durable ground. Last week's stubble looks older, a weary gold, pale as a grandfather's face hair. The roadside houses seem less peaceful today, less minding of their own business. Dogs bark from everywhere at every sound. Now that the quiet blanket has melted, they are on guard again.

I like my room at the top of Mrs. Ferguson's spare house—the warmth, the rosiness, the amazingly huge space of it. Yet in some peculiar way, I miss Auld Reekie and the anonymous reassuring city sounds, the shroud of filthy smoke. This place is both too quiet and too noisy: the dogs, the birds, the lonely limp of a buggy wheel along the unpaved road. I've never seen so many birds, and Mrs. Ferguson has two names—Latin and American—for each one.

I try to imagine living in one of these houses permanently, as Mrs. F. does, even one of the small, two-storey places, alone in the howling winter wind and cold grey light. I suppose it's all in what you're used to, and she was born here. As were her parents and theirs. But it gives me the willies just to picture it. Unless, of course, I had my husband next to me and my children across the hall.

Occasionally, before I take the path up to Mrs. Ferguson's solid oak door, I pause and look east, back to Scotland. Then west, deeper into this wild continent. I wonder what direction I'll take, where I'll find him.


3 FEBRUARY 1931

Now that the snow has gone, I see it's left behind not only color but depth, shape, size. There is a way that snow, in its silence, mutes other senses as well. The numb quiet is not restful.


6 FEBRUARY 1931

More snow falls, sticks, lingers on the hard, frozen earth, and I know I am a profoundly impatient person. Connecticut is so closed. So cold. Edinburgh never got such chill, the pavements melting from the footprints, all those bodies sailing back and forth. So different from here, where you can walk two miles and not see a soul except the cardinals and the juncos. The birds have raided the busy holly trees at the turning to Miss Higgenbotham's pond. They are that hungry. That cold. Colder than I am. This is useful to remember.

# CHAPTER SIXTEEN

# "My Life With the Windsors"

## *Valerie, North America, 1953–1990*

I ALWAYS THOUGHT MOTHER LOOKED LIKE QUEEN ELIZABETH. THE Second. Attractive, although not pretty, in that clean-scrubbed, long-nosed way. Both were small figures with swept-back hair. Open-faced, no-nonsense. The kind of woman who enjoyed giving directions, but would say straight out if she didn't know where you were going. My best friend from the fifth grade, Carol, told me one summer (thirty-seven years after the fact) that she used to think my family was rich because my mother made such large ham sandwiches for lunch.

I liked to think Queen Elizabeth was also generous with her subjects. As I grew older, I came to see that it was the other way around. They stocked *her* larder. In recent years I've been disappointed by the Queen's petulance about paying taxes. It's time for the twentieth century to catch up with her after all. There have been other disappointments: the Corgis, truly ugly dogs; those boring horses; the horse-faced children; and some of the hats. Still, over the years, I've felt a twisted filial pride in Elizabeth's dignified but pleasant dresses (both she and my mother look good in blue); her low-key, powdered-nose presence at state events; and the unflustered way she responded to the intruder she found sitting by her bed in Buckingham Palace. (I would have screamed.) So fond have I become of Elizabeth in this strange family projection that I'm always horrified when she opens her mouth and I hear that pinched, upper-class English accent.

Re

Our connection with the Windsors is first revealed to me at age six, in late May, 1953, a week before the coronation of ER II. A package arrives in our New Jersey home from Aunt Bella, a Canadian cutout book with cardboard models of Princess Elizabeth and the Duke of Edinburgh as well as beautifully colored facsimiles of the royal carriages. I remember those best—body by Fisher—impressed that this was the same firm that constructed our neighbor's car. Mom regards the gift with shifting emotions—delight, disturbance, humor, as if Aunt Bella has sent pornography through the international mails. OK, she says finally, I can look through the book, but cannot cut out the figures until the actual coronation date. This will be televised on our new Magnavox, which has recently shown us pictures of Edmund Hilary climbing Mount Everest and the American government testing nuclear bombs.

Anticipation thickens by the day. Like Christmas, this coronation reveals that our family is more than my brothers, my parents, Grandma, and myself. As Mom and I bake cinnamon cookies for the big event, she reminisces about Scotland, that Protestant place she is from, where Aunt Bella is also from. This is the first time I hear about the new aunt who lives in Canada, where we might visit one day. Once in a while Mom mentions another aunt or uncle, out of the blue. Canada, Mom explains, is not as far away as Scotland. And it is in a different direction—a northern place that's very cold.

I wonder if Aunt Bella is pretty. My mother isn't pretty, and I'm just coming to terms with this. In fact, I am becoming preoccupied by prettiness. Recently I have decided that since God is fair, He will make me pretty as I grow older, to compensate for my extreme ugliness at age six. I propose this logic to my mother, who smiles and shakes her head. "But you're a very pretty little girl. And you'll be a stunner when you grow up." This isn't true: I am pudgy and freckled and my new front teeth are coming in at a forty-five-degree angle.

Perhaps I am obsessed by beauty because of the TV actresses now streaming into our house or the omnipresence of Virgin Mary statues—another lady who looks nice in blue—at church and school. Perhaps it's those young nuns' pink faces, plucked forward by their wimples, the holy card visages of clear, piercing eyes and turned-up noses. Most likely it's the comparison I make between my thin, formal mater and the mother of my best friend, Gerry Kliemisch. Mrs. Kliemisch is as pretty as the nuns, but also warmer, looser. She smells of vanilla or pickles or hot chocolate, while my mother smells of cigarettes and Tide. She washes the dishes in Tide because it's silly to waste time on two kinds of detergent. Mrs. K.— who is always smiling in the kitchen with one of her seven children pulling at her skirt—seems the ideal, pretty mother, and for an entire week, every night, I kneel down beside my bed and pray that God will give me a pretty, Catholic mother.

Suddenly one morning when I am home sick from school, perhaps overwrought by the frenzy of coronation preparation, I realize that if God gives me a pretty mother, I will lose Mom, whom I love, in spite of everything. I don't want another mother after all. Will God let me take back my prayers? I become obsessed that He won't. From everything I hear in school, He is a make-up-your-mind kind of guy. What have I done? There are two people I can ask—Sister Margaret and Mom. But I'm too sick to ask Sister Margaret, and this heavy burden won't wait until I get well. Anything could occur by then.

And so, although I know this could hurt my mother's feelings, I confess what may happen to me, to us. She is sitting on my bed, blowing on the Campbell's tomato soup to cool it down for me. Slowly she explains, as she often does, that I shouldn't fret so much. God isn't going to trade her in for another mother. Everything will be fine. She offers me a spoonful of the bloody soup.

I am sobbing. "I'm sorry. I'm sorry." I swallow some soup and moan, not knowing whether my sin has been insult or betrayal, but understanding that my sin has been against her, not against God.

"Don't fret," she says again, "You're always worrying about something."

I have recovered by Tuesday, 2 June, the Big Day. Mom has got me excused early from school for this historical event. We've set the cookies and a large bottle of Pepsi on the living room table, our stubby altar in front of the hallowed television tabernacle.

Grandma, my Dad's mom, retires upstairs; as an Irishwoman she'll have no part of this sacrilegious tripe. Still, to this day, I don't know if her objections were religious or political—or whether for her this was an important distinction. Her room is right above the parlor, and soon we hear the familiar, almost comforting sounds of her manic rocking and muttering. Praying, Mom tries to persuade me Grandma is praying, but I know the difference.

Together Mom and I open Aunt Bella's book and leaf through every page before I pick up the scissors. Where should I start? The spectacular vestments? The bouffant silk dresses? The gleaming jewels? The fur-lined robes?

"It's not a happy life," Mom warns me, as if I'm in danger of running off to marry a prince.

I watch her carefully because I have come to know that if my mother isn't a pretty mother, she is a very smart one.

"There are so many duties."

Again, the ornate carriages catch my attention, and I wonder what progress the automobile represents. Who would choose one of those smelly, dirty, oversized bowling balls when you could ride in an airy, gilded vehicle pulled by sensuous grey horses?

"Our milk was delivered by horse-drawn carriage when I was a little girl," my mother muses.

I laugh, thinking of Mr. Munson's white dairy truck turned into a cart.

Mom is taken aback, then notes it's almost time for the ceremony to begin. Not wanting to miss a moment, we watch five minutes of test pattern before an image of Westminster Abbey appears.

"That's where Mary Queen of Scots is buried," my mother murmurs.

Because I can't tell if she's talking to me or to herself, because I know nothing about this particular saint, I peer at the screen, waiting for Princess Elizabeth in the newsreel footage.

Her size is disappointing. I have hoped for something more magical, or majestic, or miraculous in front of our altar of home-baked treats. Maybe I expected her to pop out of the television. I am painfully conscious of the royals as miniatures in the rectangular box.

The first shots, of course, are background. Even a six-year-old knows this isn't the main event. We watch Princess Elizabeth in her diamond wedding tiara with the dark sash across her strapless ballgown. The tall, handsome Duke of Edinburgh hovers nearby. Then shots of the princesses together—the reserved, alert Elizabeth and the sultry-eyed Margaret— with their sweet-faced, pigeon-bodied mother. Charles is my brother's age, but looks both younger and better dressed. Anne, with her golden curls and inquisitive eyes, reminds me of Rosemary, my favorite doll. Altogether, a family a six-year-old can identify with.

Aware of the strange silence (TV noise was becoming crucial to family conversations, as if we would talk only with a witness in the room), I notice my mother studying the screen like a difficult book. Usually she maintains detached curiosity about television and the Catholic Church.

Suddenly the TV is transformed with Coronation Day fanfare. All of London has turned out to catch a glimpse of royal metamorphosis. Half the world has joined them: heads of state from Europe, Africa, Asia. Mother points out Nehru and Menzies and Churchill.

My favorite is Queen Salote of Tonga, who rides, smiling, through the rain in an open-air carriage. At six-foot-three inches, she is the world's tallest queen. Her confident smile is cherubic in a triumphal, archangel way—as if all the traffic and cheering and cameras are for her.

Mom nudges me when the McKenzie Highlanders appear, thrumming and piping down the street in their funny kilts. "Ah, look, they're wearing our dress tartan. It's too bad you can't see the colors, such a lovely mix of blue and red."

I am puzzled. The plaid picnic blanket takes on new meaning.

"We're McKenzies. That's my maiden name. Those men are Scots, see their kilts?" She is disappointed that I haven't picked up nationality by osmosis, one more unmentioned or unmentionable thing that I'm supposed to have intuited.

Yes, of course, I understand that a long time ago, my mother came from Scotland. She still talks so fondly of the Royal Mile and Princess Street.* I nod enthusiastically, trying to warm to the sound of drums and whining pipes.

The announcer describes thousands of people lined along the Mall, Picadilly, Trafalgar Square to see the world leaders and beautiful carriages. London is festooned with images of crowns and other salutes to the new monarch. I have already made up my mind to live some day in London.

Up the streets march other bands, and with each one, Mom recalls a different sibling. Uncle Alex in New Zealand. Colin in Australia. Johnny gone to India, but now back in Scotland. With the Royal Canadian

*Misspelling is intentional. My childhood understanding.

Mounted Police salute, Mom remembers Bella in Victoria and Chrissie in Toronto.

"I thought Aunt Chrissie lived in Maine," I say.

"It's another Aunt Chrissie, dear, in Toronto. And I guess you have a third Aunt Chrissie if you count Danny's wife in Cleveland."

She says this matter-of-factly, in a that's-the-end-of-that voice.

It's all news to me. Recklessly, I persist. "How many brothers and sisters did you have?"

Her face fixes on the screen. The royal coach is pulling up to Westminster Abbey.

"How many?"

"Oh, about twelve," she says. "Don't ask so many questions. Watch this, you'll learn something."

It is now that I recognize the resemblance between my mother and the new Queen of England. Such parallels in coloring and features, but an even deeper connection in the strained dignity of expression, that serious, anxious look, even when their faces are meant to be in repose. You couldn't call Elizabeth a pretty woman.

So like a wedding: the Abbey is crowded with expectant people. As Elizabeth walks up the aisle, ladies follow, each gripping her elaborate train, as if assisting a wounded, giant bird. The old Archbishop of Canterbury looks like a Catholic priest, but Mom explains that this is a Protestant service, that the coronation occurs here because the monarch is the head of the Church of England.

Here I know something is wrong. Very wrong. I am in serious training for my First Communion and I fear that watching this ceremony is some kind of heretical complicity against the First Commandment, which prohibits attending services outside the One True Church. Is this why Grandma went upstairs?

Perhaps because I'm distracted by the state of my immortal soul—at best this is a near occasion of sin—my attention wanders from the long, elaborate ceremony in what sounds like a cold, hard, foreign language. When the comely Duke of Edinburgh kneels down to pledge his faith and trust to Elizabeth, my romantic impulses are roused again. Yet this is too brief. All that liturgical raising and lowering of crowns makes me nervous. People are droning on and on and on. Blessings. Vows. Boring commentary. My focus is drawn back to the cutouts of Aunt Bella's handsome Windsor Grey horses, the little men in black-visored hats, the amazing crown of diamonds, rubies, and other jewels frothing around a lush, purple pillow. When I look up again, it's almost over. She is leaving Westminster Abbey, fancy ladies following her train in the opposite direction. Cameras pan over throngs of ordinary bystanders, people like my aunts and uncles who have returned from corners of the empire to witness the coronation. The announcer tells us that the crown weighs over four pounds, then, at the risk of being indelicate, compliments the young queen's neck muscles. Elizabeth is concentrating hard to do it all correctly and again I see my mother's worried expression. Looking from Mom to the Queen and back again, the family resemblance is all there. Elizabeth is carrying a sceptre and an orb just like the ones in my book. These, apparently, are also heavy, and I think of my mother's admonition, "It's not a happy life."

I understand that I am meant to aim for something between the lives of Elizabeth II, queen, and Mary Gill McKenzie Miner, waitress, toward some happy medium.

This is when my life with the Windsors begins.

❧

Decades later, we recall the coronation while we are on a train or bus or auto trip. My mother and I often travel together: movement is in our blood. And we have our best talks in transit, as if leaving home frees us from our history and secrets and the web of daily lies that holds our family together in my mother's imaginative optimism. Only when Mom and I leave home, it seems, do we enter the real world together. Perhaps while we're on the road, the material pressures of negotiating gasoline levels and road directions and room prices stimulate direct, honest talk. At any rate, it's on one of these trips that she suddenly says:

"You know, I left Scotland because of the King. People should be ruled by vote, by democracy."

"Really," I say, surprised because she has suddenly swerved from the topic of my brother's wife. Surprised, too, because it seems she had more pressing economic and emotional reasons to immigrate. "Doesn't Parliament run things?" I ask. "Isn't the monarch just a figurehead?"

"The Scots don't need an English figurehead."

What can I say to this? Still, perhaps because I've always harbored this long, semiconscious affection for the Queen, I say, "Well, why did we watch the coronation, then?"

She smiles, "You remember that."

"Oh, yes," I tell her. "The Pepsi, the cutouts, the two of us visiting Westminster Abbey for the first time."

Her face softens as she thinks. One thing I enjoy about my mother is how often I find her thinking. This thoughtfulness lends itself to a distinctively old-fashioned sincerity.

Her voice is serious. "We watched because it was a historical event."

I laugh. Mom fed us historical events the way some mothers prepare fresh fruit and vegetables.

She smiles back. "Besides, I've always loved a parade."

I see the procession of all my aunts and uncles. I think about the day I learned about the three Aunt Chrissies.

"Remember the Queen of Tonga?" she asks.

I nod, "Six feet, three inches." She is laughing, that fine, merry, pretty mother laugh, and I hope that Queen Elizabeth, despite her uneasy life, has moments like this.

# VI

---

*Daniel, 1907–1908*

# CHAPTER SEVENTEEN

## Daniel, Edinburgh, 1907–1908

YOU COULD HAVE LEFT IT LIKE THAT AND KNOWING HER AS WE BOTH DO now, it's fair to say she would have had enough willpower to forget. OK, you tried, too. Even thought of a Glasgow job that would have brought more money and a change in scene. Yet Maggie said no. In her blind, sweet determination, she saw nothing of your urgency in wanting to leave. She said life was good enough here, when blessings were counted. And so you stayed in Edinburgh, too close to that wet, sticky, painful heart of dreams gone off.

I find it hard to reenter your life here, hard to summon the sympathy and elasticity to write your story as wide as truth.

You're looking at me proudly, thinking I've inherited this writing from you. Just as you recorded Mr. Menzies's business, I'm recording yours. Sometimes, inside these sentences, I do feel more scrivener than creator. This book is different from journalism, in the way that scar tissue is distinct from natural skin; it's about getting at a deeper layer of experience. You honestly tried to put Mae out of your mind until you got that cursed letter from Colin in the spring, thanking you for the scarves, saying that life down there wasn't as good as advertized, but the money was better and the landscape was bloody amazing. He'd never imagined anything like it. And that made you realize how much you'd never see because of luck and history. It got you thinking about what you had known and felt and lost. Or almost lost, because Colin's writing set you to thinking about the word *correspond,* and how some people lived the best part of their lives in letters.

So you wrote a simple letter. You had heard that Jock was teaching Mae to write. Edinburgh wasn't such a metropolis that you couldn't find out what you wanted to know. You didn't say much—because who knew if *he* might open it first—an April birthday greeting to Mae with best wishes. For the first week after you sent the letter, you felt elated. There was something wonderfully reckless, childlike, about it. Maggie half-jokingly asked if you'd been drinking. Then she put the good mood down to you hearing from your taciturn brother. She was pleased, herself, at his appreciation of the scarves.

Of course Mae didn't respond. What did you expect? You hadn't acquired Lesson One of the professional writer, that the reward of writing was the composing, itself (one can expect nothing from the reader, or at least nothing specific). I will grant you that you waited all the way until Christmas to send the next note—a card, this time with warm regards. And it's possible that, hearing nothing, you would have stopped there if Bella hadn't come home from the hotel one night in June to announce her engagement to that strange John Mathieson. Maggie was beside herself with glee, too caught up in the excited planning to perceive another door shutting.

Colin was riding horses in Australia and you were stuck in Edinburgh with the mother of the bride. Both of you quickly fading into the previous generation.

You struggled for hope the only way you knew how, by dreaming of that quiet house back in Ayr, or if it were really necessary to start over, a homestead in America or Canada. You wrote a short note, once a month, then once a week, until she felt forced to ask you to stop. By then, you both understood, she was hooked.

How much of this dreaming about running off together did you actually believe? How much was sheer, wild fantasy? Was Mae your audience or your inspiration? You were such an odd combination—a dedicated, hard-working provider with a sense of responsibility that was profound. And a passionate, willful man determined to get what he needed from life.

# CHAPTER EIGHTEEN

# "Night Lights at Earth Central"

## *Mary, New York, 1945*

MY EYES SHIFTED FROM JACK'S MOTHER'S CRUCIFIX—AFTER ALL, THIS was her home, too—to the ribbon of streetlights shimmering below on Riverside Drive.

Sounds rising from the next room—a moan, a sigh—then swift terror through my chest. Quietly, I rushed to the living room. Jack was right; John was too old at three to sleep with us, and you can't have a boy growing up in the front room. We needed a bigger home. Still, we'd had so many upheavals lately, some very painful changes, and I wasn't prepared to move. I didn't want to leave my New York City, the home I had found and made. John (I sometimes wanted to call him "Joy") lay sprawled on the cot, sheet flung aside, breathing—yes—breathing ever so evenly up and down, up and down, his blond curls inextricably, beautifully tangled. My bairn, my John Junior, was it possible to love anyone as much as this?

Relieved, I returned to solitude at the kitchen table, and looking through the thin summer curtains, I opened my empty self to midnight on Riverside Drive. The traffic had grown dimmer, but it never went completely still. Our dishes dried slowly in the drainer amid the lingering peppery, oniony aroma of Jack's famous spaghetti sauce. I wasn't really *looking* at anything, seeing specifics, just mooning, as I did when I sat alone with morning coffee. Batty behavior. Better to go back to my diary, but a diary had consequences, possible readers. No one could know your thoughts. Musing was safer, easier to erase.

A woman lucky enough at the end of the war to have a man sleeping in the next room should be lying with him. I needed rest to tend to our beautiful three-year-old boy. Yet, memories hovered; August was never my favorite month.

Loudly below, a horn honked, a slamming door followed clattering footsteps. An impatient lover? Drunken husband? So different from Leith Walk, from any Edinburgh Street. New York was one big thrill of a city where people weren't afraid to create scenes. Quite the contrary, New Yorkers *looked* for stages.

Like Jack, with his wild, sodden (well, we were just at the end of a long war) off-color stories. Don't blush, he'd tease, you've married an all-American boy. What do you expect? And so, at night, after he had slipped off to bed, I'd throw out the bottles, open the kitchen window, and air the flat. Air out the smells and feelings of the day, the confinement of three lonely years without my husband.

This heat, would I ever get used to it? So hard to sleep in steaming, breathless weather. Somehow Jack and our wee John could slip right into it, could pull up the hot, moist night and float serenely away. Both early risers, father and son. Too early for a ragmop woman who hadn't sailed off until the safety of dawn. So each night I watched the curtains breathe in/out, in/out, as if they might rock me to sleep. My bonny lies over the ocean. Not anymore. He was home. I needed to remember that. Everything, now, was going to be all right.

I had been like this since I got here, really (here being America— Connecticut, then Florida, then back to the gregarious, welcoming harbor of New York): the night waking, the morning sleeping. Did it have to do with where the sun set on this unfamiliar continent? The angle of light? Midnight here was 5 A.M. in Edinburgh, a time for watching. Insomnia didn't bear thinking about, I suppose. Just a good thing that restaurants had evening shifts. And if Manhattan were hot, I could only try to forget the wilting humidity of Connecticut, then Florida, summers.

※

I was fortunate, really fortunate, for this whole lucky country. Fortunate that my cabin mate from the *Transylvania*, Jenny, kept my Connecticut address and wrote to me about resort work in St. Petersburg. It was time to leave Connecticut's dour, reserved beauty. I was ready for Florida, for the giddy holiday people in their translucent pastels. Ready in my early twenties—was this truly thirteen years ago, how could I be thirty-five years old this summer?—eager to kick up my heels. I knew I was in the right place when I walked into the bedroom I would share with Jenny and saw those red and yellow boats sailing on white curtains. If Connecticut were a different world from Scotland, with its runny food and drawled accents, Florida was a different planet. Those shimmering people who drove sleek cars had no idea that you were supposed to go anywhere, do anything. Floridians simply lived for the day. They embodied the present tense of being American. In Florida you imagined. I imagined I could fly.

I lapped up exotic pleasures: fresh shrimp with lemon, the soft, warm light of mid-December, gaudy birds, perfumed tropical flowers, vanilla ice cream cones on the boardwalk. Still, I missed the safety of city life. One night, when I eventually fell asleep, I dreamt about a row of pink and turquoise houses, the door of each ajar, guarded by green alligators with snapping jaws.

This is what I mourned about the city: the battle of building construction and bus engines. Purposeful human voices. Interruption. Church bells. The excitement of 5 P.M. when the clerks get off work, change their shoes, and begin to live. The slow, guilty pulse of Sunday morning yawning into Sunday afternoon. Even the dull thud of the weekend ending on Sunday night, hopes dashed, head down, ironing your uniform dutifully because you suffer impossible optimism, because there's nothing else to do except listen to good swing on the radio or start a new library book. I missed the buzz and anonymous danger of rounding a city corner, like the half-conscious anticipation of turning the pages in a good novel.

So, despite Jenny's warnings, I traveled back north to my "port of arrival." I liked the sound of that. It seemed decades since I had walked off Ellis Island, and now I was back in the grimy, blaring, crowded beauty of 1930s New York.

New York. What did I anticipate? Nothing in particular. Everything. I wanted to be surprised. People kept asking why I would come to New York in the middle of the Depression. Depression? Compared to Edinburgh tenement housing, my room in the Village was a palace. And I got a job the first week. Jenny was amazed (secretly, she missed cities too), but I confessed in my next letter that landing the job probably had more to do with my accent, which people in Manhattan found either endlessly amusing or inexplicably charming.

Here I'd traveled from outer space Florida to Earth Central—New York. From history to future, Scotland to America. New York in the 1930s: Governor Roosevelt runs for president. Jazz clubs hop in Harlem. The Giants and the Yankees win the World Series right after one another. Jimmy Walker resigns over corruption. This was a place where things happened. The World's Fair. Radio City Music Hall opening a six-thousand-seat movie theatre. "State Fair" becoming a hit on Broadway.

Just as well that I missed the 1920s. Flappers. Speakeasies. Decadence wasn't really my nature. Here in the early 1930s, I heard a familiar melody—joblessness, dilapidation—always counterpointed by a beat of possibility.

New York was my future. I would enter one of those business schools and learn to type. Maybe I would marry an executive who would insist I quit work to make curtains and raise four children and fix him a martini when he came home on the subway each night.

Oh, there was nothing wrong with restaurant work, let me explain. The job was warm, dry, sociable, and they fed you (I've never been much of a cook). I appreciated the tips, the incentive they provided, and the surprise. Like when that pommy Englishman left a chocolate bar and a quarter under his plate. So good to hear a voice from home, he had said. Of course, I was my father's daughter and knew that Englishmen and Scots are different species. Still, I could use the quarter, and he was nice enough, and Father always taught me to take people as individuals.

❧

What was left in Edinburgh except a bleak, empty flat—parents dead, brothers and sisters dispersed all over the world? Yes, here was home. Here, now, I was *not* alone, this was home, with Jack and John and Jack's mother. Mother. And I was so grateful to have my husband back from the war. Of course we would get used to each other again. (Had we really known one another when we married? How could I detect if the war had changed him?) Recently we had been through so much. Fortune and tragedy and now this cavernous fear about The Move. Everything was going to be all right. He was with me. He would always be with me. Our new home across the Hudson would have a master bedroom for us, a lovely room for Mother, and two other bedrooms. One for Johnny and one for the next child. For surely that's what families did in these times: they went on to the next child.

Switching off the overhead light, I pulled back the pretty curtains, then sat facing the open window, looking straight into the silver and dark night. Different from Edinburgh lights. I had trained myself to say "Edinburgh," rather than "back home," and felt a little sad now about how natural the distance felt, even here, alone, in the middle of the night.

These New World lights were the first of many changes. Moving between cities is like teetering between railroad cars. Everything is strange. The buildings, first of all. Here architecture was new, tall, shiny. While I missed the wynds and closes, I loved the clarity of New York's east-west grid. You didn't stay a stranger here long, perhaps because people were so different from one another and that made them openly curious. Scots avoided you if you were from a certain neighborhood, dressed in a certain way. Sure, here you had Brooklyn, Queens, Yonkers, but I don't know. New York was a busy, speeding city. Edinburgh was more like an ornamented tree—graceful, reflecting different lights occasionally, but essentially static. New Yorkers gave you permission to ask, to change, to move.

Americans seemed to enjoy difference. People laughed at my strange jokes, perhaps at the foreign vocabulary. I guess I was sassy, rather than sarcastic, like New Yorkers. Jack said my humor was a life force. I don't know, I think I just expected less, found more surprise and amusement than he did.

Truth was, he'd had a hard life, an unfair one, but that was changing now. His mother had recovered from most of her mental troubles. The War was over. He had a real job. No more selling peanuts at Ebbets Field. No more hailing taxis for snobs at the Park Plaza. He had a real job with Victory Carriers, the best of the Merchant Marine. And we were moving to a HOUSE in New Jersey.

To get to New Jersey, you simply crossed the Hudson River. Still, the shift felt so dramatic. Maybe because when I came to America I had nothing to lose. I never looked back. But now I had become an individual, a person with family. With this child, I had re-entered history, from the opposite direction, my actions less shaped by my parents' pasts than determining of my son's future.

Leaving New York. Leaving the clean organization of Howard Johnson's and the classy extravagance of Schraffts. Leaving Fifth Avenue in mid-December: the shop windows dancing with angels and Santas and gingerbread men. I've never much minded winter in New York. Always preferred it to those dripping summers. I love watching the ice skaters at Rockefeller Center.

Leaving the winter sales, the postholiday crush of garments on sturdy basement tables. Women jostling for space, for the right angle, for adequate reach. Survival of the pushiest or the most patient. Democracy in action: you could wear the same clothes as the wife of a doctor or professor because they were marked twenty-five percent off, fifty percent off. The trick was arriving early enough to find your size and color. The trick was broad scanning combined with deep digging. Americans gave up too easily: often the best slip or blouse lay there at the bottom of the pile, waiting a sharp eye. Being married expanded the range of my shopping—baby clothes, men's clothes, wee gifts for Jack's mother. Now my shopping became a family mission. How would my family be dressed if I had stayed in Edinburgh? Would I have had a family? Would my husband have survived the war?

Jack used to say he liked my witty practicality, such a contrast to his mad mother and bitter sister. Mad or not, Mother Miner was on my side. I know she urged Jack to do the right thing when I became pregnant. Perhaps she thought I'd be a better daughter than her own Adele, who was, even then, marinating on Long Island. Of course, he didn't need persuading. He loved me. He was just twenty-five and about to sail out into an endless war. People say I'm a saint for taking care of Jack's mother, changing her leg ulcer bandages every afternoon, accompanying her on those halting, arthritic walks, but she, herself, had been a blessing with the sewing and ironing and child-minding when I went to work—or when I made the occasional trip down to the Village, where Teddy and I would toast our lost youths together.

If I'd had my druthers, I wouldn't have married on the cusp of a world war. Yet it *was* time—at thirty-one—to settle down. And if I had to marry, I'd pick a lively one, this exuberant, playful, younger man who swung me so hard late one night at the Bonga Ballroom that I fell bottom-first through a wide canvas drum. The memory still shoots me into fits of giggles.

This war was so different from the last one. We seemed to be losing fewer men, but maybe that was the difference between Scotland and

America—Americans naturally suffered fewer casualties than the men across the pond. And how would I learn what was happening in other countries—even to my own brothers in New Zealand and Scotland and Canada and England—for the American journalists reported an American war. Jack's destinations with the Merchant Marine were always secret, and my *not knowing* was the worst part. First a letter from Norway. Then one from Australia (Father always spoke fondly of his brother in Australia). But *where* in Australia was my Jack—such a vast country—and for how long?

Then the miraculous telegram that would forecast both joy and tragedy in the long term: "Leave in San Francisco. Meet me for cracked crab on Fisherman's Wharf." The wire was followed by a letter urging me to take the train with Johnny and join him on the Pacific Coast.

"San Francisco, you won't believe it, Patrica." He always spelled it that way, it had become a pet name. "Some day, we'll live in San Francisco, Patrica."

It was during a blissful night in San Francisco at the El Cortez Hotel that we conceived Robert—or Roberta if it had been a girl. I suspected I was carrying, really, but wasn't sure until I got back to Dr. Mulligan in New York. At that point, I knew everything would be fine. Jack would come home and one day we would set off with our babies to San Francisco.

Sooner than expected, less than nine months later, the war had ended. Jack was returning to New York. The flat had become so dreary. There I was, ballooning with historical promise, and surging with the zest of late pregnancy: sweeping and scrubbing and renovating. Mother, dubious at first about this redecoration, was soon caught up in the scheme, and agreed to make new kitchen curtains if I found good sale yardage. And then—at the bottom of the pile on a sturdy basement table: red and white and blue flowered drapery to welcome our very own hero. I had found this lovely, playful fabric, and she did . . .

Now I picked up my cup of cold coffee—was this coffee-drinking why I couldn't sleep last night?—no, it had more to do with sorrow. With conscience. Even if Dr. Mulligan said it wasn't my fault. Oh, I wished, as I'd wished a thousand times since then, that I hadn't been so bothered about a perfect kitchen.

Jack wasn't coming home to an apartment. He was coming home to a family.

If only, I often think. If only I had asked for help. If only Jack's ship hadn't docked two hours early. If only . . . But at the time I was bursting with excitement. The prayerfully baked chocolate cake had fallen on only one side. The salad was made. The potatoes were peeled and cut. Mother was reading to Johnny and he was quiet for the first time that day, poor cowboy, bless his excited little heart. I should have asked Mother's help hanging the curtains, but she had already done so much, sewing and washing and ironing them that I was determined to do this myself. What happened was my fault, a sin of pride.

You see, I was almost finished hanging them when I saw Jack running up the sidewalk. Just two or three hooks and we'd be all set. Gingerly, I moved my bare feet along the cool top of the radiator. I had to complete the task before Mother caught me.

Then, somehow, leaning over toward the end of the rod, I lost footing. Everything speeded up. No, I couldn't bend forward, didn't want to risk crashing through the window, so I reached out for the icebox, to steady myself, to right myself, but it was inches too far away. Inches. (He lost his life by inches as I went crashing to the floor.) This wasn't happening. The war was over. But I was dying. Oh, what pain. Waves of water breaking, flooding. And the red, red blood.

When I opened my eyes, Jack was standing in a hospital. I was lying in a bed. Jack was home, tired, unshaven, worried. No, it wasn't Jack. Who was this? Not the man rushing up the sidewalk. (Maybe that had been Father. Coming to meet his grandson?)

"Get out, get out." My voice. This must, must be a dream. I couldn't be awake. God was more merciful than this; He would always be with me, with our wee family.

But Jack insisted, bent over and kissed my cheek.

"It's good to see you, Patricia."

He had wakened me fully now. How could I ever forgive him for bringing me back to a world in which I had killed our child?

# CHAPTER NINETEEN

# "View from the Escalator"

## *Valerie, New York, 1954*

JUST THE TWO OF US (AND A DOZEN SILENT STRANGERS) SPEEDING INTO the gleamy city. In companionable silence, we sit together on the old Bergen County Transit bus to Manhattan. Along snowy streets. Over the George Washington Bridge. Our bridge.

As the bus ducks beneath the black-grey web of wires, I think how much I hate this ugly part. (Later "sinister" is the word I use to describe these innards, these urban life support systems.)

When we finally enter the big Port Authority Terminal, this different world is full of possibility, safer, darker, taller, faster, my kind of place. Mom and I hold hands along 42nd Street to Fifth Avenue. There, on our favorite street, each revolving door opens to a bright, foreign galaxy.

Together we hunt, careful not to lose one another. Always careful. Our family is continually losing parts of itself; I know this before I understand which parts have dropped off, which have sloughed away, which have evaporated. I see the danger if not the remedy. Yet here in New York, all we have to do is keep an eye on each other. This kind of getting lost is a real fear, easier to handle than the anxieties at home.

Store basements are the most fun: dim, hot, smelly, crowded with people in unbuttoned overcoats who are pushing, pulling, shoving, buying. Mom has warned me to be careful. Some of them are not our kind. Not so honest. Not so clean. You can't tell them by sight, she says, you just have to stay alert. Indeed, I have inherited her radar. Heroically we persist, finding a shirt for Larry, socks for Daddy, and clutching our booty as we ride the escalator up to the ground level.

Never take the elevator because you might miss something: a new style, a lady spraying perfume samples, a sale, clearance, discount, close-out, special. It is in a department store that I first grasp the concept of synonym.

First floor. Second floor. Pajamas, I remember, are on the fourth floor. Then maybe we can go up one more flight to look at the dolls. After Christmas each year, I bring my gift money and buy a new doll from the sale rack. During the fall, I like to drop by for a visit, to inspect the newcomers. In a way, to welcome them.

Suddenly we see Stuart Erwin, the TV star. We notice him riding down to the second floor as we are riding up to the third. I spot him. Them. Stuart and June Erwin, TV and real-life husband and wife. Stuart and June, she agrees. Oh, how I wish I had said something.

"Go ahead. Go on back down," she nudges me.

But what would I say? I watch him standing there in front of the men's shoes. June beside him, helping, nodding, like on the show. I've always envied their TV daughter Jackie.

"Go ahead," she says. "Tell them you like the program."

"Really?"

"Really."

"Come with me."

No, she shakes her head and lightly touches my shoulder wings. "You go ahead, by yourself."

Alone, I think. Then, heart racing, I ride the escalator down from sportswear to men's shoes. Looking back, I find her watching. Carefully.

Here they are. Headed to a different department when I say in an embarrassingly childish voice, "Are you Stuart and June Erwin?"

They could flee. They could ignore me.

Instead, each of them takes one of my hands and smiles.

Jackie, I wonder, has something happened to her, do these safe people need a new daughter?

"Nice to meet you, Valerie," he is saying.

I come to my senses. Say something else.

They are both smiling, glad I like their show. Even thank me for thanking them.

They wave, walking slowly into socks and belts, and I watch until they disappear. Then I ride the escalator triumphantly, filled with a story for my mother.

❧

Childs' Restaurant is her favorite. Today we get a booth. She orders pancakes for lunch. With butter and maple syrup. A little too rich, but I would never say so. This meal is a treat, an extravagance that will be savored for weeks. It's not every day you meet television stars.

Cold air on our faces afterward, we hold hands as the crowds gather around us at the corner. This is one of my favorite parts of New York life, the way people walk from east to west in huge gangs. Together, with the human train, Mom and I travel across the streets, her hand tightly gripping mine.

❧

The first passengers on the homebound bus, we claim the next to the last seat, which is higher than the others and better for viewing.

Our packages around us, she says, "This is a good kind of tired."

I nod contentedly.

The dark outside is spotted with yellow lights, tiny golden sapphires. Silent now, we watch together for signals from a thousand lives we will never know.

# VII

*Mae, 1909–1914*

# CHAPTER TWENTY

## *Mae, Edinburgh, 1909–1914*

SHE THOUGHT OF JOHNNY AND DANNY AS SHE UNHOOKED EACH OF HER earrings. Chrissie as she slipped off the bracelet and Jack with the hairclasp. (What was she doing—a thirty-year-old mother of four, tramping off to a seedy rented room? She should get up now and find her way to her sister's in Fife, which is where Jock thought she was tonight. Yes, there were moments of lucidity like this.) When she was in Daniel's presence, in his arms, his eyes, there was nothing but now, waves of lust and guilt and otherworldly dreaming.

Supper had been cold and rushed because they had arrived so late from the city. The owner of the room had brusquely informed them that only a sponge bath was available at this hour. Daniel had given her the loo first, and now she waited, cursing chivalry, which had left her so much time for self-reproach. She thought about escaping, ascending, disappearing.

Inhaling his scent from her hands, that smokey tart smell, she closed her eyes, which is when she learned she wasn't alone after all. (The ghostly girl was there—looking older this time, tired and mid-twenties, sitting in a church. Distracted, the girl—well, she was really a lady now—suddenly reached in her pocket for a small silver packet. Was she going to smoke in church? She pressed the packet firmly and out popped a white pill, which she surreptitiously swallowed. Sweets? Poison? The girl—lady—grew more relaxed. Perhaps some kind of medicine. She squeezed the hand of a bearded man next to her.)

Their new coming together was even more electric than before. Mae wondered if this was because they were older and more generous, older and more experienced, older and more appreciative. His body was long, loose, fragrant with soap and still lightly traced with sweat from their journey. His sweet earth odor was as familiar as yesterday. They lay beside one another for a long time, holding warmth, silent between the sweet moans. When he brushed her nipples, touching gently, then exploring—tender fingertips on the softest clay—she knew that his eyes were closed and his mouth pursed. He was memorizing her; the need for this engorged her with dark sadness. She moved sooner than she might otherwise, to the touching of him, suddenly delighted by the feathers on his chest. He shifted slowly above her, resting on his elbows until she urged his full weight down on her body. Once he was in her, she sighed with unbreakable joy. They rocked back and forth, up and down, exploding together, flooding one another.

That night, as she listened to him breathing beside her, she stared out the small, square window through the greying cotton curtains at a full moon. She had thought it wasn't supposed to be full until the end of the week. But she'd always been poor at reading the sky. She closed her eyes and the girl returned, looking queasy as she ate chips with salt, without vinegar.

Mae did cherish her family. She had come a long way since being a servant at eleven. Look at her sister Jessie, who was struggling with a drunken husband. Jessie thought Mae was the luckiest woman she knew: four beautiful, healthy children. A loving, loyal husband who had taught her to read and write. Then why did she feel so miserable? Was she mad? Why did she find this sweet family unreal, unsatisfying? Where did she get the persistent sense that well-being was not enough, that in the face of great happiness lost, mere well-being was misery? Mae didn't know how she knew this, but she did.

※

A week later, what she *did* understand was that she had no choice but to sacrifice the well-being. Returning from a truncated visit to Jessie, as she walked out of Waverley Station, she felt she was carrying Daniel's baby.

Jock welcomed her back exuberantly, saying that she did indeed look fitter than when she had left. The time with Jessie must have been a tonic. The children had missed her, but had behaved exemplarily. Johnny had been spending after-school hours watching the soldiers drill. This attraction to discipline pleased Jock as much as it appalled her. Danny and Chrissie had each made a drawing for every day of her absence. Jack did get a bit cranky now and then, but that was to be expected when a wee boy had a cold and missed his mam.

*R*

Of course Jock sensed the baby wasn't his own. Just how he knew, she wasn't sure. Perhaps it was the skinny darkness of her after the sweet, round blondness of the first four. He had greeted his other children with exuberance bordering on ecstasy—a miracle, he named each of them: Johnny and Danny and Chrissie and Jack.

When he saw this new baby, he said, "A lovely lass." Almost too quickly, he added, "We'll call her Mary, 'Mae,' after you, love, Mae II."

She regarded this kind, gentle, principled man she was lucky to call her husband and thought how he had always wanted a second daughter to name Margaret, for his mother, as Chrissie had been named for hers. Jock's naming the child as her own reminded Mae not to underestimate his intelligence.

Jock was a good provider, an attentive father. Still, she mourned those lively conversations with Daniel, his quick wit, political curiosity, appreciation for literature. If he had been born in another time or place, Daniel would have been a teacher. She looked down at dark-eyed wee Mae and saw her marrying a teacher. Did every mother do this imagining through her children? What had Mam dreamt for her? Was this a way of coping with the disappointments and concessions in her own life? Or was it an unexpected blessing of motherhood that children were periscopes to higher ground?

Perhaps fathers did this too. Did Jock dream for Johnny, Dannie, Chrissie, Jack? And Mae? Certainly he treated her no differently from the other children. He rocked her and sang to her and bought her a special sweet at Christmas. She simply understood from the expression on his face that he knew she knew he knew.

*R*

As payment for this reprieve, she stayed away from Daniel.

She tried.

But the man had a right to see his daughter. A right that superceded the right of rights and wrongs. And although she had lost her grip on morality, she retained certain instincts.

So she and Jock came to an unspoken agreement (these were the sturdiest kind) that Mae and Daniel could have one another if she loved and tended to the children. Sleeping with them all in the same house together at night was enough for this man. He left her alone on the right side of the bed. Divorce crossed her mind, but quickly. Only rich people did that.* Besides, it was unnecessary. Indiscretion occurred in the best of families.

Thus Peggy was brought in under the McKenzie blanket, too. Yet Mr. McKenzie was losing patience. Clearly the affair had gone beyond reason, reprimand, resolution; beyond any bounds of scandal.

This is when Mae made the hardest, if not the most momentous decision of her life—to leave Jock McKenzie and make a home with Daniel and their children. This was a choice freighted with loss, as any of her choices would have been, for there were children and history on both sides of the frame. Daniel was more ready for this than she. And despite Maggie's wailing and threats, he eagerly urged Mae toward their new life. It wasn't that Jock hadn't offered Mae a choice. He had told her that Peggy was the last straw. A third child she would have to bloody deliver to Daniel to feed and rear.

For the rest of her life she would relive her decision to leave, reenact it. She would return to the chair in the corner of their room when everyone was asleep, and pray to God above to help her. Rocking her body, her belly, her baby, back and forth, she asked for guidance, for an answer. A real marriage with Daniel required impossible loss. How could she give up her life with Danny and Johnny and Chrissie and Jack? How could she tear Mae and Peggy away from their wee brothers and sister?

Silently she moaned in that corner chair, hands pulling the hair on both sides of her head. Why? Why? Why? She cursed herself for exhausting Jock's generosity as much as she had eviscerated her own virtue. *Why* did she believe she had a right to happiness? Why hadn't she accepted her responsibility and her fortunate, if not perfect, life as an adult woman? God didn't hand out second-chance tickets.

---

*The year of baby Mary's birth, there were 223 divorces in Scotland. There were 234 the next year, and 249 the next. In the United States during those same years, the figures rose from 83,000 to 89,000 to 94,000.

Staring into the frozen dark, she ached with the violence she had done to Daniel and Maggie's family, too. For didn't they have seven children of their own?

Thus Mae, who had lived her whole life in Leith—Coburg Lane and Manderston Street and Springfield Street—moved from the foot of Leith Walk to the tip of Princes Street. In November, 1914 she and Daniel and Mae and Peggy settled into Union Place. It was just another tenement, really, but someone said the area had been named by French weavers in the last century. The stairs were lit by a good skylight; the wrought-iron banisters were sturdy; thick wooden shutters closed away the city at night; the loo was on their landing; and the room looked out to Calton Hill. At Springfield Street they had simply stared over the neighbor's broken shingles to another dark tenement. Mae didn't much like being in the same building as Grey's Hotel, but did appreciate the convenience of Mitchell's Market just down on the street. These neighbors were more city folk, not the sailors and industrial laborers who crowded Leith. People here worked in shops and offices. Maybe her daughters would get clerk positions when they were of age. Maybe, maybe. She tried to be optimistic.

Yet often as she left her chair to return to the warm consolation of their bed, she wondered mournfully how the capacity for love could be so closely related to the capacity for desolation.

# CHAPTER TWENTY-ONE

# "New Jersey/New Jersey"

## *Mary, 1954*

THE VEIL LEFT ME UNEASY. OF COURSE I DID WANT VALERIE TO HAVE A wedding—twenty years from now. There was something obscene or scary or both about watching them masquerade so young.

I had seen them before, when John made his First Communion, both the boys and girls shrouded in white. Yet it was the girls who gave me a start—made out like little brides. I knew they weren't playing dress-up. The children were actually pledging their lives to Christ. I suppose that was a world away from infant brides in India. Maybe I was too much of a spare Presbyterian.

"May we go to New York? May we please go to New York, Mommy?" Her voice. My girl.

"How about somewhere closer, like Hackensack?" Practical mother, a role I was bound for.

"No, please! Barbara Mirelli's and Janet Oslager's moms took them to New York. Because that's where the best dresses are." She looked at me sideways. "And the best bargains."

"OK, OK," I laughed. "Mother's daughter, you win."

It turned into an all-day shopping expedition, nothing if not thorough. I tried to do it right. Lunch at Childs' with those delicious pancakes. I was a little distracted, thinking about my sister's visit later in the week, but I enjoyed listening to Valerie's excitement about her big day. By midafternoon we were stuffed into a little shop near Macy's with half a dozen other mothers and daughters. I felt like a fraud as the women reminisced about their own First Communions. I smiled knowingly, a recent skill.

For heaven's sake, I had never been sectarian about religion, and I *was* a Christian. Yet I knew Paradise was open to all good people. Alamgir, for instance. I never worried about his being a Muslim when we were dating in Edinburgh. Muslims were good people, family people. And the Jews—I admired their long, ethical heritage, their reverence for history. I liked to think I had inherited Father's sound moral code without his narrow-mindedness. That time he followed me into Maria Ciotti's church with a switch, that was unlike him. Never before had he punished me corporally (his words were always sufficiently demonstrative). "Papists." He hated Catholics. "Lurid," he had said, "corrupt." His democratic impulses were offended by their ornate hierarchies.

Yet I was a less serious person than my father. I harbored an odd attraction to exotic Catholic ritual: the incense, vestments, statues and the formal, sometimes energetic physical movements—standing, sitting, kneeling. They had a richness we Presbyterians lacked. On the other hand, some of the hocus pocus reminded me of royalty: titles, ring kissing, ranking. To say nothing about the Pope. His Holiness, now how was that different from His Highness? It didn't make any sense that one Italian man could know more about God's will than each of us in *our own* hearts.

Janet's mother had recommended a reasonable place on West 33rd Street. Close with the pleasant odor of starched cotton.

While little girls giggled behind the curtains, three mothers chatted around the cash register, each describing the flowers, weather, holy cards of her own big day. I found my way to a corner near the boys' white socks—who could have predicted so many different kinds of Communion socks?—I should have been thinking about Larry's outfit for the next year.

Then she appeared. Christ! Excuse me; it's what came to mind. Gosh, she was lovely in the little satin and lace dress, much nicer than the dotted Swiss at the other shop. And she did look like a miniature bride.

"Mommy, may I have it? May I please have it?"

This was also five dollars more than the dotted Swiss. I could hear Jack's mother explaining that First Communion was a girl's first "important moment." Myself, I felt her first period, her first intercourse, her first childbirth might have greater weight.

Could I say no?

On the bus home to New Jersey, Valerie grasped the precious parcel tightly on her wee lap. I wondered if she might be praying. You could take piety too far.

As we approached the George Washington Bridge, I resisted a familiar restlessness. Tried not to think of the hopes we carried to New Jersey six years before. Of course that first house was a little daunting, with its chickens and ducks and fruit trees, but I was confident because we were starting a new life together.

What I didn't quite understand was that he could continue to leave me—now us—behind. He had to, of course. It was the nature of work in the Merchant Marine. Sailing away with Victory Carriers (the very name of the company made you feel safe) to Holland or Pakistan or Chile. International commerce relied on ships, on seamen like Jack. His destinations became an education for me. So many places I had never dreamed about.

I counted my blessings that Jack sent his paycheck monthly, that he supported his family *and* his mother. When he did return, he always brought necklaces and scarves and fabric from colorful places for me, a doll for Valerie, and some soon-to-be-broken (but not soon enough) musical instruments for the boys. Every country seemed to have its own version of the drum. Then, once the kids and Mother were asleep, he would take me to our cosy bedroom, lie naked next to me in his musky hairiness, and tell me how much he had missed my warm, smooth body.

Still, things could be better, he knew, and while I was lazy enough to settle for small comforts, Jack always had his eyes open. In fact, everyone *was* happier when we moved from Englewood to Dumont. The new house was still modest, no sidewalk out front, but more the kind of place a person could aspire to rather than just inhabit. Jack was a man born to aspire. He'd run into some bad luck and, as he put it—a few assholes— but Jack knew he was on his way up. Maybe he wasn't educated, however he was smart—everyone remarked on his photographic memory—and now he would make up for lost time. Someday soon, he would move our family to San Francisco. California sounded like heaven to me. Was I ready for heaven?

Looking out the bus window now, I reminded myself that Dumont was even closer to Manhattan than Yonkers. I could get downtown quickly, easily. So I hadn't really lost New York. I was lucky to have a loyal, loving husband who would always stick with me.

Almost home now. Valerie's eyes remained closed, but she looked as if she were napping, not praying. Poor kid. This First Communion was a rite of passage. I had to remember that.

What was exciting for me was that my family was about to come together tomorrow with Nan's visit. Things were a little too hectic just now. Still, I was dying to see my sister, blond, blue-eyed, petite Nan. Petite—the perfect word for her. Prettiest of the girls. And the most successful. I would be hostess to my older sister in my own family home. She was traveling all the way from Detroit—in the middle of the continent near Canada—where her doctor husband had a job putting people to sleep before operations. Of all my brothers and sisters, Nan had fared the best (although she had her heartaches, too, with Jacky, the retarded boy). Nan lived in a big house near a lake, but she hadn't forgotten her origins. She wouldn't mind sleeping in Valerie's narrow bed. I'd give up my own, if Jack weren't home. Our house might not be as grand as hers, but I felt grateful for the central heating, the little garden of trees and seasonal vegetables, including Jack's beefsteak tomatoes, the trellis of tiny red roses on the garage wall.

How wonderful that Jack would be in port to meet my sister. The timing wasn't perfect. He was still unwinding from a long voyage, and he'd had a huge fight with John yesterday. It didn't seem right, a strong man belting, strapping, an eleven-year-old boy. But Jack said lenience was no favor. Things would smooth over. And Nan might as well see my life as complicated as it was.

Home, finally. Everything safely as we left it. While I hurried into the kitchen to start supper, Valerie tried on the beautiful dress for her appreciative grandmother and her uninterested brothers. I was a little worried that she might spill something on it, or fall and rip a hem, but I was also feeling relieved to have the kitchen alone. Jack would be home by six, and I wanted to have his supper on the table.

Supper was my most harrowing time of day. Not only did Jack love to eat, but he was a brilliant chef. Still, he was so patient. The kitchen was a wife's domain, he insisted. And I was just fine, really, while he was at sea. The kids seemed happy enough with baked spaghetti or meatloaf and frozen veg. America froze endless kinds of vegetables. And we had our own electric refrigerator. The kids also liked fish sticks and raved about pizza, so Fridays were never a problem. When Jack came home I'd have a go at Chicken Fricassee. This was the closest I came to casserole. Maybe the difficulty was that, deep down, food bored me. I was an eat-to-live person, except when it came to milk chocolate bars and strawberry jam. And these were more weaknesses than foods. Also, I tended to think of cooking as a waste of time. I didn't need fancy. That said, I was grateful every night to have something to eat.

Tonight it would be hamburgers and unfrozen French fries. Onions, ketchup, lettuce, mayonnaise. Just fine. Nutritious and filling.

I guess Jack hadn't known what he was bargaining for when he married me. He hadn't reckoned on my limitations—probably because they were so unnatural. I couldn't cook, sew, drive, draw, sing, play an instrument, or follow geographical directions. (How did you get to America, he teased—did you get lost on your way to Australia?) But he didn't really seem to mind, except those few impatient times. Men like being superior to women, even, maybe especially, about domestic life.

Nowadays I realized there where numerous things I *could* do: tell jokes, dance, shop, ride buses, fill time, iron, dust, polish furniture, vacuum, add, subtract, listen, wash sinks and dishes and children and clothes. I was getting pretty good at making thick American sandwiches.

I loved to read and knew my lack of schooling wouldn't hold me back in America. Our family subscribed to *The Bergen Record, The New York Journal American,* and *The Catholic Digest. Look,* my favorite magazine, had some very good articles on President Eisenhower, Congress, juvenile delinquency, and medical advances. The news was an interest Jack and I shared. We watched John Daly together, and Edward R. Murrow, who didn't look at all like I imagined him from wartime radio. I often thought Jack and Edward R. Murrow would make good mates; they had exactly the same cranky good-heartedness. (That was one thing about Jack. He might lose his temper, but deep down, he cared about people. He had standards. You couldn't ask for a more loving, devoted husband and father.) Anyway, the news. I had always believed it was good for the children that we watched news about the world as a family.

Only part of each evening was spent in front of the TV. I tried to set a good example for the children by reading books. Serious, heavy volumes like *The Tontine, Keys of the Kingdom,* and Catholic books like *The Robe* and *The Cardinal.*

It didn't feel as strange to raise my sons and daughter American as it did to raise them Catholic. I was an American now. This was a nation where you could be who you set out to be. Where class wasn't a permanent birthmark. Heavens, I was more American, certainly more patriotic, than some of our friends whose grandparents had been born here. Of course, they had a right to criticize, where I didn't, but it was also possible that I saw the place with a fresh eye. I loved the fact that everyone in this gigantic nation—from Maine to California—was American, that it wasn't broken up into tense, pushed-together countries like Scotland, Wales, and England. Your imagination could ramble in a place like this over so many landscapes. I liked the fact that people called each other by their first names. That no one curtsied to anyone. That I was accepted as Pat Miner, Jack's wife, that they couldn't track me to Leith Walk and dig up old shame. I was happy as a stranger in this friendly place where I could imagine my own identity and people accepted me.

"What's for supper?" That was Jack's strong voice booming from the living room, through the television news.

He still excited me, this manly man.

"Hamburgers," Larry reported eagerly.

"Mmmmmm. Nice and rare," Jack said, "dripping with blood juice." He'd been drinking with Jim and Hugh, I could hear it in his voice.

"Oh, Daddy," Valerie laughed, "don't call it 'blood juice.' That sounds horrible."

"Next time we'll have them *raw*," he growled. "You'll get used to eating real meat."

I turned up the heat and hurried with the condiments. The man was hungry. I had a family to feed. In fact, he did eat raw hamburger, raw bacon, and when I fretted about diseases, he would say, "Forget it, Pat, this is America." Maybe he was right. As he was about so many things.

The next afternoon I cleaned house thoroughly for Nan's visit. Later, sitting idly over coffee, I considered how sweet it was of Teddy to invite her goddaughter to brunch after the Communion. Even making a restaurant reservation. Coming all the way in from the Village for the Mass. And I realized I should be doing more. I was the mother. This led me to worrying about the way we had hung the dress in that plastic bag upstairs, still wrinkled from the bus ride.

With Nan arriving and leaving before Saturday, the Communion on Sunday, I might not have any other time to iron it properly. A quiet afternoon stretched ahead. Why put it off?

Mother would have used steam, but I didn't dare. It could leave a long, wet streak on real satin like this.

As I started ironing, I thought how I always wanted to ask Sister Margaret (she was the friendliest of the nuns) if she starched her wimple or if it were made of cardboard. Those habits looked so uncomfortable, especially in the summer. The nuns were good, self-sacrificing women, intelligent (Irish in America were different from the sort at home), and they clearly believed in teaching discipline. So I was happy enough to say the rosary with the children. It *was* the same faith, after all, with a few curlicues added. Mary Queen of Scots was Catholic. I just continued to remind my children that the Gates of the Kingdom of Heaven are open to many.

My mind was wandering like this when I noticed that terrible smell. Oh, no, it couldn't be. Not the dress, not the *front* of the dress. All this raced through my head even as I examined the ugly yellow-brown burn. OK, OK, don't panic, I told myself. Mother occasionally scorched a garment too, and she just, that's right, she just ran the thing under cold water. Washed the scar right out.

I was in a mood for miracles. No, not quite gone.

More water.

No.

Ah, I finally remembered lemon juice.

But the scorch mark was stubborn. So damn stubborn.

Later, interminable hours later, I had to tell her. I waited until we were alone in the kitchen.

"No, no," my daughter screamed, "it isn't true."

I stood, facing directly into Jack's temper. She had inherited the quick, Irish anger, not good for a girl.

"Don't worry, sweetheart, everything will be fine."

"No it won't," she was still shouting, "my dress is ruined. My Holy Communion dress." Head lowered, she slammed her palms against the icebox. "No. No!" The tears started.

"We'll get another. We'll go straight back to New York and buy the same one."

Sobbing, she ran off to her room. To pray, I think.

After an hour, I ventured upstairs. She was lying face down on the pink comforter.

Stroking her tangled auburn hair—just like mine a life and a continent ago—I reassured her. "We'll go right back to that store."

"Really, Mommy? The same place? Really?"

I could tell now that she was as scared as she was angry.

"Ya. First thing tomorrow morning. I'll get you excused from school. Tomorrow, it's off to the city. We'll be back in plenty of time for Aunt Nan's arrival."

It was going to be all right. I couldn't bear the look of betrayal on that little face.

Both of us were silent on the bus to Manhattan. I tried to put my mind to brighter things. Oh, I looked forward to seeing Nan. She would understand this blunder, would listen to my tale with Job-like patience, nodding in the right places to absolve me. Confession was one of those Catholic rituals I envied and mistrusted at the same time. Imagine the relief of having someone tell you—as only God could—that you were forgiven! Theologically it made no sense. Another area where Catholics seemed, I don't know, underdeveloped. That immaturity ran through their language (calling a clergyman "Father," as if he were a parent). I preferred "Reverend," which honored a minister who had achieved some degree of wise goodness. How was a priest, who couldn't marry, a model for anyone normal? Still, Catholics were Christians, which is why I didn't object when Jack explained that he couldn't marry me unless I vowed to raise his children Catholic. He was the man of the house, the family provider. Sometimes, though, I felt the Church held my children ransom.

The clerk in the dress shop, where we had been so happy last week, looked offended, maybe even annoyed.

"Oh, no, we don't *have* another one," she blurted in astonishment. "We sold out of that design days ago. It was very popular, so feminine, you know." Valerie turned toward the shop window, eyes filling.

"It's not our fault," the woman nattered on. "The churches do this every year—hold First Communion masses at the same time. And they never give enough notice."

Valerie was pretending to study a woman walking her large dog along West 33rd Street.

For a moment, I imagined it was my fault because I wasn't Catholic. Ridiculous. The scorching had been an accident, not a punishment; clumsy ironing was one of my unnatural limitations.

The clerk was talking to Valerie. "I do have one or two dresses left in your size, dear. Would you like to try them?"

"Yes," she said bravely. "Thank you."

We had seen these dresses before—a high-buttoned linen one and a rather plain ivory cotton with touches of lace at the collar and cuffs. The first one looked ridiculous on my lassie's plump little figure. The second was OK, but nowhere as nice as the dress I had ruined.

Wordlessly, we agreed on the second.

As she changed back into her clothes, I stared out at the busy street. Yet all I could see was Valerie. Valerie in the veil and creamy dress. I saw her processing up the aisle with dozens of other white-clad communicants. She would look lovely, a little too saintly for her own good. She would be praying. Perhaps for my immortal soul.

# CHAPTER TWENTY-TWO

# "Slut with a Vacuum"

*Valerie, California and Washington, 1962*

IT IS A HOT, DRY, EMPTY CALIFORNIA JULY AND I KNOW I AM A MISERABLE failure as a woman. I am fourteen. It is already the summer before my sophomore year. And still, I don't have my period.

I am vacuuming my parents' bedroom and, as usual, cleaning gives me time to ponder personal defects: I have never been on a date. I have only one friend in this hot, new state. My braces will never come off. Clearasil does nothing for my pimples.

Vacuuming has always made me dizzy. I can't explain it. Suddenly, I am yelling at Mom. "Why can't I do this tomorrow?"

"Just get on with it," she shouts back from the kitchen, where she is doing her best to can tomatoes. Maybe she has a headache. She's been getting tired and tense during Dad's trips out of town.

"But I hate vacuuming," I whine.

"You're turning into a lazy slut."

Huge silence moves into the house. It's as if someone has turned off the world.

"Oh, I don't know," she rushes in apologetically, wiping her hands on a beige terry dishtowel. "You don't have to do this today if you don't want to. I'm sorry I called you that."

I know better than to ask what "that" means. After thoroughly vacuuming the bedroom (she's right, compared to her, I'm lazy, very lazy), I hurry to the living room and look up the word "slut" in the dictionary. Sitting on the couch, I page through the Ss. She never gets mad like this, doesn't blow up as my father does, and I feel strangely gratified by her anger.

"Slut."

The definition makes me laugh. Quietly. Such a ridiculous name for me, who can't even have a period. Her confidence in my womanhood is a little cheering.

I *am* prepared. Poised for action. Years ago, I memorized those flower-covered "Personally Yours" Kotex pamphlets. Consulted my mother. Stocked up for the big day. All set to be a full-fledged female. And nada. In P.E., the other girls get to skip a couple of showers each month during their heavy bleeding days. Perhaps they think I always start bleeding on the weekends?

They're not thinking anything, Mom has told me, you've got to stop thinking that people are thinking about you all the time. Somehow I find it even more alarming to imagine that they are ignoring me.

ℛℯ

Damn, why is Dad always uprooting us, moving us on? Our school is in one town and our parish in another because Dad has settled us in yet another unincorporated neighborhood to avoid taxes. It's hard to meet people. Put another way, I am lonely.

I ache to go back to my friends and school and church and home near Seattle. Even after a year in California paradise, I miss my girlfriends. I long to visit. But Daddy has no time for vacations and Mom would never let me take the train there by myself. Even though I've saved enough from my regular babysitting jobs. How much longer will I be a prisoner of her fear?

I ask her permission to go to Seattle. It is 1962. The World's Fair. A once-in-a-lifetime educational opportunity. I cajole her, expecting nothing. I have to try.

"Well, I don't see why not," she shrugs, perhaps fearful of homicide if we spend another summer week together.

I imagine riding, all alone, by the window, up the West Coast.

"You'll find another job when you get back. You're a good worker."

I beam at one of her highest compliments.

ℛℯ

Of course the first night of our Washington reunion, conversation turns to pads and belts and nosey brothers. My friends argue about whether you should exercise during your time of the month—obviously they don't mean swimming (how could you do that?)—playing baseball and volleyball and running. Diane, who has been bleeding for a year, comes down on the side of practicality, of just getting on with your life, and I decide she is right. Once my period arrives, I will continue as usual, regardless of the pain or inconvenience, because menstruation is a natural part of adult life.

But I am not natural.

At the World's Fair, my Sacred Heart girlfriends and I ride the monorail and visit international exhibits and eat and talk from morning until after dark. Maybe I won't have to go back to California. Maybe Carol's mom will adopt me. They have a big house.

Then, suddenly, one painful morning in Seattle, nine hundred miles from my miserable California summer, I discover blood. Beautiful, dark red blood on my turquoise underpants.

Deirdre's mother gives me a hug. She asks if I need pads, if I want a cup of tea.

I am a little bewildered, mostly proud, and distractedly wonder if giving birth is anything like this.

"Oh, your mother will be so disappointed," says Mrs. Knowles. "This is the sort of moment you want to share with your daughter."

I know for sure, now, that although I am a woman—perhaps because I am a woman—I will fail my mother.

# VIII

---

*Mae, 1916*

# CHAPTER TWENTY-THREE

## Mae, Edinburgh, 1916

ON UNION PLACE, IN A SMALL, DARK TENEMENT AT THE END OF AN exhaustingly long set of stone stairs, Mae and Daniel now stayed with their three children. Arthur Conan Doyle had resided in the neighborhood in better days. Neighborhood, Mae thought to herself as she sat alone by the window one night, what now smelled like a slum had once hummed like a neighborhood. Daniel, perhaps inspired by her thoughts, determined that they would read Sherlock Holmes together in the evenings. To her surprise, this was a pleasant enough distraction—the arrogant London sleuth led such a preposterous life that you had to laugh, to forget troubles or at least be diverted.

Mae felt grateful Colin was a fit baby, eager and happy, more robust than any of her children, although he did remind her a little of Danny's spirit in the first few weeks. They named the boy after Daniel's adventurous brother Colin in Australia. Colin Campbell. No McKenzie, this one. Maybe young Colin would one day meet his uncle to ease the acrimony in Daniel's family. Surely Daniel's brother had sided so wholeheartedly with Maggie that the fraternal rift might never be bridged. It didn't bear thinking about. Daniel was frantic and frayed, working to feed these new bairns while still supporting the children with Maggie. Even though Matt and Alex were at the Front now and Bella was married, that left Donald, Nan, Chrissie, and the other wee Mae at home.

Maggie had tried to poison the young minds against their father, calling him all manner of names, saying he loved his pleasures more than his family. And Donald and the girls did seem strained around Daniel, but she was sure that would pass. If Maggie had any sense she would blame this whole mess on the Scarlet Woman. Certainly, that's how Mae, herself, saw the picture. If only she had had more discipline or sense.

She returned her attention to the sewing, thinking about her basic Gill trait of endurance. You just got on with things. And, after all, she had a lot to be thankful for. Seven healthy children. Two men who had cherished her. A solid roof over her head. She'd come a long way from being a dockworker's servant. So what if she and Daniel would never live their quiet dream in Ayr (although, Daniel, bless his heart, still held forth about this after a couple of drinks). They had a sound, loving life here and no one could take that away.

Mae had stayed up late, working under dubious light, to complete the dress for Chrissie's birthday. Strange to think of her four eldest bairns living with Jock, without her, all the way down Leith Walk. Daniel had a right to expect her to warm his bed after a long day. Morning through night now that he was working for two families. Still, she understood how important *her* two families were. He just hoped, he had told her, she wouldn't get sick cleaning other people's houses half the day with three small children in tow, then coming home to do for him and staying up late making amends gifts for Jack, Chrissie, and Johnny.

They weren't "amends gifts," she had informed him, just bonnie wee nothings with tassles on the ends—presents to remind them that she was still their mother, although she could see them only on weekends now. Besides, this was Chrissie's birthday, and an eight-year-old girl expected something special for her birthday. The lamp seemed to be growing dimmer. Too early for her eyes to go. She was still a relatively young, vigorous woman. The children kept her that way.

On Saturday, as Mae rode the tram down Leith Walk to Springfield Street, she fretted about leaving the children with Daniel. Colin was colicky and his father seemed nervous about how to tend the baby. It was beyond her how a father of nine could still act like a giraffe around his children, but there you had it. He would be fine, she told herself, and there was sturdy Mrs. Craig next door if anything went truly wrong.

Tentatively opening the parcel on her lap, she pressed the white cotton trim between her fingers. The deep red flowers in this pattern would bring out Chrissie's high color. (She was sure Chrissie understood that she missed them, that they were still her beloved bairns, that she had had no choice but to leave them behind for the sake of the babies Mae and Peggy and now wee Colin. It was Mae and Peggy she worried about—old enough to remember Chrissie, Danny, Johnny, and Jack, yet far too young to accept the breach in family, let alone to understand it.) Och, how she missed those quiet blue eyes of her eldest daughter. Chrissie, as young as she was, had become a support at home, helping with chores, keeping peace among her brothers. Becoming to Mae, well, almost a little friend. Now Mae grew more and more excited about seeing them as the tram cut through Leith. This long, long street had become a strange bridge between her two lives.

At first when no one answered, she assumed her own absentminded-ness—perhaps she was meant to come later. She waited in the dark cor-ridor, then decided she would feel less conspicuous outside. Mae paced the wet pavement up to the corner of Leith Walk and back to the house. Up and down past the Volunteer Arms, one of the less inviting names for a pub. Strange how nostalgic she felt for these grey and beige stone build-ings. After an hour, she returned to her old doorway and, hands still shak-ing from the cold or nervousness or both, scribbled a note that she would return the next day.

⌇

Again, no one answered. Mae waited. Tried the neighbors' doors, but even they were out. Odd, she thought, eerie—no, she and Daniel had been reading too much Sherlock Holmes. The next day, it was the same. Her note gone, no one there. On Tuesday, about tea time—after she had finished her cleaning jobs and arranged for Mrs. Craig to look after the children until Daniel returned from his late night at the office—she found herself pounding on their door.

Pounding, screaming, not caring if the whole bloody building heard her. Which they must have.

Danny answered, fresh-faced, hair slicked back. "Hello," he said stiffly, ages older than the twelve-year-old boy she had seen ten days before. "What are you doing here?"

"I am your mother," she said, the terror of her sleepless nights forging into fury with this impudent, innocent lad. "And I've come to visit you."

"No, you're not," he lowered his placating voice, speaking slowly, as if to a mad woman.

"Not what?"

And, as if in sincere and courteous response to her perplexity, he answered, "We have no mother."

"Daniel McKenzie!" she shouted. "How dare you?" Her voice broke. She was weeping.

He continued stiffly, "Father explained that you loved Mae and Peggy better than us. We all understand."

"What? What?" she spluttered.

And finally, *he* appeared, red-faced and mean as she'd never seen him. It was inconceivable how she could have wed this devious, obscene little man.

"All the children understand," he said in a loud voice, loud enough for the downstairs neighbors, let alone for her daughter and sons. "They know why you've gone and left us and they accept that." He began to close the heavy door on her.

"No, Jock, no," she called, and, on hearing her shout, Jack and Chrissie ran out from the table.

"Mammy," Chrissie wailed, but Danny held the girl's arm tightly. When she screamed louder, Jack set to beating on his sister.

Neighbors opened their doors.

Jock stared at her, livid, silent.

She set the precious package on the chair by the door.

Her second son spoke for them. "See what trouble you're causing. Shouldn't you want to leave now?"

Suddenly she saw that stranger again. The girl-woman now had shorter hair and wore dark blue trousers. She said nothing, but held up a small, square box, inside of which Mae watched Daniel trying to calm a screaming baby while the two girls tugged at his grey socks. "Where's Mammy? Where's Mammy?"

Mae knew she was going crazy and gripped the cold, black wrought-iron railing for balance. As she fled down the damp, stone stairs, past the reeking toilet, she noticed someone holding open the outside door to the cool sunlight. The woman in the trousers nodded sadly as Mae passed out to Leith Walk.

# CHAPTER TWENTY-FOUR

# "A Habit of Vanishing"

## *Valerie, Edinburgh, 1990s*

THE MORE I MEDITATE ON THESE LIVES, THE MORE I STARE INTO THE gaps between details. Curiosity is a progressive affliction, and lately I've been wondering about my grandmother's family. I find them in book nine of the 1881 census. Grandmother is one year old, living with her parents, Archibald and Christina, and her three siblings. Their neighbors are a clerk, a housekeeper, a van lad, and a dairyman. I want to know more, but she has disappeared by the 1891 census. I can't locate anyone except her father, Archibald, and he is on a merchant ship. (Odd how my mother and her grandmother both married merchant sailors. Mary is the patron saint of seamen.) I spend all day searching.

Finally, late in the afternoon, I see a listing for Mary Jane Gill, aged eleven, living without her family. The only other detail is an address near Coburg Lane, where she was born. Racing to find the census microfiche before the library closes, I do locate her. "Mary Jane Gill, age 11, Servant." She is living in a one-room tenement with her employers, George Dallas, a forty-five-year-old dockworker, and his wife, Martha, aged thirty-five.

An eleven-year-old servant. It fills me with amazement, then sadness. I knew she must have had a hard life, but it never occurred to me that it had been this tough for so long. When did she start the job—at age nine or ten? No wonder Mother felt such equanimity about her own life. After all, she didn't have to go out to work until she was fourteen.

I walk through Leith, trying to identify the tenements where my grandmother was born, where she worked for the Dallas family. Coburg

Lane is torn down, taken over by several shipping businesses and a big office firm called Coda Technologies. Some coda. This section of North Leith is perhaps the poorest of the neighborhoods I've seen in Edinburgh. I walk down dead-end streets and into vacant buildings, stupidly feeling immune to harm in this, my family estate. Of course, Mother was happy in her seventies living in a studio apartment across from the cafe where she worked because San Francisco's Tenderloin, for all its problems, is much more comfortable than Leith.

From the 1890s map of this neighborhood that I dig out of the National Map Library, I know that Coburg Lane ended near the Water of Leith, Edinburgh's River. These days, there is a concrete public footpath and benches. What was my grandmother's experience with the river? I wander around a graveyard, searching for McKenzie and Gill stones, until I realize that people this poor can't afford headstones. I search through the car parks and vacant lanes and find one boarded-up building that dates back to the 1870s. Its location could be the corner of Quayside and Coburg Lane. I take some photos of the desperate old thing.

Then I wander up to Manderston Street, where Grandmother lived before she married Mr. McKenzie. Most of Manderston Street seems to have been blasted for modern council housing, replacing one disaster with another. But I do take photos of the Victorian buildings there as well. Manderston is just a few blocks away from Springfield, where the McKenzies lived when Mom was born.

I already know that most of Springfield Street has also been torn down. The McKenzie-Campbells had a habit of vanishing. Not quite without a trace. When I first found Springfield Street two summers ago, I was so distressed that Mom's building had been destroyed. I was also a little shy. Today, I have come prepared to look closer. (I have been to libraries and map rooms. I know that Springfield Street is one of the oldest roads off Leith Walk, and in the 1780s Mr. McCulloch of Ardwell, Customs Commissioner, entertained the writer Samuel Foote here. Leaping ahead a century, I have scoured the Post Office Directories for the years Mom lived there. Although the McKenzies couldn't afford a listing, I do learn that when Mom was born, the neighbors included Jane Dobie, James Robb, and John Dickinson. And the establishment of Stenhouse, Williams and Sons.) Today I do find one building that dates back until at least 1910. Sturdy, grey, cold, low-storeyed, it has thick recesses for windows. I take more useless photos.

Then I venture into the Volunteer Arms to see if I can find out if the pub was here in Mom's day. There's a public house on the corner in maps dating back to the mid-1800s, but was it this public house where Mr. McKenzie drank his pints? Inside, the place smells as if it hasn't been cleaned in ninety years. Three rooms are packed with grey people who are smoking and drinking and some of whom are watching a match on the telly. Shyly, I approach the bar, but the publican ignores me. I walk further down and catch the eye of a second bartender. "Can you tell me when this pub was built?" I can hear my foolish American accent and my trivial question drowning out all the conversations and music and TV buzz. I know everyone in the pub is staring at me, this busybody with academic questions. I want to tell him I'm not a stranger. I'm not here for history, but for family flesh and bones. It takes him years to answer. "No," he says finally, barely containing his smile. "No, dear, I haven't a clue."

OK, I have some sense of place. I have visited the streets where my mother and her parents and their parents lived. I have birth certificates, marriage certificates, death certificates. From the census I know that no one in my family was "Deaf, Dumb, Blind, Lunatic, Imbecile or Idiot." I know they did not speak Gaelic. But what have I really learned?

Saddened, horrified, I am also simply astonished by this un-Scottish opera. Poverty, child servitude, proliferating babies, desertion, early death, diasporic expatriation. As I face my grandparents' daily difficulties, I understand the impossibility of the choices for which I'm holding them culpable. Still, I can't comprehend how they could have allowed all this pain.

Why did they have so many children? I don't feel them to be particularly religious. They weren't stupid. What contraception was available then? Was it too expensive? Were they too bloody-minded to use it? How much of the problem stemmed from simple, complicated lust? I don't seem to *feel* very much about my grandmother. Maybe because it's easier to be mad at my grandfather. Since I can be angry with him, I sense a connection. For her, I have mainly sorrow, incomprehension.

Then my friend Susie, a Scottish historian, lends me a book on Marie Stopes, who struggled with family planning for years and finally managed to set up the first birth control clinic in Britain—six years *after* my grand-mother's last child. Marie knew, ". . . there is nothing that helps so much with the economic emancipation of a woman as the knowledge of how to control her maternity."*

Yet it's really T. C. Smout in *A Century of the Scottish People, 1850–1950*, who clarifies the most for me: "Artificial contraception could have made some contribution (to the decline in the birth rate): from the 1880s the use of the rubber sheath in particular became better known, as a conse-qence of the much publicized trial of Charles Bradlaugh and Annie Besant for distributing 'new-Malthusian' propaganda. Contraception was evidently first practiced by the middle classes, among whom the birth rate fell first and fastest. Already by 1911, there was a well-marked class differ-ence in family size. Artificial contraception was sternly denounced by all the churches, not least by Presbyterians, who spoke of 'the withering blight cast over humanity' by its practice and demanded that the manu-facture and sale of anti-conception materials should be 'rigorously repressed.'"

As the Reverend Norman Maclean declared, "If the British race refuse to multiply and develop the resources of its vast empire, other races, not yet weary of life will inevitably displace it. If Australia and New Zealand are not occupied by the British, the yellow man cannot be shut out."†

In fact, Grandfather and Grandmother did produce many pink-faced people who did go to Australia and New Zealand and India (as well as to Canada and the United States). Reverend Maclean would have approved of their proliferation if not of their morality. And I, who have no qualms about their morality, now acknowledge that my grandmother was more powerless than naïve. Any judgment I make has more to do with my priv-ilege than her innocence. Because my moment has followed hers, I have had a chance to pursue my loves and lusts and passions with relative impunity. Childbirth, backstreet abortion, syphilis, AIDS—I sneaked through the window at a small, safe time. My grandmother was also a woman of her time and class. We all live (and die) in history.

---

* June Rose, *Marie Stopes and the Sexual Revolution* (London: Faber and Faber, 1992), xiii.
† T. C. Smout, *A Century of the Scottish People: 1830–1950* (London: William Collins Sons and Co, Ltd., 1986), 174.

# CHAPTER TWENTY-FIVE

# "Learning To Swim"

## *Mary, California, 1966*

I GLANCED OUT THE BUS WINDOW AT THE CARS STREAMING PAST. MOSTLY men drivers. Heading to work. A few women behind the wheel. Young women with children. Several my age, not many though. Yes, I was afraid to drive. Also, however, I *liked* the buses. They were a public convenience.

Or was it a public conveyance? I would look it up. But where? Well, I would ask VJ, she knew that kind of thing. It was a journalistic sort of question. I'd have to find the right time—lately I always seemed to call when she was studying, or rushing off to work at the cafeteria.

Mid-November and still hot. Well, that would change; these yellow California hills would drink in the late fall and winter storms, would turn as green as home by March. Odd how often I was thinking of Scotland as home, now that Jack had left.

This was the way to think about it: *He* had left. It was nothing to do with me. I wanted to believe that.

What a strange dream. It didn't really bear thinking about.

*(I am in my favorite seat, the middle by a window on the driver's side, in one of the newer AC buses. Unusual being the only passenger. The bus turns left and the driver is lost. He drives faster, careens around turns. Suddenly we are being followed by a fire truck. Faster. The siren. Faster. The firemen try to pass the bus but our driver is in a panic and he steps on the gas. We go faster. Faster. We are speeding into a mountain. I recognize this place: the High Street, no wonder these hills are so green. We are headed directly into Arthur's Seat. The driver comes to his senses, but can't halt the speeding bus. Hurry, hurry, he calls,*

*jump. He opens the door. But the bus is going too fast. Enraged at my cowardice, he leaps out, himself. The fire siren is louder. We are going faster, faster, straight into the mountain. I feel the front end crash, then the back as the fire truck plunges into the rear. The bus is an accordion, a collapsing accordion. And I am all alone, sitting straight in a middle seat by the window.)*

No, I shook myself and looked down at the apartment ads I had circled in the *Oakland Tribune*. I was not alone. There were at least half a dozen other people on this bus—and many more in my lucky life. I was a mother, a grandmother, a sister, a friend, a hostess at the Athenian Nile Club. And a wife—I was still, technically, and *would always be* a wife.

This is how he planned to do it—he would go away on Friday, tell them he was loading ships in Bellingham or Port Angeles. Then on Sunday (or maybe Monday night), when it was obvious he wasn't returning, I was supposed to explain to our children that their father and I were separating. He had it all figured out. A master planner, our Jack. I should file for divorce, he instructed, that was how it was done.

I remember when he proposed this scenario—we were sitting on the living room couch, drinking morning coffee. A custom I used to look forward to. I stared at him (of course, this wasn't the first time he had talked about separation, I had been staring at him for months now) and suddenly I really looked at my husband. At the boyish certainty of his chivalry.

"That's the way it's done, Pat. To protect the woman."

"Funny kind of protection," I whispered back. We really shouldn't have been having this conversation in the living room. Just a wall away from Valerie's bed. Good thing she slept like a lumberjack, like a Campbell. But still, well, we shouldn't have been having this conversation at all. We were husband and wife. Parents. We had made a life together and carried it across the entire country. Divorce was preposterous.

"Well, I'm leaving. One way or the other," he declared. "It can be on your terms or not . . . as you like."

"My terms are marriage."

"I've been telling you for months," his voice swelled. Then he checked himself, lowered the volume. He was, if nothing else, a good father. "I need a break. Some time on my own. To think things out."

One minute he was saying divorce. The next, separation. I let the contradiction hang between us. He didn't notice, just speeded along.

"A break will be good for everybody."

"I don't understand," I said. "What have I done?"

"Pat—for Christ's sake—I've told you a hundred times. You haven't *done* anything. It's me. I'm, I don't know, changing in some way. I'm fifty years old."

I stared at my empty coffee cup, not daring to get a refill because he would use the opportunity to leave the house. This was already later than he liked to take off. He'd depart at 5:30 A.M., just to beat traffic into the City. He'd get to work an hour before everyone else. Habit, after all those years of getting up early on the ship, he would say. He couldn't break it once he got a shore job.

"But you're the same man I married." If he was fifty, I was fifty-six, maybe that's what he was afraid of. "Strong. Handsome."

"Damn it, Pat," he slammed the cup down on the table so hard, Friskie started to bark. Could I hear Valerie stirring on the other side of the wall? Of course this was ridiculous. These were thick walls. In our sturdily built house, dogs barked, people talked, TV blared, children slept.

"Look, I've done the best I could, waited for Larry to graduate from high school. Waited until Valerie recovered from that nervous breakdown."

"Jack! Lower your voice."

"Well, she . . . 'worries' too much."

He looked at *me* suggestively, but surely she got this anxiety from the nuns'—*his nuns*—stories of sin and guilt.

"Waited," I blurted. "Waited alone. You didn't tell me. I mean, it's not like we've gone through this decision together. What say do *I* have?"

"But it's not about you."

It was about *her*. We both knew that I knew it. That red-haired slut he met in a bank somewhere. He'd never directly added her to the picture, but I'd found sticky strands of her coiffure on his shirts, I'd picked up the phone extension a couple of times—accidental, wrong times, but listened long enough to register that vague, high-pitched little voice.

He stared at the empty cup.

So-and-So wasn't getting any younger and she wanted a man. My man, my husband, my children's father.

"No," I answered suddenly. "*You* tell them." I felt panic, and at the same time, a stillness.

He looked at me, shocked.

"I'm not picking up after you on this one. It's your decision. You break the news."

"But Pat." He reached for my hand.

How dare he be so familiar? I never wanted to hear him use my name again. Then what would he call me, "Mrs. Miner?"

Tugging the sash of my robe tightly, I walked back to the bedroom. This ragged, old maroon chenille robe, I should take more care with my appearance around the house.

Maybe it was Robert, I thought. Maybe if I hadn't lost Robert. Maybe we never would have moved from New York. Was that the last time our marriage was truly happy?

I sat in the bed, among our still-warm blankets, then pretended to read. The July sun was shining, strong, bright. Already I could tell the day would be a scorcher.

He'd never had a gentle way with that back door. And the car. Sometimes he was steering a rocket ship when he zoomed out of the garage in the morning.

%

Our bus slowed down to let off the Bayfair Mall workers. San Leandro, so soon. I'd better pull myself together, concentrate on the day ahead: two hours of apartment hunting before work. It gave me a lift just to think of a new place. Then working lunch at the Athenian-Nile Club, I loved the classical-sounding name. We had two birthdays today: Dr. DeWitt and Mr. Seward. Mr. Seward had remarked on this red dress the first time I wore it. I wondered whether he would notice it today. Of course, such thinking was nonsense. Mr. Seward was at least five years younger than me *and* a "confirmed bachelor." Such a strange identification, as if he had gone through some ceremony, been slapped on the back—sports style— by the bishop. Besides, Mr. Seward was a businessman. If I married again, I had more in mind a professor. Lewis Stone, Ronald Coleman, that type. A grey-haired professor. I didn't care what his subject was: history, chemistry, Greek, I had a lot to learn.

And there was no hurry. Here I had a good job at a prestigious club, somewhere I felt at home. Capwells' Roof Garden Restaurant had been a fine place, of course. We got a nice type of shopper. Ladies who wanted a leisurely lunch—not the assembly-line tuna sandwich with potato chips they served in the store's basement cafe. Still, I had always dreamed of working in a dignified place like the Club, with its winged leather chairs and formal, dark hallways. It was the kind of club my father would have belonged to if he hadn't been so sick. A retreat where men came in, of an afternoon, to read the paper or chat with business associates. No problems with lunch reservations in our huge dining room—of course, if you wanted a special table, it *was* wise to book ahead—we never turned away a member.

I did contribute something special. The members had commented on it. "*A joie de vivre,*" Dr. DeWitt proclaimed. I appreciated this compliment, got the gist of it from his face, but was especially pleased when Valerie translated it for me, helpfully correcting my pronunciation. "*Joie de vivre.*" People at work were always commenting on my "personality." Mr. Seward called me their "good sport." Something had happened to my old Scots reserve.

Since going back to work six years ago, I'd felt a lift in my spirits. I mean, I was perfectly happy being a wife and mother. I loved our home. Yet, outside the house—on those social occasions with other mothers—I felt stiff, formal, a little odd. Maybe because I didn't drive. Maybe because I wasn't Catholic. I don't know, let's just say I wasn't designed to be a den mother. Other moms led the Brownies and Girl Scouts to sewing and culinary badges. I couldn't drive or swim or cook or sew. In fact, it was wee Valerie who taught *me* the blanket stitch. Anyway, after returning to work, I had discovered a sense of myself. My voice seemed stronger. I recognized an old self from Howard Johnson's and Schrafft's and Fairley's. A younger self. It's true, these days fifty-six was hardly old. I was in the prime of life.

Turning back to the classifieds, I noticed some of these apartments had air conditioning and dishwashers and swimming pools. It would kill Jack if I wound up with a swimming pool.

℞

I did try one more time. The night before he told them. He planned to leave on Saturday afternoon. We lay stiffly in our bed of twenty-five years. I couldn't imagine how either of us could sleep on a night like this.

He said, "Oh, don't be silly, what else would we do?"

I thought of Mary Queen of Scots at the eve of her execution in the cold tower, praying. One thing about Northern California summers, the air always cooled down at night.

I had to try. In my Presbyterian way, effort was a form of prayer. I knew it wasn't the geography that ruined us. We *had* been happy in Washington State. Frustrated about his tomatoes, that's for sure, but happy with the *space*, with the more temperate weather. With paneling bedroom after bedroom. I took it as a *sign* that the Giants moved west the same year we did. And then, finally, as he had always promised, we came to California. His dream was materializing—a lemon tree and more paneling and regular trips to Candlestick Park. We did have hard times in the West, too, with Mother's death, the debts, John's adolescent pranks. Valerie's nervousness. Life. On the whole a good life. Or so I thought. "Was it me, was it something I did, something I didn't do?" It sounded pathetic to ask yet *again*, but I *had* to know before it was too late.

"What?" he said drowsily. I could smell the whisky on his breath, stale cigarette smoke on his white t-shirt. He had stayed at that bar down near Lucky's until 11 P.M. This was our last real chance for communication.

"We should be able to do something about this."

He was silent.

I leaned on my elbow, facing him in the moonlight. "Jack, because if it's something I've done . . ."

"Something you've . . . " He rolled over, facing the wall, that great warm whale of a man. Smelling of sweat and booze and cigarettes, but also of anniversaries and blood and children. How could he leave? What had I done to deserve this?

"No, Pat, no," he mumbled, pretending to be sleepy.

How could anyone rest on a night like this? We *never* really talked. I should have pressed him before now.

"Look," he said, sitting up, suddenly alive there in the bed with me again.

I bent closer so he wouldn't have to raise his voice.

"Look, I've explained it's not *your* fault." He started out gently. "Not about you at all." He was growing agitated, petulant. "It's just me, my fault, *mea culpa*, I need my freedom."

"You. You." I startled both of us with my spluttering, "It's *always* about you. Our whole life together. Our whole marriage. Your kids. Your mother."

"My mother. You always told me you loved Mother." His big brown eyes widened.

He wasn't going to silence me. I would feel guilty about that later.

"Your house. Your bloody paneling. Did you ever think we might *paint* one of the walls?"

"You said you liked the paneling. I picked out the ash for you."

This wasn't the conversation we needed to have, but I couldn't help myself. "You dragging us around the country for your job."

"I am the breadwinner."

"Were."

"Were." He farted. "I was the breadwinner until you got that Mickey Mouse job at Capwells', making less than $2.00 an hour. Embarrassing me in front of my friends."

"Is that it? Was that it, really? My job?"

"Come on, Pat, I'm tired. We need to sleep for tomorrow."

I thought about how his voice came to life when he argued.

Jack rolled back toward the wall. "Not about you. Not about you at all."

❧

The Fruitvale bus stop. A lot of people transferred here. Sunny, as always in Fruitvale, or was the sun my imagination? I lived in my imagination these days. Fruitvale was a nice neighborhood. I could picture renting a small house here. Lots of shops, schools, churches, families. But at this stage of my life—that's what this was, a new stage of life—a convenient, comfortable apartment would be just the thing. Strange how one stage could follow so fast on another. Just ten years ago I was setting up house on the far side of the continent. Washington State would be home to me, my three children, my mother-in-law, and my husband, who had finally found a shore job that would allow him to spend time with the family.

Now, in 1966, Mother was dead. Jack was gone. John was father to two girls. Valerie was rooming at Berkeley. Larry was the only one living with me. Wee Larry, bless his heart, studying so hard in those classes at

Cal State. One day, he would be gone too, off to a marriage or—God forbid—the war. Meanwhile, I had to find an apartment with two bedrooms. Yes, I quite liked the idea of this one with the swimming pool. "The Jackson Lake Apartments," it had a ring. I mean, on a hot day, after work, it would be pleasant to dangle my paining feet in the cool, turquoise water. We were headed to downtown Oakland now.

Fine, I was going to be fine. I just had to get used to this new state of affairs. I had to stop crying. That's why I cut out those martinis before I went to bed.

I needed to stop running the divorce through my mind again and again. I had to stop phoning Valerie so often. Of course she was impatient with me the last time, after all, she had her own problems. And this separation-divorce-whatever-it-was must be hard on her. On all the kids. He was their father. Yes, I had to stop calling and stop crying. The last thing I would ever want to do is be a burden on my children

Perhaps the silver-haired professor would teach me to swim.

I pulled the cord. Thanked the driver. There was never too much common courtesy in the world.

# IX

*Mae, 1917*

# CHAPTER TWENTY-SIX

*Mae, Edinburgh, 1917*

SOMEWHERE BETWEEN THE BEGINNING OF LLOYD GEORGE'S ADMINIS-
tration and the end of Tsar Nicholai's rule, Mae and Daniel conceived
again. On the scale of historical events, this was a minor note, Mae understood. She was just a common city woman with too many children. She
had seen this often enough—in her own building, in her own family. Look
at Mam. Look at Jessie. This was woman's lot. And the luck of the draw.

Still, at first, she denied the belly. Not only would this bairn be a cruel
stroke of Providence but he/she/it was biologically impossible. You weren't
meant to conceive when you were nursing. Everyone said so. The milk
prevented it. Colin was a hungry one, always eating. It embarrassed her
sometimes, how these breasts had swollen. Most of her life, she had fea-
tured herself as unwomanly. More of a tow-haired waif or gamin. But she
was thirty-seven now and the recent years had filled her out. Daniel said
he found her curvaceous. That's what mattered. She had the love of her
children and a fine man. Yes, they had normal relations, but she *couldn't*
be pregnant. Not again.

When she missed her monthly in October, she decided it was nerves.
Anxiety over money and that spot of trouble Daniel had with his coughing. What a cold, long November it had been. She began to take the children for walks up Calton Hill. How proud she was of her three wee
bairns. Old women would stop and declare about Colin's beauty. She
thought he resembled her own brother Willie, at that age, Willie now
dead from a mining accident ten years.

Sometimes she pretended their story was as simple as this: she was an ample woman, mother of three, wife of Daniel Campbell, a bright man ascending fast at his office. This is what she told the ladies at the Greenside parish. This is what she told her children. A version of this. As much as they could understand.

She tried not to think on just how much young Mae did understand. She was a bright lass who loved to sit at her father's feet when he read. It was a pleasure to see their natural loyalty. She was Papa's girl in looks, in temperament, affection. Mae didn't feel jealous exactly. No, she was happy for the two of them and dreamily wished she had had such a connection with her own father so long ago.

Sometimes she almost believed her story was this uncomplicated. That the years with Jock (and Johnny and Danny and Chrissie and Jack) had been an imaginary life, a slipped life. Of course she missed the children terribly, but tried not to dwell on pain. She felt heavy guilt, although she understood life wasn't chosen from a set of alternatives. In this case, it wasn't a situation of either/or, but rather this/then/that. The hike up Calton Hill would do them all good. Shake loose the cobwebs. Provide a little fresh air. Oh, they had to move from that stuffy house soon. She didn't like sharing the address with Greys, a drinking hotel. Meanwhile, the walk wouldn't do any harm, might even get her plumbing running.

Mae loved to stand on the hill looking down at the High Street and Holyrood House and Arthur's Seat. Loved to tell them stories of the graceful city where they had all had the luck to be born. Mam had warned her about sentimentality, had told her directly that she couldn't afford romanticism. Yet girls who become child servants need a natural elixir like sentiment, safe and free for the taking. Lately, little Mae, who had been listening closely to her father, had begun to relate her own stories about Mary Queen of Scots.

The weather broke colder. All the more reason to take the children out of the house, to get some exercise. The hike became more arduous. Colin was filling out—it was much harder to push the pram—and so was she broadening. Mae knew from the tightness of her dresses and the chaos in her stomach that she *could* well be pregnant. Yet she had lost one baby, that ghostly child who had caused Jock McKenzie to marry her. God forgive her, she hoped she would lose another. Everyone knew the first month of pregnancy was the trickiest. You should be careful, especially if you were taking exercise.

Oh, it was vile of her to hope against the babe. God's will be done. He never gave us anything we couldn't bear. And yet, and yet, maybe He had erred this once. For how was she to cope with *four* small ones in that tiny space? Could she carry Colin and another bairn up the dark, stone stairwell? The skylight gave them no help on these grey winter afternoons. Already their clothes were piled in the coal bunker—folded, yes, but still a mess; the children's bed was part shoved under their bed. There were seventeen people who shared the hallway toilet and sink. How would they feed, clothe, another child? This was the fifth time she had gotten pregnant with Daniel. Plus four more times with Jock. How did women cope? How did you avoid carrying? How did you deny your husband? Birth was, after all, a natural process. God knew what He was doing.

She couldn't burden Daniel with this. He had so much on his mind at work. He was worried about his sons Alex and Donald fighting in Europe. Strapping youths, who should have been home courting girls, getting married, having children of their own. Yes, Daniel was at a time in his life to be a grandfather. He had had enough strain with these three wee angels underfoot. No, God was merciful, loving. He wouldn't do this to Daniel.

Peggy was a pretty one, with eyes as blue and bright as Jessie's. A playful, daring little flirt, unlike her serious sister Mae. She'd adapted more easily to the move from North Leith. Seemed to forget her brothers and sisters there. Whereas Mae would often ask after them, particularly after her big brothers. Is Johnny any taller? How is Danny's school? Brief queries in a flat, young voice.

Mae was ashamed, really, when she thought of it, but if this daughter weren't so inquisitive, she could pretend better. Just the five of them, a happy wee family. She was coy in answering questions from the women at church, and what they didn't ask, she didn't tell. At home, Daniel stayed off the topic of Maggie's rage. He did mention her children, occasionally, just as he would mention his own. That was natural. Yet he was always careful, somehow, to know the right moment, a time when she could remember the children without weeping. Oh, Lord, what had they done? Between them there were *fourteen* children in all. Surely this was enough.

She waited until December. Waited patiently, impatiently, numbly, for the blood that would release them. Instead, she swelled and ached, grew by the day more exhausted and seasick. No amount of climbing hills or hot bathing or praying would relieve her. She felt so crowded. So alone.

No one on God's earth was alone. Mae had Mrs. Guthrie. Mrs. Guthrie, who had helped in the birthing of Colin. Mrs. Guthrie was a woman made for emergencies.

Mae considered keeping it from Daniel. What need had Daniel of women's news, with his mind full of war and work? Then she realized that if she were to send the children to Jessie for a week, "for a holiday in the healthier environment of Fife," as Jessie was always bothering her, she would have to tell the truth to Daniel. Besides, it would be just as well to have someone home that afternoon in case any caretaking was needed. Not that she imagined there would be, the baby just started. Mrs. Guthrie did this all the time. Yes, women did this all the time.

Who knew, with the children on holiday and after a couple of quiet days to recover, she and Daniel might even find themselves walking along Princes Street, admiring the holiday windows.

# CHAPTER TWENTY-SEVEN

# "Ghostwriter"

*Valerie, Berkeley, 1966–1971*

THE PHONE HANGS ON THE WALL NEXT TO THE DOOR. TECHNICALLY ON my roommate Susan's side of our dorm room. The phone I neglect to use when I avoid calling my mother for five weeks.

Susan and I are so happy to be at Berkeley, after our freshman years at the more homogeneous campuses of Davis (*moi*) and Santa Barbara. My first college year was so claustrophobic I became immobilized in the looney ward, then so tanked up on meds at Davis that my parents finally relented and allowed me to transfer to radical Berkeley. After all, I'd be rooming with Susan, my sensible, straight-A friend from high school.

My parents are right, of course, in worrying that the move will change me forever. I drop the meds, and if I'm not thoroughly happy, I'm excited to be alive. Berkeley is large, cosmopolitan, stimulating, and blessedly anonymous. No one notices me here.

Mom and Dad aren't adept, themselves, at staying put. My mother is an immigrant; my father is a sailor; and our family is always shifting from one place to another. So, in July when Dad announces that he is leaving my mother, I am shocked and terrified, but not completely surprised. And while Mom acts stalwart at first, she falls apart by my nineteenth birthday in late August. I am relieved to be away from the house now. At Berkeley. Finally.

This place is so far beyond my dreams—the top school in the country, they tell us—that I don't even think about graduating. English from Crews; Anthropology from Washburn; Physics from Karplus.

Rabble-rousing from Mario Savio and Bettina Aptheker. Just being here is enough. I have no further aspiration.

At night, Susan and I take off our contacts and peer at the Berkeley hills, imagining all those lights are stars. I had wanted a room overlooking the vast Bay, but Susan persuaded me that the hill view was preferable. This reflects a difference in our temperaments—my hunger for mobility versus her appreciation of context; her generous curiosity about where we had been (history major) versus my urgent focus on where we might go (incipient journalist)—that will last for at least thirty more years. After savoring our fuzzy view and gossiping across the room about dorm neighbors and cute guys and our dining commons jobs, we say good night and turn toward our separate walls. I try not to think about my mother.

"He's your father, no matter what happens between him and me," she calls the dorm to tell me. "It's important for you to remember he loves you. He'll always be your father."

A refrain we have heard before.

"You shouldn't be cross with him. He did what he thought he had to do."

I am too filled with hurt—for her and more obliquely for myself—to be angry with him.

She is noble. For the first few weeks she is also tough. Then she begins to sob.

Her expression of pain embarrasses me. I am lost. The worst suffering from her I've ever witnessed was her once-a-year splitting headache. The worst suffering I've ever consciously witnessed.

"I can talk with *you*," she says, on another day, between sobs. "You're the girl."

I don't know what to say.

"You don't have to say anything. Just listen."

But I have trouble listening. She doesn't understand that *my* family is falling apart. He left *me*, too. Us. No, I don't fully accept this either. I just know I'll go crazy again if I have to keep listening. Maybe because we never discussed Grandma's mental illness. Crazy scares me more than anything. Always has.

One afternoon, after a bad midterm and almost late to my shift in the cafeteria, I answer the phone and hear her now familiar weeping.

Not now, Mom, I want to say.

Instead, "I'm sorry. I'm late for work."

Silence.

And somehow I manage to ask her to stop calling for a while.

Affronted, she says she will wait to hear from me. I wait, she waits, five weeks.

Five guilty weeks. Five quiet weeks. Five relieved weeks before I call.

Ever since, I've been ashamed. Because she was right. She didn't have anyone else. I'm the girl.

❧

BERKELEY, 1971

Dad is still not paying his alimony or back child support. He has moved out of state to escape the law—to Nevada. Years later I will learn that this is part of a social epidemic, this syndrome of stiffing the ex-wife. But right now, at age twenty-four, I am ashamed of my father. Ashamed he is my father, fearful that I have inherited his genes, angry for my mother. Worried about her. Mom can't afford a lawyer. But she does have a daughter. A daughter who followed her advice and learned to type. (Mom still thinks she'll take that up in retirement.) So her daughter sits down and writes a threatening letter to the man who will always be her father.

October 10, 1971

Dear Jack:

I am once again writing to ask you to send me the money you owe me which amounts to almost six thousand dollars. In fact, it probably amounts to more than that when you consider the interest I could have accumulated.

My attorney has assured me that he could procure a judgment immediately. I have no desire to go to court. I will not hesitate to bring suit, however, if you evade this letter. In fact, rather than pay an attorney, I shall apply for legal assistance (for which I am qualified due to your debt to me.)

I am very much in need of the money.

Sincerely,
Pat

cc: my attorney and myself
*Ghostwritten by the girl.

℞

Twenty-five years later, after both Mom and Dad are dead, I find the following letter from the IRS among Mom's papers:

30 October 1971

Department of the Treasury
Sixth and Lenora Building
Seattle, Washington 98121
District Director
Internal Revenue Service

Mary G. Miner
1525 Jackson Street, Apartment 312
Oakland, CA 94612

Dear Mrs. Miner:

In the process of the audit of another person's Federal tax return, we find we need answers to the following questions. Will you please state whether you received alimony in 1970; and if so, how much? If you did receive alimony in 1970 did you report it on your 1970 tax return?

Please also furnish to us: your social security number and the address that you used on your 1970 tax return.

Very truly yours,
J. Swanson
Auditor

# "The Light Should Last Forever"

## *Mary, California/Edinburgh, 1968*

I HAD BEEN WAITING FOR THIS. I DIDN'T KNOW HOW OR WHEN, BUT I knew she would leave one day. I was suspicious when she called from Berkeley to say, let's have dinner Thursday. A weeknight away from the library? This meant something. Like all of us, my girl worked too hard.

It was a lovely French restaurant near Lake Merritt, a little pricey and a little saucy, but the nice waiter gave us a private table by the wall. She stalled nervously until salad was served.

"I've applied to a summer program at the University of Edinburgh."

Not—May I go? Will you let me leave the country? Not, I'm going back to your home, is that OK?

I ate a roll to absorb this news. Well, she *never* asked permission these days. I hadn't been able to tell her a damn thing since she was eighteen. What had I done wrong? Was college responsible? Her generation? She never seemed to ask anything, except those infernal, nosey questions.

"Isn't that expensive?" I finally responded.

No, she explained, besides, she had money in her savings account from all those jobs. She could get a student charter flight. Being my daughter, she had the economics sorted out.

"And I kind of hoped you'd come over." She was finishing her second roll. "Maybe before classes start, you know, to show me Edinburgh and to visit Uncle Johnny."

Said with the evenness of, "How about a trip to Ghirardelli Square this weekend? She did not, of course, know what she was asking. This dream: to bring back my daughter. This nightmare: to return to all that fearful sadness. What would I recognize? Would the place be thick with ghosts who could trap me there?

"Too expensive." I shook my head and picked at the salad. "It's the wrong time. Someday. But not just now."

"You get a two-week vacation," she said, "and charter flights are cheap. Britain is cheap, especially with the exchange rate."

"No, I don't think so."

"I'll help you. I've saved a lot of money."

"Oh, don't be silly. I have some money saved too, I . . ."

"Then it's settled. June in Edinburgh. Think about the light, it should last forever that far north."

She sometimes forgot, I sometimes forgot, who was the mother here. By the time our fish was served, she had added London and Paris to the itinerary. I told myself it would be good for her to get away from her pleasant, but unimaginative, boyfriend for the summer. I may have failed as a wife, but I had raised three lovely children—bless their hearts—and my Berkeley-educated, French-speaking daughter was about to take me to the Eiffel Tower, Royal Albert Hall, and back home to Union Place.

Well, she was twenty. The age I was when I left Scotland. And if she had to cross the ocean in the contrary direction, this was probably the right time.

℞

We met in London. Different charter flights. Cheaper that way. We had booked the first night at the St. James Hotel (a recommendation from one of the members of the Athenian-Nile Club). After this, we would stay at cheap B and Bs. Seventeen dollars a night was an extravagance, of course, but I knew we would both be exhausted the first night and I wanted to start out on the right foot, at least in the right mood, because we *could* bicker (like any mother and daughter) when we were tired.

She was a good little traveler, full of ideas. Start with a tourist coach. Soon we were perched on the top deck of one of those teetering buses, oogling, blinking at the London fairytale: Big Ben, Parliament, the Thames, Trafalgar Square, Picadilly Circus. Was it possible? Had I really crossed the earth and thirty-eight years in one day?

The first night, VJ's friends—Londoners who had gone to Berkeley, where did she pick up all these people?—took us out to the Tower of

152

London and a green brocade pub where a tipsy fellow tried to hold my hand. I wasn't too old, at fifty-eight, to blush.

The next day we visited Westminster Abbey, which seemed eerily familiar because VJ and I had been there fifteen years ago, front-row guests at the Coronation. I've never been one for Anglican extravagance, but the main altar *was* stately. And you couldn't help being impressed with the coffins of so many famous figures: John Milton, Jane Austen, Thomas à Beckett, Mary Queen of Scots.

&

Paris was a bit scary. That syrupy language was tricky as quicksand. I'd never been in a place where I didn't understand the words (OK, there had been New York for the first two weeks).

Then the hotel: red draperies and a bidet in our room. What kind of establishment had she found?

"Economical," Valerie grinned with the ignorant fearlessness of youth.

We did sleep well, through breakfast the first couple of days, and I came to like the wry, mustachioed clerk who winked as he gave us our key each night. Picnics on the Seine. Notre Dame. The Flea Market. Elegant shops of scarves and perfumes. Did I deserve this?

I shouldn't have drunk so much in Paris. "Everyone does," my world-weary daughter assured me. Regardless, it's possible I *never* would have been ready for Edinburgh.

&

Yes, I know it's taken me a long time to reach this part—the whole *purpose* of the trip. All right. On the train from London to Edinburgh, despite my buzzing head, I tried to prepare her. We sat beside one another drinking British Rail stewed tea and cello-wrapped biscuits. I mused at the speeding countryside, so strange to take this express train straight back to my past. Glancing away from the window momentarily, I caught her eye and began my confession.

"You know, something I've never told you . . . but you're old enough now."

Her face lit with worried curiosity.

"Well, when I was born, well, my mother wasn't married to my father." I couldn't look at her. I had to finish the story. "You see, she was married to Mr. McKenzie. That's why I'm a McKenzie, not a Campbell like my father. And, you see," I rushed ahead to forestall questions, "Uncle Johnny and I have the same mother. But different fathers. And Aunt Bella and I have the same father, but different mothers." I was afraid this all sounded more complicated than it was.

She seemed to be taking everything in. Then suddenly, forlornly, "You mean Aunt Bella and Uncle Johnny aren't related?"

"Well, no, of course they're *related*, I mean, we never thought about things like that." Flustered, I plowed ahead. "So, you see, I was waiting until you were old enough to explain." Already it was a huge weight off my shoulders. I hoped she wasn't too ashamed.

Valerie looked surprised, concerned, but not ashamed. She said that it must have been hard on me growing up. She told me not to use words like "illegitimate" and "bastard." I was as legitimate as the next person.

I had turned back to the window. I hated it when she treated me as if I were naïve.

So hard to talk about; so much Valerie couldn't possibly understand. Yet before she met Johnny later that day, I *had* to explain. No, this wouldn't come up directly in the course of our visit, but I didn't want her confused by oblique references and then thundering forth with questions.

"Well, what side is Aunt Nan on?"

A whole new world had opened to her, God help us.

"My father's," I said tersely.

"And Uncle Danny?"

"My mother's. He was/is Johnny's brother." To curtail the entire inventory, I said, "That's enough for now. I really don't want to go into it."

Outside, rain had started, a fine June mist that I hadn't seen for almost forty years. God, I felt so happy and sad.

"But, but . . ." she flushed and got that about-to-explode with curiosity look in her eyes, a desperate expression, really, that made me nervous. She seemed to believe in urgent answers to difficulties rather than practical, gradual solutions.

I held my silence.

Then she assumed the wise-before-her-time expression. "It's all right, Mom. I mean, marriage is just a social convention. It doesn't *matter* that your parents weren't technically married when you were born."

Doesn't matter! I held my tongue. Doesn't *matter* that the result was two, no three, fractured families. Death. Separation. More death. Doesn't matter? Oh, not that I blamed my parents. We all have urges. It was simply sad. An accident. I was an accident and a source of guilt. Not my fault, either, of course, but shaming nonetheless.

"It's only a legality, Mother," she spoke patiently, reassuringly. "Marriage is just a ritual."

I continued to keep my counsel. Just a ritual, my quarter century with Jack. Our family. Wife. Mother. Not a ritual. A life. This girl didn't know. This silly girl lived in her head. One day she would grow up, calm down, come to understand, one day. Meanwhile, I changed the subject, to something that would occupy her mind.

"Did you know," I asked, "that Johnny was a drummer in the McKenzie Highlanders, that he went to India in World War I?"

"World War *I*?" she blanched.

Rain threatened more loudly now. Real rain. I imagined it on my thirsty face.

℞

We had an hour in Edinburgh before the train to Fife. Good thing we would be heading out to Johnny's straight away. Just one glimpse of Auld Reekie had filled me with disbelief and regret. Disbelief that I had ever lived in this tired, beautiful city, disbelief that I had deserted it.

"Do you recognize anything?" She asked excitedly.

Regret in going. And in coming back. I was too full to express any of this to Valerie.

How could I answer such a question, "Do you recognize anything?" Recognize. Anything.

Looking at Edinburgh now was like opening my eyes after four decades of darkness. I had left at age twenty. It was an ancient city then, now. Nothing had changed. And everything.

℞

Johnny and Jean lived in a tidy, old stone house overlooking the green, rolling hills of Burntisland. Everything was comfortably familiar. I *supposed* this plump, grey and pink old man of sixty-eight *was* my brother. He looked enough like, well, a little like, Johnny as a young man. Why do we imagine people as ever-young? My brother had been stolen. He had lived a whole life since he'd seen me—he and his stalwart Jean. Was my brother the young man who he was or the old man who he became? And if he was this stranger, what business had I of being here at all?

As this nonsense distracted my brain, VJ was busily chatting away with gregarious Johnny. I might need her as a translator here more than I had in France.

Over tea, he was happy to reminisce about India, how he had run away and lied about his age to enter the military.

"Pass the *chini*, love?" he said.

I stared.

"Sugar, oh, I forget, sometimes slip into Hindi."

Valerie wanted to know what job he had retired from?

"Security guard," Jean explained. "Never pilfered a *penny*, although there were some that did."

"Och, that's behind us now, hen," he dismissed her complaint, her compliment.

ೱ

Jean, being a woman, knew what I wanted—I hope I hadn't been too obvious—a *bath* and a towel fresh from the warming rack. (At $2.50 a go, we had avoided the tub in Paris. But French sponge baths had their limits.) Nothing more comforting than a hot bath.

Then there was food.

Tea with coconut cake, gingerbread, shortbread.

A tour of their sweet garden, bursting with peas and tomatoes and leeks and peppers.

Then food again.

Supper—on a fresh tablecloth every meal: a newly laundered, hand-embroidered cloth (and the nicest one—I truly think this—was made of World War II sacking). On the mantle of the artificial fireplace, between the clock and the transistor radio, there were three framed photographs—Johnny's children (poor Una had died early of rheumatoid arthritis), Chrissie in Toronto (Had I ever mentioned her to Valerie?), and someone whom I knew, yet did not know, was our mother.

An odd picture—black hat, black coat, and between them curly blond hair, a full face. Mouth closed over protruding teeth; eyebrows plucked over fair eyes (blue? green? hazel?). Of course, maybe she wasn't wearing black. Maybe it was deep red. Or purple. I can't imagine green. A handsome woman, not pretty because of the sour expression, maybe dour. She looked so formal, so sober, as if she had dressed for a funeral, but surely they didn't take portraits at funerals. This woman had a lot on her mind; she was a serious person. Oddly, she looked fiftyish, although she died in her thirties. I wanted to remember, tried all the angles of this single photograph, but she was no one I knew.

I returned to the conversation about how Johnny made Jean immigrate back from Canada because of the cold. Jean complained that she missed the drama of winter landscape. His skin was turning blue just thinking about it.

VJ kindly listened to us rattle on. Then again, this encounter was a feast for my girl's big curiosity. I could tell she was frustrated that we talked more of our grown-up lives than of our childhoods (we already knew quite enough about our childhoods), more about each other's children than about our own brothers and sisters.

In Burntisland, days passed like that—was it months?—eating, talking, walking along the beach, eating, talking. Johnny and Jean had strung a line of peanuts across the kitchen window, and each day's headlines concerned bird sightings: types, coloring, frequency. Astonishing. He must have inherited that taste from Mr. McKenzie. Definitely not a bird person, I was happy to live downtown, free of such morning racket.

℞

I summoned the courage for a day in Edinburgh. We took the train back across the Firth. Then walked from Waverley down Broughton Street to the old neighborhood. Fast. Valerie walked fast and carried a map.

First, I saw St. Mary's—how could you miss it—still as regal after all those years of walking by St. Patrick's Cathedral on my way to work in New York.

Then a sweet shop—from the old days? Judging by the dust on the penny candy jars, quite possibly. We stopped for treacle, caramel toffee, and chocolate-covered snowballs. Valerie was fascinated and disgusted. The indulgent daughter insisted on paying.

As we proceeded toward Union Place, my heart raced.

Valerie was sampling a smidge of treacle; she declared it "interesting."

Interesting: too much education, this girl. Treacle was more like thrillingly crunchy or blissfully sticky or even cloyingly sweet. Interesting was a silly, dismissive response.

Union Place appeared before us. I was busy savoring the toffee. And, there it was—just a building. How little I felt. Just another multistorey tenement. Then a rush of memories—the cold metal railing along the stairwell, the lavatory in the corridor, the way we called our one room a "house." This had been my house, my home for over ten years. Other people lived there now. I felt safe. All I had to do was turn away.

"That's it," she said excitedly. "That's it." She had taken the precaution of asking the address this morning. And why did I have to remember it? Why did I have to tell the truth about what I remembered?

I stared at her now, my new world in my old life. Smiling with her red cheeks and wide grey eyes. I wondered at this legacy of reproduction, wondered why she needed to remember what she hadn't experienced while I needed to forget what I had.

"Yes," I admitted to her, that was my home. Where Colin was born. Where our mother died. So long ago. I was beyond that—had found safety, had created a whole new family—we were all beyond that. It was simply a building. A shell. Enough. Time to go.

"But don't you want to step inside?" she looked at me, amazed. "To look at your apartment? To see what you remember?"

"No."

"Come on."

She didn't know, couldn't know, for who would have told her, that the "apartments" here were one or two closet rooms with very little light. We had a window, I remember seeing folk coming and going from the shops, from the church, up and down Calton Hill. I hooked the wooden shutters at night, to close out the cold and noise. I loved that time of day, all of us safe inside, cosy, not cramped. Which did I dread more—her seeing it, or visiting it myself? Well, I could do something about the latter.

She went up alone. Up to the second floor at the corner of the stairs.

I paced back and forth on the pavement, praying for her. What would she meet in the stairwell? Who would answer our door? But this kid had a will. There was no stopping Captain Valerie once she set sail.

Sooner than I had dared hope, she was returning down the steps. Irritated, dejected, she explained that no one (thank God!) had been home.

So we explored the neighborhood. This was safer, even fun. I recalled the local stores, like Mitchell's and the shop where our neighbor, Mr. Thompson, was the assistant butcher. So many ghosts, whose stories I hadn't remembered for years. Mr. Matthew, the postman. Mr. McConochie, the waiter. James Stevenson, the tailor downstairs. "How about this one?" she asked outside a Pakistani greengrocer.

"Well, management has changed, but, yes, yes, I'm sure this is where Father would send me for chipped fruit and *The News of the World*."

VJ seemed to be enjoying this, too, and clutching that map, alternating as voyeur and guide.

*Ro*

After a few more days at Johnny's, we did visit town again. I wanted to show her Princes Street, but it had seriously deteriorated since the twenties. Yes, there was Binns, Jenners, Forsyths. But look at these cheesy chain shops and tourist stores. Of course I realized we were tourists; I even felt a strange freedom in that.

Everywhere we saw such good buys on woolens. I bought Christmas gifts and had them shipped back home. Home *from* Edinburgh. As if this city were someone else's fable and not the wellspring of my life. America was home. "Interesting," as my diplomatic daughter would say.

We had always shopped well together. Co-conspirators, something in the blood. Here on Princes Street, she was charmed by the clerks who negotiated without cash registers, who still made change through vacuum tubes along the ceiling (now that brought a person back). The clerks referred to us as "love," and "dear." The ones who called us "hen" got to me. I kept gulping my breath, trying to feel it go down. I told myself just to keep breathing.

On the Royal Mile, we stopped for tea and biscuits (biscuit, not cookie, the word had returned automatically). Did I ever think, those days at Fairley's that I'd be taking my daughter to tea on the High Street? We walked afterward—downhill toward Holyrood House—sauntered, poked in shops, paid a visit to St. Giles.

Then, we stumbled on Milton House School. I didn't remember it being this close to the Tollbooth. My nostrils swelled with the rich, damp smell of those wynds and closes I took on my shortcut to school. The two-storey school building was just as imposing and as ornate as I recalled.

Valerie pointed to a stone laid in the neighboring building. The 1612 inscription read, "Blessit Be God in all His Giftis." Aye, I remembered that.

And I could never forgot the handsome Victorian school next door, the holy grey and red stone building. Here, she did cajole me to step inside, explaining that school was dismissed for the day and we wouldn't cause a disturbance. (I said to myself, OK, VJ was going to be a teacher; she knew about schools. This would be fine.) The narrow hallways were redolent with familiar polish and mildew. The back windows still looked out on the Salisbury Craigs and Arthur's Seat. Altogether, an aristocratic setting, even if I do say so myself.

As we walked further down the High Street, toward dinner, toward tomorrow, I thought how once upon a time I did live here. Many years ago, I was real here.

Next a longer excursion, one I had really looked forward to, alone with my daughter. Crammond, the seaside resort where Nan had taken her younger sister before she sailed forever to America. Valerie and I rode the coach down to Charlotte Square, then over the Dean Bridge, along the Queensferry Road, and forty-five minutes later (it seemed longer in 1928, but transport was slower then) we were at the top of a familiar hill. Down we walked—a trek that felt strangely longer than it did when Nan and I had had short, young legs. There it was.

I suppose Crammond didn't amount to much, really, a tiny village on the Firth, with white houses and tiled roofs. Years ago, I imagined that Nan and I had gone to Spain. Now the frame of reference had changed. California. This looked like the California coast, like those pretty houses Jack would never buy because surely the roofs leaked. Mexican, he shrugged. I had pictured Spain, then, too. Never recalling Crammond.

I remembered. Nan and I were on an outing alone. My older sister wanting *my* company. Eating lunch on a bench overlooking the harbor of small boats. Walking along the pier to toss crusts to the dignified white swans. This is how it had looked four decades ago, right? Well, these ancient white houses must have been here. But the swans? Had they been swans or gulls then? How much did I really recall? How much did I imagine? What was the difference?

Something mysterious about this place Valerie was now calling the Scottish Riviera. Nan simply loved it, and that's why she brought me. This village felt *so* familiar, although I was sure I had been here only once before. Crammond was a between-worlds sort of place. Clearly Edinburgh, but not.

ℛℯ

Our last day together, 30 June. (Scotland in June! she had exclaimed, the light will last forever. Already it was diminishing.) June, when I was born, was one of those miserly, short-a-day months. For our final adventure, I took Valerie—or she took me, it was hard to tell after two weeks here— to Portobello.

Such a busy place—as it had been then. We walked past tiny, neat beach houses. New people in mini-skirts and bellbottom trousers wore familiar red faces and blue eyes. They patronized the same sweet shops. She insisted on stopping. Yes, chocolate-covered snowballs, caramel toffee. VJ bought a bag of each. Suddenly, she had grown sentimental. But I insisted we eat lunch first. So, carrying vinegary fish and chips wrapped in newspaper, sweets melting in their little white paper bags, we traipsed to a beach looking out to the sea.

This wasn't the beach—you needed an ocean for a real beach—any more than Crammond was a beach. Here was only a sea, the Firth of Forth, the North Sea separating Scotland from Holland and Denmark and Norway. I was no longer the dutiful daughter. By now, I had crossed the Atlantic Ocean, had lived one life with a man who sailed to Japan and China and Australia. I had taken automobile journeys with my family up and down the coast of the Pacific Ocean from Vancouver to Los Angeles. I knew oceans. Still, whenever I dreamt of the beach, it was of these lapping, Portobello waves.

After lunch on the sunny sand, she dragged me out to the water, offered to carry my shoes if I'd walk with her on the hard, grey crust between land and sea. So we strolled for a while, cool water tucking in under my tired feet (if God would grant me one exchange, I'd turn in these feet). Such a *physical* sensation, all of it, the sun, that tart, salty smell. It brought a person back. We talked about other beach promenades, when she was a girl and I was a wife and mother, when I was doing what a woman is meant to do with her life.

"Do you remember when we took you to Spring Lake? I guess you would have been five or six?"

"I remember the sunburn," she laughed.

Coos Bay, Oregon, I recalled, Santa Cruz, California.

"And do you remember Long Beach, wandering along the shore after that Elvis movie—just the two of us?" she smiled.

Returning to the present, I registered the Scottish figures: a hawk-faced, gaunt older couple, a short woman pushing a pram with her two tow-haired children. My first son had been blond, a little god in golden curls. Both VJ and LJ had dark hair, but John took after my mother. Looking at this terribly young girl with her wee bairns, I counted my blessings. That I had lived a life before I married. That I had three healthy, grown children. I was luckier than this young thing and luckier than my blonde mother. I was a Scottish woman walking along the Scottish coast with my Scottish daughter.

"What's that putrid stuff?" Valerie laughed as a small boy walked by, sucking a bright pink stick.

"Edinburgh Rock," I answered, laughing back at her and at the laddie's greed. Curious, how some words can be buried in a person, ready to call up a whole life. I hadn't thought about Edinburgh Rock in decades.

"Should we buy some on the way back to town?" she asked in a humoring-the-mother voice.

I wasn't quite listening, the rock putting me half in mind of another journey, one Father and Colin and I took to Portobello. I remember Colin burying himself in the sand. I think it had been a grey afternoon.

Back to town. Yes, I was very tired. A long day, a long journey. Six thousand miles. I could use a cup of tea. A moment to put up my miserable feet.

☙

That was how June ended, and along with it the trip. Still, this expedition felt fantastical—perhaps more than ever as I perched in the airport bus by the window (she had instructed me to board the bus early, to secure a good seat), waving good-bye to my daughter. I was flying home to America and she was studying in Edinburgh. My daughter attending literature and philosophy and history classes at the University of Edinburgh.

We hadn't done so badly, we McKenzie-Campbells, if this had happened in just one generation. She would be staying at lovely hostels off Craigmillar Road. Taking the bus home along the street that changed from North Bridge to South Bridge to Nicholson to Clerk to South Clerk to Newington and on southeast to the hostel each evening. *I* always felt more settled, when I knew my bus route.

But this was *not* me, I reminded myself. This was my daughter. Going to University as Miss Geddes promised.

No, no. NO! I looked out through the cold, nasty rain. I couldn't do it, couldn't leave my wee lassie in Scotland as a reckoning for some long ago promise. No. Although I had dreamed about bringing her to Scotland, I had never considered *leaving* her here.

Valerie was smiling unaccountably, waving that crooked left arm while she gripped her schoolbooks with the other. School.

Just summer school.

I had responsibilities at home. A good job. A nice apartment. Sons. Grandchildren. It was time to go home *from* Scotland.

I could still get off the bus.

Our driver started the motor, an ugly, deafening noise.

She was blowing kisses, getting soaked, waving widely.

I could still get off.

The bus began to move.

My job, the rest of my family loomed large, so I stayed put, fretting for her safety. I waved back.

She *would* return to me. Absolutely. I willed this. I refused to lose another soul to this damned and blessit city.

# X

---

*Daniel, 1917*

# CHAPTER TWENTY-NINE

## Daniel, Edinburgh, 1917

YOU WERE TOO NUMB, IT'S UNDERSTANDABLE. OTHERWISE YOU WOULD have greeted Jock. Such a warm December day, you wondered—although you tried to stop yourself—if her body would begin to smell before they lowered it into the ground, into this painfully sweet earth.

You had to tell him about her death, if not about her way of dying (That was hers and yours, the last thing you'd share, her way of dying). Notifying him was a human thing to do. But you hadn't expected him to attend the service, to bring along the children.

"Their last chance to see her," he answered the unasked question that was so clearly marked on your astonished face. You didn't say they'd have had more memories of her if only he hadn't barred Mae from her children's lives. You nodded at each other; enemy soldiers observing Christmas truce.

As you sat stiffly in the pew, you thought of Alex and Donald fighting in France and prayed they would come home alive. You offered your life for theirs, although you knew the Creator wasn't much for bargaining. You'd tried that again and again since her death. Your life for hers. Your life for one more year together, one more day (enough time to say good-bye), another hour.

It had all happened so fast. When the old woman, Mrs. Guthrie, came out to the steps and whispered, "We've lost her," you thought at first she was speaking of the baby. You'd had a feeling it would be a girl.

Clearly the news hadn't registered, so the crone bowed her spikey, grey head and spoke more loudly, "Your wife."

The world was revolving in slow motion.

"I'm so sorry."

Your mouth opened to contradict her.

"She didn't make it."

No, you wouldn't credit the silly cow. Mae had enough life for ten people. You knocked against the stupid woman on your rush into the kitchen table.

"No, no, Mr. Campbell, I wouldn't . . ." she bleated.

You weren't going to allow her to die, anyone would know this. And perhaps here was your mistake. You weren't humble enough. You didn't say, "Please God," or "If it is Thy will," or "Just let this be a warning, dear God, oh, dear God." No, instead you barreled into that blood-spattered room as if you were the Lord, Himself.

Mae was a cold color, alright. For a moment, you didn't perceive anything except the chilly cast of her skin. Then you smelled iron, blood, witnessed traitorous crimson soaking the sheet over her belly and legs, saw the bright spatters on the chairs and floor. The old woman's accomplice was rushing about mopping, wiping something off that God-awful midwifery instrument. You thought of the metal rod entering her, as a poker would meet a fire, rearranging, putting out the flames.

"Christ!" you exploded, pulling the weapon from her, raising it high above her cowering head. "Christ almighty, what kind of barbarians are you?"

"Hush, now."

You swung around and glared at the wretched old woman.

"Stop that ranting this minute." Mrs. Guthrie stood, thick paws on her enormous hips. "Do you want a charge of murder on your head, the children losing two parents at once?" The woman's voice was certain, instructive, experienced.

You lowered the poker.

The girl scurried, mopping faster, faster.

"How *could* you do this?" Tears coursed down your unshaven cheeks. She watched you.

"You're nothing but butchers, murderers."

"Hush, now, and be respectful of the dead," she whispered. "Your wife's body was tired, worn out, truly. She couldn't have made it through another childbirth. There was nothing we could do."

"Nothing you could do! You did *this*," you pointed at the gorgeous red blood, "you evil, evil woman. You killed my wife, my children's mother." She ignored you now, let you wind down, explained that she would have her shifted to the hospital, how they would report her death: "Complications of a six-week-old fetus." She offered to help you "move the body."

Horrified by the image of that witch's cold fingers on Mae again, you said you would carry your own wife to your bed.

After Mrs. Guthrie attached the last button of her jumper, she mumbled something outrageous about sympathizing with your loss.

"Out," you muttered.

"You shouldn't blame yourself. Mae wanted to lose the child. She knew the risk. Women know."

"Out," you were shouting now. The young helper, already through the door, scuttled down the steps.

The old woman stood her ground, staring at you almost kindly. What was she waiting for? She had had the cunning to be paid before she commenced her black task.

"Pull yourself together," she turned, wearing unimaginable dignity on her face. "You've got children to care for."

"The children, Lord, they would be home with Jessie soon. Bloody Jessie. You were sure Mae's sister had put her up to this. Someone was going to pay for this death, this crime, this tragedy. Someone besides Mae.

Mae's arms and legs were cold, but what made you saddest was the warmth you could feel along the spine. You smelled sugar and yeast and saw her golden head peering at you over the bakery counter. You had already known death with your parents, but that wasn't the same. They were old, on their way out. Here Mae's sweet face was almost without lines. Her lids were lightly closed, as if she were taking a short nap to freshen up for your next twenty years together. Even as you missed your parents, wanted to turn and ask advice or inquire about a piece of family history, you had always known you would face their deaths one day. But Mae was springtime, strength. How could this skin be so pale, this body so still? People were always surprised when a spouse or a child died, as if the deepest source of love for them was not their perishability. Yet this you did know as you stood holding her body over the table, you were grateful she did not have to bear more pain. A husband caressing his wife's fine fingers, you still found it incomprehensible that your love for each other had caused her death.

Before the service, Jock kept to himself, huddling with his children, their children, the siblings of *your* children in a corner of the stuffy church vestibule. You understood him nesting like this, but it was unnatural the way he kept his children apart from their Campbell brother and sisters on the walk into the sanctuary.

"No talking now," he reprimanded when Danny started to answer a question from Mae. He scooted the children in front and planted himself, fencelike, between the two families as they walked up the aisle of the nearly vacant church.

Unnatural was the word Jessie used, her weeping only half done, to describe the way you had laid Mae out in the bed. After arranging for the coffin, she moved the body, herself, much more ready to leave Mae behind and think of what remained as a body. It was Jessie who explained her death in birthing to the children. She, who called on the undertaker and the minister. There were moments you half hoped Jessie would take the bairns home with her so you could quietly kill yourself.

It crossed your bleak mind that Mae had willed her death, for you had made her life that miserable. Yet this notion was your grandiosity speaking; she was a lot stronger than you, and she would never have left without saying good-bye.

To you, now, suicide was impossible because of the children. Wee Mae had grown so numb, so inward these last few days, as if she were spending all her energy erasing memories. She would sit by the window, pretending to read, her eyes fixed on the same page for half an hour. You needed to live, if only to thaw out this favorite child.

Once the pastor finished intoning his words of empathy and redemption, once he stopped imploring God the Father to harbor Mae's immortal soul, and, finally, once his orchestrated moment of silence had passed, Mae's brother and sisters moved to the back of the church in an unseemly rush, as if the door of Jenner's sale had opened.

In the vestibule, people gathered around you and the children. Jessie patted your shoulder gently and you thought about how she had used to sleep with Mae in the Gill's back room. Jessie and Jock and yourself, you had all known her sleeping rhythms, had all witnessed her unfurled surrendering at night, her struggling to commence each day because, despite years of hard early labor, she was never a morning person.

Jessie nodded you and the other men on to the cemetery. "I'll just go back and start receiving people," she took your hand. "You stay at the cemetery as long as you need."

You must have answered. Maybe you said, "Ta, I'll see you back home."

"The children can come with me."

No, no, they shook their heads and you could feel the little tremors as you held hands with Mae and she with Peggy and she with Colin, who had just learned to stand and nod.

She consulted with her family, some of whom you had never met until today—because of the scandal, because of the busy difficulties of everyone's lives.

"We'll wait until they're ready," she said.

The McKenzies were leaving, too, Jock and his children, the rapidly growing Danny and the demure, pretty Chrissie and wee Jack. You wondered when young Johnny, all the way in India now with the McKenzie Highlanders, would know about his mother's passing. You would never have figured that Johnny for a traveler, a soldier, even a drum-toting soldier. But then you were just beginning to realize at age fifty-two how little you knew about these people. It made you more than sad. You wondered if, as much as you had rebelled against religion in the past, there was some reason for commandments, maybe not to the whole institutionalized folderol and dogma, but to guidelines for navigating the tightrope between individual will and collective survival.

Little Jack was acting up, making faces, hiding behind the legs of Mae's brothers, and Jock was fully occupied minding his youngest son. So he didn't notice, couldn't stop Danny and Chrissie from staring across the fence.

Their eyes quickly passed over you, as if lancing a boil, and fell on Mae and Peggy and Colin. You were touched to notice, perhaps to imagine, that while Danny stared with wide curiosity as if at zoo animals, Chrissie's eyes lit with recognition.

# CHAPTER THIRTY

# "A Scottish Opera"

### *Valerie, Toronto, 1970–1974*

"HELLO, AUNT CHRISSIE, THIS IS VALERIE, MAE'S DAUGHTER, YOUR NIECE from California."

Breathlessly I recite the prepared words, my identity. The careful order: Mae's daughter, *her* niece (a dubious claim, perhaps, since we've never met), then California because there are two Maes in that generation. I don't know if Aunt Mae in Florida is related to Chrissie or not.

"Oh, yes, your mum wrote that you were moving to Toronto." Her Scottish accent is thicker than Mom's, more like Aunt Bella's.

"Yes," I repeat, to make sure I am still breathing.

"Well, welcome to Canada, Valerie."

I love the way my family says Valerie, with that moist sound in the middle—as if they have been sucking on hard candy—as they hit the "ler," "lar," actually. They say "Vularie."

The next day my new husband Web and I are riding the tram east, endlessly east, across this dark, brick, northern city to "the Beaches." I think Aunt Chrissie has said "Beeches," until the map reveals she lives close to Lake Ontario. I get it, this is the shore, an inland Canadian beach.

I've been married three months now and am a responsible adult daughter repairing the seams in our family. This is why I am going: a sense of blood duty. How could you move to a city and not meet your own aunt, even if she is a half-aunt, from a virtually unknown half of the family? Yet I have met her brother Johnny in Fife. I am going to the Beaches on this fiery fall afternoon for my mother. (She expects the visit. Maybe that's why she birthed me—as emissary to the Campbell-McKenzie commonwealth. Surely my brothers wouldn't do this.) I am also going out of curiosity: every new aunt and uncle discloses a different chapter of our story.

Over the last twenty-three years, the myths and lies and half-truths and forgotten details about the McKenzie-Campbells have fuelled a wild curiosity that is, no doubt, the source of all my writing. Right now, however, I want only to meet a new member of my family.

Web and I walk up a path to the modest brick house.

A small woman waves from the door.

As I approach, waving back, I see she has Mother's eyes and jaw. Otherwise Chrissie is a stranger in her short, plump, grey, brownness. Makes me wonder how many of my aunts and uncles and cousins I have passed ignorantly on the street. I still do not know how many of them—us—there are. Chrissie is wearing a flowered cotton blouse and smells of cinnamon. I am in my best dress. She beckons us into the busy, hot, little parlor. There, waiting craggily, is a tall, thin man.

Already I feel easier.

"I'd be your Uncle David," he booms in a whisper of advanced lung disease.

The hushed voice is musical, Glaswegian.

"Aye, I'd be a Glasgow Keelie," he grins, "your mum is right on that one."

"Now have a seat," Aunt Chrissie instructs, carrying the offering of shortbread and cinnamon toast. "What's your pleasure? Coffee or tea?"

"Coffee, thanks," answers Web, shyly settling on the couch, just across from Uncle David's throne. He is a quiet—sometimes silent—young man studying for a Ph.D. in engineering.

"Oh, let me help you, Aunt Chrissie," I fairly leap forward.

She smiles at the familiar family choreography, then says her line with feeling, "Oh, no, make yourself comfortable."

"No, I'd love to." This dialogue is gene-encoded.

"All right, then, we'll leave the men to chat and be waited on," she sniffs humorously.

I walk through the small dining room where she—like my mother—

has spread a lace tablecloth and—unlike my mother—has cluttered the sideboard with dainty teacups and figurines.

Aunt Chrissie's kitchen is as spotless as Mom's, more so. The sink is shiny stainless steel. The tea towels stiff in their linen newness. Of course Chrissie knew I would follow her into the kitchen, and this perfect scene is part of her self-introduction.

"Does he drink it strong?" she asks about Web's coffee.

"Medium," I answer safely.

"So how do you like Toronto?"

I tell her about our flat upstairs in the house of a Portuguese family. Uruguayans live on the floor above us, and we all share the bathroom.

She approves. A safe, central neighborhood.

Web's graduate advisor. My job hunting. Teaching jobs are tighter than I was told. Twenty schools in two weeks, and no luck.

She sympathizes, silently nodding approval of my Scots diligence. "Aye, David and I had a hard time when we came—in the 1920s, of course—a bad period to immigrate."

I think of Mom disembarking on Ellis Island in 1930, the middle of the Great Depression. Of course it was tougher on them, with no education. This movement is in my blood. Was there ever a *good* time to immigrate, to emigrate?

**Emigrate:** To remove or go away. Wander. Roam. Trek. Flit. Ramble. Traipse. Exit. Crawl.

**Immigrate:** To enter. Emerge. Land. Unload. Infiltrate. Embed. Attain. Reach. Finish. Start.

"But you'll do fine." She is arranging the cups on a tray. "We did. Fancy our family moving to Canada—you from the west, us from the east—so many years (forty years, isn't it?) apart. It's lovely to meet you, Valerie, just lovely."

All I hear at first is the word, "family." This is what I came for, a word that has so confounded me. In my own contradictory way, I've always thought I might find home somewhere else. Here in Toronto, I hope to understand a little more from Aunt Chrissie. Formerly Chrissie McKenzie, one of the children Grandmother left behind.

Aunt Chrissie is still talking about coming to Canada. "We did just fine, until Uncle David's chest wore out." She sits down, suddenly tired. As deflated as his lungs. "Emphysema," she says. "And I could live with that, if only he would behave himself."

I smile, imagining the bickering between them over cigarettes and exertion and diet. Is this what Mom would have had to look forward to if Dad had stayed with her? Combative years as a greying nursemaid?

"Enough of this." She stands energetically. "Let's serve the coffee before it turns to ice."

In the living room, Uncle David is lecturing Web on the superiority of Canadian hockey. Never much of a sports fan, Web reveals a shaky grip on the lesson. They both brighten up as we appear. Ladies' men.

Shortbread and toast are passed again. Coffee poured.

Uncle David tells a vaguely vulgar joke. Chrissie is amused in spite of herself and that high, spluttering laugh expresses all there is to know about their love.

The devotion is clearly mutual. Chrissie is the dumpling. He the spiced mince.

He enjoys recounting his career as a runner in Glasgow. (At a race, she fell in love with the lean, tall, bush-haired man who would develop a raspy voice and die one afternoon in his patched tweed recliner chair.)

She draws the conversation back to Canada, to their early hopes, first jobs. Yes, she is still working at Simpson's Department Store after thirty years. Can we believe it? She can't.

Mom told me they had lost their daughter, my cousin, to cancer, just like Aunt Bella's daughter Winnie. And after she had had a child, too. A little girl named Linda. This grandchild became the light and bane of Chrissie and David's lives, the second daughter they raised. We look at Linda's wedding pictures. She is a pretty girl, blonde, like the McKenzie side of the family.

Chrissie won't talk about the McKenzies or the Campbells, of parents dead or siblings living. She slipped the memories overboard that trans-Atlantic ship.

"Do you remember what your mother looked like?" I venture.

"Oh, aye, small and blonde."

"Mom doesn't remember her at all. Was she pretty?"

"Oh, aye, pretty enough."

All that I need to know about her, about her brothers, Johnny and Jack and Danny, about their mother, my grandmother, who died thirty years before my birth, all that will take time, and more visiting, to reveal.

"Was it hard for you to leave Scotland?"

"Och, you do what you have to do." What connects us is the movement. There to here. Then to now. What matters is now. The reality we construct. The new Canadian lives. Not the dim—and best forgotten—past. Bad feeling doesn't bear thinking about.

David drives us home through the shadowed foreign streets. Such a different route from the one we traveled by tram—tall rowhouses squeezed everywhere.

He watches me peering out for the pastels of California. He doesn't know *what* I am missing, but *that* I am missing. Missing someone, some place. Web sits silently in the backseat. Uncle David isn't comfortable with my husband. But he teases me, asks if I inherited this forlorn expression or if I invented it.

We laugh. I am pleased that he likes me. I know the feistiness, not the frailty, defines him. He talks about his many years working as a trainer at the Y and, again, about his early days as a runner in Glasgow. A champion runner.

My father was a runner, too. For years Mom wore the silver ring he won racing for the Seventh Regiment of the National Guard. At the armory in downtown New York, I think. Both Mom and Aunt Chrissie have chosen men with strong legs and a sense of direction. Unfortunately, Dad had to keep moving.

※

Some weeks later, we return for Thanksgiving dinner. Here in Canada they celebrate Thanksgiving a month earlier than in the States, otherwise, everything is uncannily familiar: the overheated house, the overstuffed table, the conversational lulls. We are family. A little boredom is natural.

Again it is the imagination of a Canadian life that occupies our conversation. If I am ever to learn about young Chrissie, I will first have to get acquainted with the successful expatriate, with the steady job, comfortable house, sound automobile. We talk about sports and politics and television.

"When is your mother coming up for a visit?" Aunt Chrissie asks, almost offhandedly.

"Spring," I guess, knowing that Mom would be terrified of this snow.
"A long time," Aunt Chrissie reflects.

I am touched that after forty years she is feeling impatient.

Later, I drop by Simpson's with their Christmas present. Chrissie greets me in the demure brown waitress uniform with a spotless white apron. She looks larger in this setting and more official, but also smaller, one of a half-dozen grey-haired ladies who could be my Aunt Chrissie. How do I know for sure this is the woman to whom I'm related? Although she offers me tea and a scone, I understand I should decline, that this is just a courtesy. I kiss her rouged cheek—rouge being the one cosmetic women in our flush-faced family surely don't need—and almost say I love you.

❧

When Mom arrives in the spring, I am busy being the married daughter—showing her *my* Toronto, my apartment, my job, my husband. (I have married up, into a middle-class, college-educated family. Mom approves of this, even though she thinks Web is a little quiet. After too many years of my pugnaciously loud father, quiet is not a problem for me.) Now I am eager to introduce her to my aunt.

"Oh, Chrissie and I already have a plan for lunch," Mom says kindly.

"Really?"

"You have work to do," she says. "I'll just take the subway down to Queen and Yonge."

"But how will you recognize her?"

She is puzzled. "We're meeting outside, right in front of Simpson's."

"On the street?"

"Yes," she laughs. "Don't you think it's a respectable time of day?"

"Of course, but . . ." I stumble because age is a touchy issue between us, "but I mean Queen Street is crowded with shoppers, how will you recognize each other?"

Startled, she asks, "What do you mean?"

"Do you want me to come along, just to introduce you?"

"She's my *sister*, of course I'll recognize her." There's determination in her voice, anger, almost, as if I have called her senile or crazy.

I feel like a character who has been kicked out of a story. If I have any part in the margins of this drama, it is in a very muted subplot.

As rain streaks down the front window, I watch my mother walk toward the subway. She carries a hideous, fold-up, orange umbrella someone failed to reclaim from the lost-and-found of the restaurant where she works. No doubt Chrissie has a similar one. Ye shall know each other by your umbrellas. I don't want to see her go, but watch closely as she walks out in the rain, down the shadowy street, toward the subway station.

So I am not there. But this is what she tells me:

Aunt Chrissie and Mom recognized each other immediately—one little grey coat hugging into another. They went back to Simpson's for lunch—not to the restaurant, but to the glassy cafeteria with a lovely view of the old City Hall. And they talked, for two hours.

"About what?"

"Oh, Edinburgh. Childhood. You know."

I don't know. She will not tell me. I shall have to imagine them in that place, at that time, as those people. Perhaps this is Mom's legacy to me—the questions that create a writer's passion for clarity.

Indeed, when Web and I take her out to the Beaches for dinner with Chrissie and David, they talk about now, about Canada and California. One reason is politeness; they want to speak a language everyone can understand. Trudeau. Nixon. The coming of summer.

Shortly after she gets back home, Mom starts writing me letters about her possibly moving to Canada. She sees my point about it being a saner country. She likes Toronto, a real city with public transportation. And it would be nice to live near a daughter and sister.

Selfishly, I do not encourage this line of thinking. I am beginning to realize that I had needed to leave more than Nixon's State Department behind when I immigrated to Canada.

℞

Mom visits Toronto a second time, with Aunt Nan. They stay—Nan's treat—at the Royal York, a hotel where I can't even afford coffee. I love Aunt Nan—how can you not be fond of this tiny, bow-legged, blue-eyed fireball who emigrated from domestic servant to rich doctor's wife, who cheerfully raised a retarded son on baseball hats and balls and programs from the Detroit Tigers—ever genial Aunt Nan. Still, somehow, I think I prefer Aunt Bella, whose hard work was laced with a certain sour humor, and Aunt Chrissie, bickering with Uncle David about the cigarettes.

Several days after Mom and Aunt Nan arrive, they take the tram out to the Beaches. Web and I arrive later for dinner.

They are sitting at the card table. The four of them playing pinochle as if nothing has happened—fifty years, children, marriages, migrations—as if Nan's father hadn't stolen Chrissie's mother. As if those two passionate people had not produced Mom, then death and orphanhood and years of silent estrangement.

My relatives are playing cards, drinking tea and laughing as if they had done this every Saturday since 1930. I watch these aunts from both sides of my Scots family, Mom in the middle, and Uncle David charming each of them with his hoarse laugh. I don't remember when I have seen my mother so happy.

The last time I visit the Beaches is just after the big decision. Four years after immigrating to our new Canadian life, Web and I are separating. (Of course I still love him. I have never understood how you could *stop* loving someone with whom you have shared dreams and fears and sex and long Sunday newspaper afternoons.) So what's happened? I am just beginning to grow up, to know the pleasure of my own accomplishments. Gradually I've realized that although Web helped me escape my family, I no longer need him, and, in fact, now it is *he* I need to escape. I have hurt him. *What happened?* As a twenty-six-year-old, I have few answers, but strong doses of exhilaration, guilt, confidence, and terror.

This is what I tell them: I am going to Britain for a while.

What I do *not* tell them is that I have discovered sex and ambition. No more wholesome nice girl image for me. I am fresh with the erotic tension of two affairs, which have taught me that maybe I shouldn't have married the first person with whom I slept, that "open marriages" like ours close down swiftly. This is the 1970s and I am filled with postrevolutionary ideas. Morality is historically relative.

There's a world out there I want to write about. I plan to settle in London to write short stories. Then a stay of several years in Tanzania to fight neocolonialism, support national liberation, and write novels. With the sweet, naïve arrogance of youth, I believe that all I need are possibilities. And I know there are beds waiting for me. I won't use my body for anything except my own pleasure. There will be quite a lot of that.

Uncle David says he was worried when he saw me today. But one long look and he knew I'd fly on from here.

"Truthfully, Valerie, I never thought Web was lively enough for you."

I blink, thinking that Mom has said the same thing.

(*"Why didn't you tell me?" I asked her.*
*"Because you wouldn't have listened," she said.*
*And I knew she was right.*
*She was wiser than I about holding back truths from closed ears. I had not learned what all the other Campbells and McKenzies seemed to know instinctively—that you had to save your breath.*)

"You know, the truth is, dear," Uncle David continues, leaning close enough that I can smell the coffee and cigarettes generating his voice. "I never did take to him all that much. A girl like you needs someone with more *oomph*."

Maybe I'll travel to Glasgow and find a handsome young runner.

"Enough now," Aunt Chrissie warns, setting down the tea tray. "What Valerie needs is a rest. A holiday. A trip to London is just the ticket."

I want to protest that I am ready for "life," not for a rest, but I know she is being generous. As is Uncle David. They are on my side. We are not a family of judges. More a clan of rueful survivors. They are both, in their own ways, giving me permission, a permission earned by family sacrifices. Since I have never learned to disentangle responsibility from opportunity, the inheritance is not uncomplicated.

This visit is short. I really don't have the time to be here—I'm behind on my students' grades as well as on my book deadline, and I'm scheduled for some probably inconsequential breast surgery, which I don't tell them about, no point in worrying people—too much to do before the flight in two weeks. Grades. Book. Breast. Get it done in order, the Scottish way. Don't spend too much time thinking about your problems.

We sip tea and reminisce—still not about Edinburgh, brothers, sisters, parents—but about *our* history over the last four years. Visits back and forth. Mother's trips north. Playing cards with Aunt Nan, whom Chrissie calls "your Aunt Nan."

As we talk about my trip, they insist I must go back to Edinburgh, to visit Chrissie's brother Johnny. I am to take their love, invite him to

Canada. We chat about my half-half cousin, their granddaughter, Linda, whom I still haven't met. Yes, yes, we'll all reunite again. One day, not in Jerusalem, but in Auld Reekie. We discuss Mom's new apartment, right across from her job at the all-night coffee shop. Then it is time to leave.

I don't want to go.

I look at Aunt Chrissie and Uncle David, who have become family in just four years, after four decades of silence. I kiss each of them. And in our family way, I disappear, perhaps never to see them again.

# CHAPTER THIRTY-ONE

# "Yesterday"

## *Mary, San Francisco, 1975*

NOW I KEPT MY EYES OPEN TO REMIND MYSELF THAT THIS APARTMENT was safe, lit with streetlights and pulsing red neon from across Taylor. I stayed awake to see, not to see. Not to see the eyes peeking from that blue knit helmet. Blue eyes, made familiar, bluer, more memorable outlined in navy wool. These macabre ski masks were getting popular for winter. Young people prized their anonymity, I guess. Yet for me it was the opposite: aging made me ache to know, be known, be at home. That's why I looked into people's eyes. Gazing more directly than most, it seemed.

Now, with my eyes open, I could hear better: buses, trucks, even the occasional shout up from the pavement. I listened to my daughter's steady breath beside me in the Murphy bed. I thought I could hear the occasional sigh from her boyfriend, Andrew, his tall frame scrunched on the couch. I had long ago stopped apologizing for modest hospitality. If people were welcome to what you had, they didn't want more. Yet, with Andrew, I had wondered if I should give him the bed because surely they slept together. Still, that would have led to another embarrassment.

Listen, it wasn't a bad life when the worst you had to fear was being embarrassed. That's why I stayed at work after it happened. Embarrassment—I didn't want to break into their private time. Didn't want them startled, worried. More than anything, I hated other people's worry.

Also, I knew the incident reflected badly on me, on the neighborhood, on the work, which was really quite a respectable position and a damn good one for a sixty-five-year-old woman. I don't know. I also stayed on tonight at the cafe because it *was* my job. Nothing wrong with me, really, and I was happy to continue working for my pay.

❦

"Mary, Mary, what happened, Mary?" Hennie waddled swiftly toward my cash register. What had she seen? The gun? The money? His heavy paper bag? His eyes?

"You're ashen," she exclaimed. "Have you had a heart attack? Are you OK?"

Relieved that she hadn't seen anything, I was also disappointed. A witness would have made me feel better, could reassure me that I hadn't had a choice. No, that wasn't it, from the time I took the cashier job, I had known it would happen one day, just a matter of time, really. And I always knew just what I would do: hand over the cash politely, without a fuss. A fair transaction. Their money for my life. I was an honest woman, a dedicated worker. I kept my hands away from other people's pockets. But I was no fool. Here, take it, I thought. Go away. His eyes went vacant above the silent lips.

He was out the door and into an automobile (black? brown? dark. large.) before I had a chance to scream. Of course I didn't shriek, but the "Oh my God" was enough to get Hennie's attention. Then Kimiko. The two of them fluttering around me. Demanding to know if I was OK, who he was, how much he got, what kind of gun—of course I'm worse at identifying firearms than at distinguishing cars, so I laughed at that question. They decided I was hysterical—laughing at the robbery—but truly, they were the batty ones, overreacting like that.

Then Mr. Patterson came up, with a long, puzzled, is-this-scene-really-necessary kind of face.

Luckily there weren't many customers. Never are at 9:30 P.M. One couple mooning over each other in the corner. Daft Mr. Clancy, drinking a fourth cup of coffee and engrossed in his mystery novel. Two middle-aged lady tourists studying a map. A quiet time.

The robber's planning had been flawless. Almost. Swift, clean, virtually undetected.

Mr. Patterson took my elbow, said he would call the police, said I should go home now. Yet the very idea of it, leaving work because of a little scare, a little scare that would turn into a bigger scare if I went home to brood on it!

Paula knew what to do. She ambled from the bar and took my hand. "We're getting you a drink, Mary. What will it be—a brandy?"

Mr. Patterson foiled my protests. "Yes," he said gravely, "I'll take over the register."

At the horror on my face, he said, "For a while, dear. You go with Paula, just for a while, until you get settled, dear."

Valerie wouldn't like his calling me "dear," would find it as patronizing as when he calls me "Mary" while I address him as "Mr. Patterson." After all, he was two-thirds my age, nothing if not precise, our Valerie. But she didn't understand—maddeningly flushed by her father's belligerence—that knowing your place wasn't demeaning, but rather a mark of maturity and self-respect. Mr. Patterson was the boss. Acknowledging that didn't diminish me.

Paula reminded me of Valerie, although the poor girl hadn't been able to get an education like my daughter had. Practical. Generous. I trusted Paula's bluff manner in a way I couldn't Hennie's or Kimiko's nervous chatter. So there I sat in the dim, empty bar, explaining to her and to the instantaneous—but too late—policeman, how it happened.

I was rolling up the pennies, thinking how useless they had become in the last five years, how a half-penny was wealth when I was growing up, how I used to go on treasure hunts through the vacuum cleaner bags with my kids. Joy in finding just five pennies each. Now what could five pennies buy you? Not even a local phone call. It was usually quiet from nine to ten and I didn't like to waste company time, so I always started tidying up at this point in my shift—packaging the coins, checking the stubs. This was partially selfish, of course, because it let me cut ten to fifteen minutes off my wind-up time in the office, go home early enough for an another chapter in that new biography of Mary Queen of Scots and a bit of chocolate before I fell asleep. So I was meditating on the damn pennies and neatly making bank rolls when he approached.

The policeman recorded carefully, although I said nothing worth noting. His pen paused; he looked at me.

"What did this guy say? Exactly."

I could feel my feet sweating, as if I were on trial here. Maybe it was the brandy. I tried to remember his words.

"Please clear the cash tray and put the money in the bag."

"Did he say 'please'?"

"Yes," I smiled.

"Was there anything unusual about his voice, a stutter, an accent?"

In fact it seemed unusual that a person in that position *wouldn't* stutter. And I wasn't great at noticing accents. You needed Valerie for that. I was failing, miserably, the poor young officer, who was only trying to do his job.

"Age? Height? Coloring?"

I answered these as fully as I could. The ski mask hid a lot of sins.

I waited. He didn't ask if I recognized him. What he didn't ask, I didn't tell.

"Blue eyes," the officer was taken aback.

I didn't say that another time, or another place, he could have been my brother Matt or any of a dozen regulars in this cafe.

It made sense that a regular—not one of the friendly ones who give you their nickname the third time they come in, but someone who often ate here—would know the quiet period, would understand when the waitresses took their breaks. The officer didn't ask.

Paula offered a second brandy.

I said no thanks, there was still another hour of work. The policeman raised his eyebrows in amusement.

Of course I recognized the fellow—not by name or job, but by eyes, curve of jaw, height. That tall blond man who drank iced tea by the back door on Tuesday. What was more important was that he recognized me. Knew I would like a "please." Knew I wasn't as dedicated as crazy Jeanne, who ran down the street after those two big women when they left their cheque unpaid. Knew that although I was honest, I had perspective. I could detect hunger. I remembered despair. I understood that $400 wasn't worth my life, his future.

So the policeman shrugged and interviewed Mr. P. before leaving. Paula was explaining her plan to study computer programming. A profitable career. I couldn't imagine this vivacious girl tied to a keyboard—unless it was a piano keyboard in the lobby of the Algonquin Hotel and she was belting out Cole Porter. No, something more contemporary, of course, the Beatles. Still, if there is one thing I've learned with Valerie, it is that you daren't forecast a life.

"I better get back to the register," I said.

Paula laughed, "Go for it." Mr. P. did relinquish my stool. He had to correct some storage problems in the kitchen. And no one else really knew this fancy register yet. I was glad to feel necessary. Especially after having lost the restaurant $400. *This* work is what I needed, not another drink. I did have to pull myself together for Valerie, who would ask better questions than that policeman.

God, my girl could inquire, and she made it almost impossible to turn the tables. I did not understand why she would leave this warm country—California, for heaven's sake—and go off to that grey, unheated island. Why would someone with her education want to subsist on lentils and beer in a crowded North London house? What did misery have to do with being a writer? If she inherited anything from me, it wasn't common sense. Still, Andrew's appearance last year was a good thing. He wanted her to move to Scotland with him. Now *that* I could see. A man to support you, a nice flat on Broughton Street, Edinburgh on your own terms. Since Andrew had entered the scene, I had thought more about returning home to Britain—not to move in with them, of course. I'd find a small flat in their neighborhood. It would be a comfort to have a mother nearby when the babies came.

Rajiv rushed in at the start of his shift, as soon as he heard the news.

"Mary, Mary," he shouted, "it's terrible. How are you? Why are you still here?"

"This is my job," I replied, more primly than I liked, but Rajiv's intensity made me nervous.

"Yes, yes, I understand," he smiled ironically.

I was very fond of him. His bluster was armour for a soft heart.

"You wouldn't waste any company time recovering."

Rajiv wanted me to be more active in the union. I'd rather have a nightmare than go to a meeting.

"Nothing to recover from," I shrugged.

"Look, I'll escort you home." Then he winked slyly and glanced at his watch, "but not one dutiful minute before the end of your shift."

Of course I let him do this—although I walked home alone every night at this hour. I lived just across the street. He would find the trip reassuring, and it wouldn't keep him away from work too long. I hoped Mr. Patterson didn't think I was making a fuss.

Riding the apartment elevator to the third floor, I decided just not to mention the robbery to Valerie and Andrew. No sense worrying them. The worst was over and it hadn't been that bad.

They were watching the news. Andrew politely switched off the TV set and took my coat. Valerie asked if I'd like a cup of tea or a drink.

"A drink, thanks."

This was my mistake.

She set down the Manhattan and studied my face.

"You OK?" she said—even her way of asking questions was like giving orders.

Nodding, I sipped the drink.

"You look a bit peely wally."

I laughed, perhaps too much, comforted by this old expression, the drink, the idea of being safely locked in my own apartment.

I enjoyed the simplicity and spareness of this place after years of marital mahogany and brocade. The kids were shocked that I preferred plain, hotel-like furniture to the family doings. But there were no ghosts in these chairs or under the bed. In fact, the bed was securely folded into the wall until night. That's my idea of housework: shove the Murphy bed into its closet. My fake ficus tree annoyed Valerie, but it was so much more dependable than a real one in this dry apartment heat. I *could* dust it, though, she was right about that.

"No, really," she persisted. "Did something happen at work?"

She sat beside me on the green couch, her arm around my shoulder. It all spilled out.

Andrew asked, "What did he look like?"

They waited.

"Well, he was wearing one of those ski masks. I couldn't see much besides his blue eyes."

She relaxed. "Blue eyes. You see," she said to Andrew, to me, to San Francisco, "people always assume these guys are black."

"That's not what I meant," Andrew rushed in.

"No, no, but in this country . . ."

I took another sip of the really quite soothing drink and closed my eyes. Was this my legacy, training an intelligent daughter to make a decent Manhattan?

"I was just wondering if the bloke were big, you know, intimidating your mum."

I had never told her that the man who had pulled a gun on me in the elevator last year was black. She never inquired.

But now she asked something else, damn her, bless her: "Did you recognize him?"

She could come back to America and get a good job in law enforcement. Luckily her question came an hour after the clueless police interview—and I had thought of an answer.

"I meet so many people in a day. It's hard to recognize someone behind a ski mask."

"Fair enough," said Andrew, who had the same instinct—was it a Scottish impulse?—to put unpleasantness behind and move on. "Now tell me about this Fisherman's Wharf you're taking me to see tomorrow. What time are we going?"

Valerie shook her head in mock exasperation. I thought this cheerful earful was just the man for her.

"Let's try to catch the 10 A.M. cable car," I declared. "That will give you a flavor of San Francisco." I kept chattering, watching Valerie's expression of frustrated curiosity turn into a more sensitive understanding of what I did and did not care to discuss.

She joined in with ideas of shops and cafes. Andrew asked ever more charmed, charming questions. By the time we went to bed, the ski mask had vanished from the room.

Almost. I did have trouble with ghosts. They stuck around. Returned at odd moments. Ordering iced tea *was* odd. In December. My husband Jack used to drink iced tea constantly. This guy was so unlike Jack. Timid, and in a certain way, deferential. "Please." Maybe he was Southern. Those people were very polite. "Please clear the cash tray and put it in this bag." Cash tray. Did he have a restaurant background? In cashiering?

Stop. Enough questions, speculation from the cop, from Rajiv, Valerie. The entire incident was over. It was not my fault. It didn't bear thinking about.

Instead, I considered what I had to be grateful for: A loving family. A decent job. My health. Concerned—if overwrought—friends like Hennie, Paula, Kimiko, and Rajiv. A generous boss. A comfortable studio apartment. Valerie fretted about the location; OK, it was slightly seedy. She complained it was hard to sleep on this busy corner with blinking lights and farting—she could be quite picturesque—buses. How did

I get any rest? she asked. Yet to me the compact studio was a perfect size, and the noises and lights were signs of life. I lay tucked next to my sleeping daughter tonight. Safe. For now.

I had come to appreciate memory. The past was safely contained—in how things were, not how they might have been. It was the future that produced worry. Since the past no longer had a future, I always returned there before I fell asleep, enjoying a walk in the Princes Street Gardens with Father and Colin, or a New Jersey afternoon, watching the kids play in our backyard, or a silly, laughing conversation like the one about Hennie's ridiculous hat yesterday.

*Yesterday*, that was the pleasure of the night shift. Time passed swiftly at the end of a day. When you got home, you closed your eyes and soon it would be yesterday.

# XI

*Daniel, 1920*

# CHAPTER THIRTY-TWO

## *Daniel, Edinburgh, 1920*

IT WAS A BONNIE SATURDAY MORNING WHEN YOU TOOK THE CHILDREN to Portobello. The air was ripe with saltwater and sugar, and everyone under four feet tall sucked determinedly on ghoulish pink Edinburgh Rock. The day radiated warmth, normalcy, well-being.

(Now that the War was over, there was more good feeling to go around. Alex and Donald had come by last week. They both looked hardy, even Donald, despite his leg wound. A happy reunion. That's the origin of this framed image—the only picture we have of you—slightly bent between your vigorous sons. One of them glancing off to the left and the other to the right, but you staring straight ahead to the viewer, bequeathing a gaze that would last eighty years, as if you knew we would need to meet. Sadly, your Campbell reunion was temporary. Oh, you might see Donald again, he was traveling only as far as England for work. But Alex, bold Alex, was returning to New Zealand. You tried to persuade him toward Australia, where he at least had an uncle. Yes, you were developing more of a family sense these days—penance or wisdom in your old age. Fifty-five, how had it happened? Yet Alex was set on New Zealand's South Island, a Kiwi soldier in the war, he longed to return to those glacial mountain lakes. So you had your photo taken with them, one in soldier clothes, the other not. You in your funeral and once-a-year-to-church suit.)

And this morning, in the spirit of times changing and hopes lifting, you finally acquiesced to the younger children's summer-long pleas to go to the beach.

Ice cream. Rowboat rides. Circus-colored sweets. A right big family outing, and you were having a fine time with these children who taught you a pleasurable fatherhood that you had been too busy, too distracted, to experience with your first family. Thrilling to see them blooming into full-blooded individuals. Spunky, wee Colin, the ladylike Peggy—both bairns heartbreakingly beautiful in their mother's coloring and softness.

Mae was more like you altogether—thin, dark, reserved. And from somewhere she got an intelligence—a real scholar, that one, brilliant at sums, her teacher, Miss Geddes, said. Mae was touching in her motherliness to the other children, even to Peggy, just a year younger. You had hoped they might grow as close as their mother and her devoted sister Jessie. They rocked their little heads to the hurdy gurdy music and watched open-mouthed as the costumed jugglers exchanged balls and sticks. Just three miles from Princes Street and yet a world away.

Perhaps now *was* the best time to raise Mrs. MacGregor's invitation. Here, in the open air, sitting on the warm beach, away from it all. You had thought this out carefully, believed a decision should be made with all the children around, for it was a family matter. You waited until they had finished the lunch Mae had so competently packed. Not a delicious meal, but filling. Your dear, wee Mae cooked the way she sang and sewed, badly and with enthusiasm. The children lay back on the blanket, spent, faces as precious and shiny as shells they had collected that morning.

You cleared your throat carefully.

Mae sat up.

The other two lay still, soaking in the blessed sun.

"Children, there's something we need to talk about. As a family." In spite of yourself, you coughed. This was not the time to be sick or vulnerable. *Paterfamilias* was the order of the day. Especially this day.

Mae frowned, "Are you sick, Papa? Are you sick?"

"No, love, this is good news." You took a long—if not deep—breath as Peggy and Colin reluctantly rose from their cosy earth. "An opportunity," you pronounced all the consonants precisely, as if giving a lesson.

Mae leaned forward warily.

"I had a visit from Mrs. MacGregor a fortnight ago."

"When?" Peggy demanded, propping herself back on sandy elbows. "Did Ellen come?" Ellen, who was just Peggy's age, had been your youngest daughter's best friend until the family moved to a better part of town. Good neighbors were always moving away from Union Place.

"No, dear, just Mrs. MacGregor."

Colin began to dig in the sand.

"Oh," Peggy looked down to her feet and wiggled her toes, as if exercising control over a manageable corner of the universe.

You cleared your throat once more, covertly snatching a breath at the same time. "Mrs. MacGregor was telling me what a good house they have over near Craigmillar Road. With an extra room."

You did your best to avert your eyes from Mae. Still, you felt her little body tensing.

Peggy sat up, staring impatiently. Colin was busily burying his body in the sand. This earth was warm, so welcoming for September.

"It's quite near, their house, that is, to an excellent school."

Mae's hazel eyes rounded.

Your voice accelerated. You needed to get through this. You had survived a lot in the last decade, the loss of one family, the genesis of another, the butchering of your beloved wife, dread fear about your soldier sons. You could handle this. It was for her own good.

"And Mrs. MacGregor has invited Mae to live with their family, to attend school there."

"Oh, no," Mae spoke slowly, shocked, then recovering, as if you had accused her of a crime.

And, to forestall the girl's rashness, you escalated with unintended words. "It's generous of the MacGregors to want to adopt, I mean, welcome you into their family."

Her wee face was seized by alarm.

"Adopt," damn, you had resolved not to use that word.

"Of course the move would be just a technicality . . . you'd always be one of us . . . generous because the MacGregors are comfortable, but they're hardly a wealthy family."

You were Abraham, I know that, she knew that. Asked to sacrifice your favorite child, you railed and resisted but eventually gave in. Most of all, you knew this opportunity should fall to Mae because she had a head and would go far. Mae was the child who might live out your dreams. Of course, with one gone, the money would stretch further. The children were thin (but didn't seem to have rickets or coughing), thinness ran in the family. Pathetic not to know if you were adequately nourishing your own children.

Beyond this, you weren't so very sure how long you would last, and you wanted at least to see Mae situated. The others, too, of course. But maybe Bella, now in her thirties, could come through, would take them in. You sighed, suffering a chill between your ear and shoulder, and looking up, you found the sun beating steady, hot.

Colin had managed to cover his thighs in sand and was now working on his hips.

"Oh, no," Mae said again.

"It's a lovely opportunity," you persisted feverishly, "And you could take the tram to see us every Sunday."

Peggy looked almost as stricken as Mae. Abandoned by her best friend, and now by her sister. Of course she couldn't say "why her, why not me?" because she didn't want *any* of these separations. Peggy burst into tears.

"No, I won't leave you," Mae recited the family mantra. Sliding next to you, she took your arm, a life raft that would freeze into an anchor.

You, the case of mistaken identity that persisted throughout her life.

Peggy continued to weep.

Colin shifted suddenly at the tense noise of it all, dislodging his right knee.

You looked into their miserable little faces and turned cowardly. "We'll just think on it, shall we?"

Peggy sniffed back her tears.

Colin resumed his burrowing.

Mae patted your hand, gently, as if reviving a patient. (Maybe she would be a doctor, she was that smart for a female.)

"I only want the best for you children," your voice was deeply reassuring, but also vaguely pleading. (Who *were* you petitioning? The God you had denied? The forces of nature that were, after all, set to conserve life? Your children—were you hoping that in some future time they would understand?)

The sun, quite unnaturally hot and direct, seemed to be eating through their reddening skin. What kind of father, you scolded yourself, would leave his children like this to blister?

"We'll think on it as a family. Everything will work out for the best."

Now this dangerous optimism was more malignant than any sunburn, this innocence you inscripted in their (my) genes.

ℜ

Eventually, everything did work out. Together, as a family, you made the plan.

Not much time left, you knew this from your coughing. You did what you could.

ℜ

**Tuberculosis:** An infectious disease caused by the tubercle bacillus and characterized by the formation of tubercles in various tissues of the body: specifically tuberculosis of the lungs, pulmonary phthsis; consumption.
**Consumption:** (a) a consuming or being consumed.*

**Tuberculosis:** Fundamentally, tuberculosis consists in an inflammatory reaction of any particular tissue to the invading bacilli and since tubercle bacilli are relatively little virulent, this tissue reaction is subacute in character. It consists in the formation round the bacilli of a microscopic agglomeration of cells constituting the so-called 'tubercle.' . . .

Such persons establish the greatest concentration of infective matter within the home, and the smaller, the worse ventilated and the more crowded the home, the more massive the infection and the more serious the danger to others. In the home contact with susceptible persons is most likely—for the home is the nest for infants and young children. It is upon the homes and families of infected persons that preventive measures must be focussed.†

ℜ

The day she left they were trading scraps. You had splurged and bought her a whole new page of those cheerfully gaudy paper dollies.

---

*  *Webster's New World Dictionary*, Third College Edition (Springfield, Mass.: Merriam-Webster Inc., 1988).
† *The Encyclopedia Britannica*, 14th edition (London: Encyclopedia Britannica Co., 1929), 532.

Peggy feigned imperturbable concentration while Mae cut out the figures slowly, precisely.

Colin cuddled next to you in the big chair as you read everyone poems from Robert Louis Stevenson.

The perfect happy family.

When the knock sounded, you thought how there were so many routes to family betrayal.

Colin ran joyfully, innocently, to open the door, and you were half-surprised to see not a tall man in a back cape and mask, but rather the relentlessly affable Mrs. MacGregor, who was born to middle-aged ruddy cheeks and good works. She carried a basket, from which she produced a tin of shortbread that she and Ellen had baked that morning.

You felt another twinge of inadequacy. So many domestic skills Mae would never learn.

"Ellen wanted to come," Mrs. MacGregor was sighing nervously. "But she had her piano lesson this afternoon."

The former neighbor was standing there in her hat and coat.

You should have made her comfortable, offered her a seat, fixed her a cup of tea. Instead you stared through her like a madman, as if she were trading her tin of sweets for your daughter. In the depths of your agonizing self-doubt, you considered yourself capable of this bargain. How had it come to this?

Mae—ever alert, kind—sensed your pain, Mrs. MacGregor's discomfort, Peggy's excitement and fear, and she knew just what to do. She brought out Peggy's coat and handed her sister a secret, farewell present, which she was not to open until she woke next morning on Craigmillar Road.

You knew now, that Mae had a life companion, her romantic willfulness. She would never leave you. Mae had persuaded everyone that Peggy would flourish at the new school, would make a better friend to Ellen (friend, she said, not sister, because she had no intention of losing her sister Peggy). You settled it with promises of weekly visits.

Peggy accepted Mae's secret gift and clasped her only sister tightly.

What else happened? Weeping, hugging, plans for tea a week Sunday. Then she disappeared.

You had a frightful coughing spell that evening. Still awake at midnight. Mae brought you a hot toddy. The girl was a miracle. Wasting her life with you, with what was left of you.

Finally you slept, you had to. After all, you needed to work, to support your children. The night Mrs. MacGregor took Peggy away, you dreamed, fitfully, of your second wife, the love of your life, who was also ripped from you in this mean, crowded flat.

Two years later, when the MacGregors moved to Fife, Peggy, torn but eager for adventure, asked your permission to go. Yes, you said, suspecting you would never see her again.

# CHAPTER THIRTY-THREE

# "Ritual Meals"

## *Valerie, California, 1977, 1989*

MOM AND I ARE EATING LUNCH IN MY CUTE NEW BERKELEY APARTMENT. Finally, things between us feel almost balanced. We are developing a friendship. I am mature enough now to admire my mother. She is beginning to understand me, or at least beginning to relinquish some expectations. Shopping, of course, is a major bond. I visit her in San Francisco, where we scout out sales at the big stores; she takes the bus to Berkeley to hunt with me through the quirky boutiques. Today we have been talking about our jobs, her customers at the Yum Yum Room and my students at U.C. Berkeley.

The perfect setting for a good talk: sun pouring through the big living room window, comfortable chairs. Heaped in a basket on the table are French rolls, her favorite bread. I have prepared Salade Nicoise, something simple, healthy, elegant. For dessert, I've bought chocolate truffles.

"You seem a little nervous," she says.

"Oh, no," I answer, spearing a piece of tomato and putting it in my mouth. But I *am* nervous, because this is the day I have planned, with excruciating care, to tell Mom about Pat, my lover, to tell her I am a lesbian. I want an honest relationship, a solid friendship with this wonderfully brave and witty and vulnerable mother. Months have gone into the planning of this lunch: the salad, the rolls, the truffles, the gentle conversation.

I breathe deeply, reminding myself that I have done everything right, for once. Finally, at age thirty, I am living back home. I am publishing stories and essays, working on a novel. She still urges me, every three or four months, to consider a more secure job at the Telephone Company, holding up cousin Billy as a model. Yet she likes the idea of her daughter teaching university, even if only as a lecturer.

"It really is a lovely apartment," she says, looking around, happily, from her perch on the chair, "and so convenient to the buses."

"Yes," I smile. I am renting my own apartment, after years of what were to her morally dubious housing collectives. This year I have had my ears pierced, learned to drive, and even bought a secondhand car. I should know that for her this is enough. She doesn't need any more news.

She picks around the funny little olives, but is enjoying the rest of her salad.

I take another breath, look out the window for courage. We need to talk.

"That was delicious," she says, filling the silence, putting down her fork.

Serving tea in the flowery china cups I have bought second—or sixth—hand at the Leeds Market and Covent Garden Market in my adventurous youth, I begin tactfully. "I have something to tell you."

She sips the tea.

"I want us to be friends, to share our lives. But, well, this is something that might upset you."

"Then don't tell me," she suggests, shrugging her small, sturdy shoulders.

But I have spent so much time shopping, cleaning, practicing my disclosure, getting advice from friends. I have spent all my life preparing. I hate her denial, can't see it as just different approach to truth.

"Where are we shopping this afternoon?" she asks.

I roll my eyes at her deflection, feeling both guilty and angry. I don't yet understand that one difference between us is that while Mom negotiates difficulties, I believe in conquering them.

Suddenly the chocolate truffles feel like a stupid, gross idea.

I sit back on the couch, inherited from Mom's recently dead friend, Mrs. Decoto. Honesty, I remind myself, is the only passage to trust. Then I reveal yet another thing she does not want to hear about my life. When I come out to her, do you know what she says?

My mother, cashier at the Yum Yum Room, looks at the ceiling and says, "There are more things in Heaven and Earth, Horatio, than are dreamt of in your philosophy."

Then Mom puts her head back against the chair and asks, "Is it my fault? Is this because of something I did wrong when you were growing up?"

### 1989

We're having a drink at the Claremont. One of her favorite things to do on a Saturday night is to take BART from her stop in San Francisco to my stop in Oakland, go out to a cocktail lounge overlooking The City, her city, have a meal at Norman's (taking half of it home in a doggie bag), and watch *Golden Girls* and *Empty Nest* on TV before going to sleep in my spare bed.

I like the view of San Francisco Bay from the Claremont Bar. I love watching the sun set over the ocean and witnessing my mother loosening up over a margarita. I don't like the smoke or the executives visiting from Los Angeles. Or the jars of tastey, fattening pretzels-seaweed-nuts marinated in soy sauce. We both enjoy the broad-hipped, no-nonsense waitresses and like to think that Martha and Monique and Molly—are they hired for their names?—remember us, although it's such a busy place, they probably don't.

On this hectic, crowded night, I curse myself for not planning better. We're too late for our usual window table. I'm not sure which of us is more disappointed, but Mother will never show it, will never indicate directly that I have failed. *Mom,* she prefers me to call her Mom and I try to remember. Here in the middle of the bar, we can look past the two thin young men sipping Heinekins, out to the butterscotch ball dipping slowly, irrevocably, toward the Pacific. What is it like for her to watch the sun set over an ocean she could only imagine as a Scottish child? I was shocked to learn that she never saw the Atlantic Ocean, either, never knew waves larger than those of the Firth of Forth, until she was already on the ship from Glasgow. She had read about waves, of course, she thought she had read about everything.

Now I want to ask if she finds this confusing, distressing, magical, the idea of day dropping into Asia. But she will look disturbed or impatient at yet another oddball query. Lately she has given me to understand that there isn't time for silly questions. She's not interested in "theorizing," prefers to spend her time remembering our life: family Christmases; the delinquent dog, Friskie; fabulous sales at Magnarama. Or recalling provocatively disjoined fragments of *her* life—those first thirty-seven years before I was born.

Abruptly, the sun disappears, leaving a yellow haze over the water, just below the slate sky. Off to the south, a jet streaks its white trail of possibility, contradicting the day's surrender. I imagine myself on that plane now, heading away.

"Days like this remind me of Peggy," she muses.

"Who?" I ask.

"Peggy," she repeats impatiently.

"Who's Peggy?"

"My sister," she answers, sipping the margarita pensively. Then a strange expression crosses her face, a new look that has come to Mother in her late seventies, a face of shame and relief that another secret has slipped from the war chest.

"Who is she?" I am alarmed, excited. "Whose side of the family— your mother's or your father's?"

"Peggy, my sister," she is annoyed with me, with herself, with the whole unwieldy experience of family. Making herself even smaller, she pulls in her elbows tightly. "No *side*. She was born between Colin and me."

As she explains, I wonder if it is impertinent to believe these stories are mine as well? How can it be that I am forty-two years old and have never heard about my aunt, who is not even a half-aunt like Bella and Chrissie, but an aunt who was born of both my grandparents, who lived in the same apartment with Mom for ten years?

"You never mentioned her. Ever."

Mom pauses to fish for a cashew from the jar of marinated goodies. "Oh, you've just forgotten. Remember the family who wanted to adopt me?"

"Yes."

"Well, Peggy went instead," she says matter-of-factly.

I watch this small woman picking the cuticle on the side of her corrugated thumbnail and I wonder how many other secrets she has. When she dies, will I discover answers in the bureau drawer, or carefully slipped into that cardboard box between old bills and Christmas cards? Whom has she been protecting with this silence? Perhaps for years she did manage to forget her sister Peggy, her closest sibling. Mom's secret making has shaped and fortified her optimistic keep-on-keeping-on-with-the-world view. She has constructed a story of the cosmos as intricate as Milton's theology, a universe in which she is both innocent and sinner, a life in which what you don't remember can't hurt you.

"But, well, did you stay in touch?" I finally ask.

"No," she stares at the last yellow shimmering. "I never saw her again."

A familiar, awe-filled sadness silences me.

She barely knew her mother; her father would "always be with her;" and her sister had just disappeared for sixty-eight years. Mother is losing a grip on her imagined life. The characters are beginning to seep back. So much for the power of fiction. The family history is deep in her body.

"Enough of that," she wipes her hands on the small magenta paper napkin. "I'm getting hungry. And I don't want to fill up on these silly nuts."

I am tempted to explore this new opening, press another margarita on her, but I can tell she will admit no more questions.

"Dinner, Madame?"

She looks out at the dimming sky, then smiles coquettishly, takes my arm.

No more reminiscing.

I leave a big tip for Martha.

And we hurry out the door, because Mom is right, we don't have much time left. We might miss our reservation.

# CHAPTER THIRTY-FOUR

# "Slipped Lives"

## *Valerie, England, Scotland, USA, 1974–1995*

WHEN THE TRAIN PULLS INTO FALKIRK, I'M NOT QUITE READY TO GET off. The sunny Saturday afternoon ride from Edinburgh has gone too fast. Hurriedly, I gather my presents for the children, the bottle of good wine for my hosts, the black overnight bag. I'm keeping Andrew waiting yet again, so I hustle down to the platform.

Here he is, tall as ever, a little larger, waving. I smile, thinking about this familiar gesture between us, and wave back in excited greeting.

*It was nineteen years ago and I was leaving him. I phoned Scotland from my London kitchen in tears—to confess uncertainty about returning to the States, to apologize. One more cup of coffee for the road before my jolly housemates escorted me to the ship. I was trying to find home, going back to see if I were still American. Also on the cusp of thirty at that time, Andrew understood those kinds of questions.*

As he ambles toward me, I am enveloped by affection and a keen intimacy, although we haven't slept together for two decades. Andrew smiles tentatively, his eyes focused elsewhere as if peering into the distance of youth. As always, he is a little formal at first, and looking all the more so today, in his suit and tie. On a weekend afternoon? Here I am in a shirt and casual summer pants. All I have in the overnight bag besides the gifts are my nightgown and a book.

*We met at a London Pub. A smokey place he had suggested during the first nervous phone call. "Welcome," he said. And I took him seriously, almost married him. His brother had been a friend in Canada and knew I would hit it off with Andrew. Andrew—a tall, smart, gregarious Scot with a generous heart and the most stirring blue eyes.*

"Sorry about the suit," he says. "I've just driven in from an archery match."

I stare.

He explains. A neighbor's party, big fete, posh people, a social obligation. Fun for young Emma. In fact, Emma and his wife Claire and their new son Donald are still at the fete.

Good, I think, we'll have some time alone with one another. My father's second wife used to disappear like this when I was visiting Dad. Out of sensitivity or hostility? Maybe indifference.

We drive fifteen minutes, through the suburbs, to his mansion. Really, a mansion built by a famous Victorian architect.

*That spring and summer of 1974, Andrew became the ever-ebullient guide to London. We had fun, worked hard, argued about how to make a better world. A man of principle, Andrew worked for various groups, fighting homelessness. I made an equally paltry salary as a freelance journalist writing about social issues for* The New Statesman *and* New Society *and as a member of the radical Writers and Readers Publishing Cooperative. We shuttled between his flat in Crouch End and a house I shared with five new friends in Tufnell Park. When he took a job in Scotland, we commuted on the train between King's Cross and Waverley.*

Eight bedrooms. The burnt orange foyer is larger than our California cabin. His world is grand now: nanny, housekeeper, two cars, beautiful view. This weekend I have a wing of the house all to myself.

We drink tea in the sunny, open kitchen. The phone rings and Andrew fends off a call from Claire's mother. Meanwhile, I play with the cat. Does Andrew remember I hate cats? Well, Buttons, or Bobbins, or whoever, *is* charming for its species.

*I photographed him at the funny sign by the "Temporary Gents" down by the Liffey in Dublin. Forever after, Andrew would be my temporary gent. Other pictures: Holding hands, one evening, we strolled along Amsterdam canals. Walking together through the bright sun of a Covent Garden weekend. Flying home to California at Christmas.*

*As predicted, Mom loved Andrew, saw him as a beaming lighthouse in our storm of short, cranky relatives. Back in Scotland, I spent weekends with his family. And this made me wonder what life would have been like if Mom had stayed here, if all our family spoke this thick Scots talk. My mother was hoping the wedding would be soon.*

The others arrive.

Everyone is charming. Emma, absolutely beautiful, has Andrew's oceanic eyes. Little, red, wrinkled Donald is well behaved. Claire welcomes me in a cheerful, tired voice.

As Andrew prepares dinner, we chat about politics, parents, former flatmates, current jobs.

Once or twice I hold Donald and pretend he is mine. Emma, too. (That nice woman Claire is visiting us.) We are safe, cosy. In and out the window of our spacious kitchen, an insistent breeze reminds me to savor the long, warm Scottish night. Emma asks me to read her a chapter from Enid Blighton. She writes a note to the Tooth Fairy and goes off to bed. I sigh at my immeasurably happy life.

*Mom didn't get her wish. Instead of marrying, I continued wandering. I traveled to Tanzania to interview President Julius Nyerere, who had been a long-time hero. In Dar es Salaam, I looked for work, hoping to live there as a teacher or even as a government information flack for African socialism. I visited Ujamaa villages and small industry collectives. Alone, and without the required permit, I traveled on the Tan-Zam railway to the border of Zambia. Later I stayed in an almost deserted hotel and roamed through the cloves and lemon grass of Zanzibar. As a journalist, I was covering the Summit of Southern African leaders from Mozambique, Angola, South Africa, Namibia, Zimbabwe. I wrote about the ANC and FRELIMO and UNITA. And I got a scoop: in an interview with me, President Nyerere was, for the first time on record, publicly critical of Henry Kissinger. That journey was a heady, scary, exhilarating time and I knew I would return to Africa soon.*

*But I didn't because I learned that Tanzanians didn't need any more white, middle-class Western idealists at that moment in history. I didn't belong there. I returned to the United States, my mother's daughter.*

Finally, about 9 P.M., Emma in bed and fantasies concluded, Andrew and Claire and I sit down to our tastey veg and overdone lamb chops. We talk about mutual friends and what used to be mutual families. About Rose and Kath in Edinburgh, about my nieces in California.

Andrew and Claire work as business consultants. They ask about my last novel and about this new book on Mom's family. We also check in on the Labour Party and the Royals and gossip about the current U.S. president, who went to Oxford with our friends Mandy and Sara. Then it's television—are we really talking TV?—sharing inside stories about *Fawlty Towers*. In Spain, Andrew says, the character of Manuel, the befuddled Spanish waiter, is dubbed in Italian. Is this middle age: chardonnay and gossip and TV chat? No, I promise myself. I tell them about my plans to teach in Sri Lanka, about how Helen and I hope to spend a year in Latin America soon. Deep down, I wonder if I've become a deluded bourgeoise, wonder how many principles I've surrendered to the small, irrevocable compromises of time-present comfort.

Claire asks me to write a note in the persona of the Tooth Fairy. Because, she says kindly, Emma will not recognize *my* handwriting. Meanwhile, Donald is dozing in Claire's arms. Andrew and I are feeling our three glasses each of Australian wine. Claire is feeling her abstemious, breast-feeding, one glass. All of us used to drink more and talk faster.

*Back in the States, I landed a job teaching at U.C. Berkeley. It wasn't the perfect job, but I would make it into one. My fiction was starting to be published. I investigated ways to return to Africa. I missed Andrew, but the time ahead of us seemed endless. Somehow, I had an affair with Henry. Then with Pat. Then with Joyce. Gradually, I understood that I was more real in California. I took Mom to the movies, on road trips. This was home, the place where I was meant to write and teach and love and agitate and sleep at night. Still, some days I was sure I would go back to Britain, to Andrew. Why did I assume he would be waiting?*

At 11 P.M., Claire yawns, handing the baby to Andrew. She needs to go upstairs for a few hours' sleep before the first feeding.

Donald is wide awake, and Andrew grins, cradling the heir in his big arms. I wash the dishes while Andrew tells his jokes and anecdotes. The house is silent, save for running water and our quiet laughter.

Andrew rocks our baby boy. Our beautiful daughter sleeps upstairs. I love this man and this life. All will be well when that strange woman leaves.

※

The next morning, as I stumble from the guestroom, aching for coffee, Andrew stands at the front door. In another suit. He's heading off to the service at the local Church of Scotland. Church?

He reads my face. Well, they are going to have Donald christened there, and besides, he enjoys the sermons.

At this point, I realize that this life is far too make-believe and far too grown-up for me: God, archery matches, historic architecture.

If I am relieved to be free of Andrew's conventional life, he must be grateful to have escaped my wackiness. I respect Andrew and Claire, who work hard at being good parents, doting, but responsible. In contrast, I would have been a nightmare mother—impatient, guilty, overprotective. The marriage would have ended in divorce. Here Andrew flourishes—in the good company of Claire and their fine family.

*Back in California, I continued to teach, to write more novels. And I fell in love with Helen. We've been partners now for fourteen years.*

*Still looking for home, I knew it had come down to making some decisions about sexuality, job, country. I couldn't float in the ether forever. Thus I decided I was a lesbian, a fiction writer, and a reluctant American.*

*I was lucky to find smart, beautiful Helen. Even my mother loved Helen, who was, in some ways, a better daughter to her than I. She appreciated Helen's gentleness and liked having a philosopher in the family. Of course, life with this American lesbian would neither be as Scottish nor as respectable as the future Mom envisioned for me. Once in a while, Mom asked about Andrew. She had imagined the wedding would be in Edinburgh.*

Claire and I sit in the kitchen, eating orange marmalade toast, drinking coffee, and discussing baby brain development, a fascinating subject. She tells me about Emma's private school and their plans for an upcoming visit by Claire's mother, something of a state occasion. I admire Claire's intelligence and versatility and grace and will always be a little jealous of her, of what I imagine her life to be.

*Over the years, Helen and I visited Andrew and Claire in their various Edinburgh flats. Finally I learned how lucky I was. Lucky to be afloat professionally; lucky to be healthy for the moment; lucky to have a loving life with Helen. Andrew and Helen immediately liked each other; Claire and I became friends, gleeful allies in teasing voluble Andrew. In the 1980s and 1990s, Helen and I visited Scotland often, wandering Mom's old neighborhoods as well as hiking in the Shetlands, and the Hebrides. Always, at the end of the day, we flew west, back home.*

When Andrew returns from church, he offers me a ride to the train. I am all packed. Ready to leave. Still, questions linger, as well as observations, regrets. We have time for one last conversation in the car.

Perhaps this is why Claire urges Emma to join Andrew and me on the way to the station.

I don't remember what we say on the road, just Emma's protests about having to sit in the backseat. Andrew gently placates her, explaining that she'll get to ride beside him on the way home.

We are, of course, early for the train. Andrew's Volvo purrs loudly in the Sunday-empty parking lot.

Andrew insists he will wait, to make sure I get on.

No, I look at his beautifully restless daughter, no, best to take her home.

From her rightful throne, protected by the sleek black seatbelt, Emma smiles and blows a kiss to the incognito Tooth Fairy.

I wave as they drive off, wondering what I would say if I could. Then was then. Now is now. But then is part of now. I would thank Andrew for showing me my slipped life.

# XII

---

*Daniel, 1925*

# CHAPTER THIRTY-FIVE

## Daniel, Edinburgh, 1925

YOU MISSED THEM—MAE, PEGGY, BELLA, YOUR BROTHER COLIN, EVEN
your estranged brother Robert. You were an old man, ancient at sixty from
too many jobs: iron worker, insurance agent, pit sink pumper, commercial
traveler. Too many children. Too many bad decisions.

This is what you did not accomplish: Fidelity to Maggie or to your
first children. You never saved enough money to move to a comfortable
place. You never took an accountancy course. You never found the right
job.

Of course, you never did these things either: Take a boat down the
Guilin River. View paintings at the Hermitage. Watch hippos bathe in
Ngororo Ngororo Crater. Attend a production of *The Mahabarata* in an
Adelaide Quarry. Hike over arctic blue glaciers. Smoke pot in a half-
finished hotel in the Moroccan Sahara. Stroll through the July-fragrant
Lodi Gardens in New Delhi. Climb Azetc pyramids in Tikal. Barter in
the souks of Ancient Jerusalem. Walk barefoot through Buddha's Tooth
Temple in Kandy. It was I, your restless granddaughter, who did all that
wandering. You never left Scotland. You didn't even travel to the
Highlands or the borders. Yet you had dreams, and you told the children
that a person could do whatever he set his mind on. Then you watched,
astonished, as your children proved you right, almost.

The older ones visited occasionally, now that Mae and Maggie had
both gone. You were relieved to see Nan taking an interest in both Mae and
Colin. You were living these days for the children: for your reconciliation
with Maggie's offspring and especially for the welfare of the wee ones.

Colin emerged as a lively, sweet, independent fellow, not unlike the good-tempered uncle for whom he was named.

And Mae, still a wonder at school with her recitations and papers and lightning mathematical answers. Miss Geddes spoke confidently about a scholarship. Mae fairly shone at being favorite pupil. For some girls, this would swell their heads. But Mae had little self-confidence. Such a serious child, apologetic for her imagined faults, fretful about Colin and yourself. Too often thinking and worrying on others' welfare first.

Dr. Bell advised you to cut down on work, to rest more, to drink a wee bit less. But you had a family to support and you were determined to keep Mae in school, to give her a chance for that scholarship. One more year and away she would go.

What would you have done without her? She always had something nourishing—soup, a stew—on the stove when you returned from work. (To be sure, her cooking still resembled her singing, and you knew you had yourself to blame.) What you liked most about a day occurred after tea, in front of the fire, where you read to Mae and Colin. Colin, it had to be admitted, liked the distraction of marbles or drawing. Perhaps one reason you got on so well with Mae was that she was the girl. You'd always had luck with females, always wished you had a sister. Mae sat at your feet as you read.

❧

Although this small tenement family wasn't the world to which you had aspired, it was a rich life. A life with more rewards than you thought you deserved. You enjoyed giving Mae half a crown to run down for chipped fruit and *The News of the World*, a mindless journal, yes, but all the attention that contemporary events warranted. For profundity, one waited for people and places seasoned in literature. The best moments were when you knew you could spare a few pence for Mae to get more of those colorful scraps. Such a treat to see her behaving like a real wee lassie and not a girl weathered before her time.

She missed Peggy something awful the first year—moping around during the day, her eyes never far from a tear, sleeping fitfully at night—pining for her sister's Sunday afternoon visits. Strangely, when the MacGregors moved to Cupar, so far out of reach, you all gradually stopped talking about Peggy.

You tried not to worry at how you were spitting blood. Edinburgh's air had been oddly dry all winter, and you remembered terrible nosebleeds as a boy. A passing nuisance, no more.

Bella visited to say farewell, and your heart sank. You knew that John Mathieson was strange, but to travel all the way to the end of Canada to some mountainous frontier called British Columbia to tune pianos was more than strange, it was demented. Who knew what the wet, cold climate would do to a sensitive instrument like a piano. Still, one had to let children live their own lives. Bella had been your best hope for Mae's welfare once you were gone. (Clearly "once," not "if," now that you were hacking so much.) Nan was too young, really, to take care of a half-sister, and she was always talking about America.

On the McKenzie side, there was Danny, who, despite Jock's temper, called by every month or so. After all, Mae had been his wee sister for her first few years, when she was a McKenzie. And Danny also treated Colin like a brother, now that Johnny was gone to Canada and Jack was in reformatory. His mother's death had brought out a family feeling in the lad. Maybe he was trying to make up for the way he had treated his mam in the last years. You had difficulty warming to Danny, because you could picture him in the doorway of Springfield Street, calling his mother a traitor. Maybe, also, because he resembled Jock. Yet he had been an attentive brother to Mae, lately concerned about her schoolwork, charming in his teasing way. A loyal, decent lad.

That February morning, early and cold as it was, you knew you had to go to the Infirmary. Breathing shouldn't feel that bad. There had to be some kind of pill or maybe a vapor treatment in the miraculous cabinet of twentieth-century medical science. People often recovered from lung ailments. You had already had enough ill fortune in your life. Even if God wouldn't be inclined to grant *you* a reprieve, He would have to see that your children had struggled more than their share. Once you were gone, who would take care of them? No, God would *not* take you so soon. Although you had long ago surrendered hope for your own comfort, you believed in justice for the children. It was with confidence, if not vitality, that you rose that dark morning, leaning on the wall for support, and made a pot of tea.

"Father, you're very ill." Mae peered through morning-bleary eyes.

"Nothing much."

How you loved this Mae, and how you regretted the first few years she had lived in that other man's house. Hated the fact that her legal name was McKenzie, but what could you do—break into Register House and erase it from the rolls? Formally setting the record straight would just have caused more pain. Someday, somehow, you could tell her the story. Meanwhile, every chance you got, you reassured her, "You'll always be a Campbell." Whatever that meant. And she knew enough never to ask why her younger brother had a different surname.

"Last night, all night, I heard you coughing," Mae persisted, tugging you from reverie. "Are you all right?"

"Fine, love. Fine. Still, I may just drop by the hospital for a bit this morning."

"Hospital!" Alarm swept her face. "You're ill, Father. Very ill."

"Och no, it's a wee thing. The doctors will set it right and send me on my way to work."

"I'm coming along."

"Not at all. You have schoolwork. I won't have you missing your classes."

She didn't even humor you with argument, rather she surmised your next line of defense and intercepted the objection. "I'll ask Mrs. Craig to look after Colin."

Together you rode the tram though that winter dark morning to the Royal Infirmary. You sat at the rear, because it was a long ride and so as not to disturb the others with your hacking. You patted Mae's clenched fist and told her Dr. Lister had conducted his most important experiments at the Edinburgh infirmary. This sparkling facility treated cases far more complicated and advanced than yours. Patients traveled from the Shetland Isles, from the North of England. You began coughing more deeply and, fearing blood would show again, you told her you needed to sit quietly alone for a while. She nodded, wide-eyed with worry, and moved a seat forward.

"Ah, dinna fas yourself, I'm a tough old bull," you wheezed. "I'll always be with you."

⸎

It was a beautiful building, more like a church or college than a hospital. And elegantly situated on the Meadows. You tried to ignore the pain, the discomfort, yes, that was it, just temporary discomfort. With all this green grass, the sheep grazing, you could be on a country holiday.

She sat beside your bed in the ward, holding your hand, fetching water. You didn't mean to, but you drifted in and out of sleep, in and out of dreams, memories. At one point, hours or minutes later, you looked up to find your mother sitting beside you. How had she gotten there? "Mam?" you asked in a small voice.

Mae's face grew longer, more serious. "It's OK, Father, I'm just here."

The drugs—it must have been their medicines that brought such sleep—made you imagine. You had stopped imagining long, long ago. Will you always trusted over imagination.

Gazing into her hazel eyes, you willed yourself to get through one more year. If only there were a bank where you could store breath. After this reprieve, you resolved to conserve oxygen. One more year and she would be in that school. Peggy was taken care of. And Colin—well, it was easier for a boy. Not easy, but easier.

She cradled your hand, ran her long, competent fingers up and down yours. "I'll always be with you," you said.

"I know that," she whispered. "Save your breath. Rest now."

Thus you drifted away and back, always waking to her imploring wee face. You tried to send her home, and she refused to leave. You said Colin would be lonely, tugging at her responsible little heartstrings. She answered that Mrs. Craig would see to her brother. You did not deserve this loyal daughter, this fruit of love and lust.

If only you had been able to start over again when Mae was born, establishing a wee family a little further down Leith Walk. If only you hadn't borne such guilt. How could an act of love bring such a terrible rift in your families? Reason. Logic. Persistence. None of these old virtues weighed as much as they used to. Perhaps this was your problem: negotiating twentieth-century desire with nineteenth-century currency. You had the wrong character, the wrong instincts, the wrong instructions for life.

"Would it be too much trouble—" you pretended not to notice her closed eyes. "Would it be too much trouble to ask you to get me a *News of the World?*"

"And maybe a piece of broken chocolate?" she added hopefully.

A man in the neighboring bed groaned.

"Aye," you spoke softly, "a small piece."

"You must be feeling better," she whispered to your cue, "if you're up to eating. I'll be back straight away."

"Take your time," you said. "Find some tea for yourself. Something to eat. The coins are in my pocket there."

She nodded.

"Then, after that, think on going home."

She shook her head.

You squeezed her hand. "Mae, love, I'll always be with you."

"I know," she said and kissed your brow.

You must have slipped off to sleep again. So hard to keep your eyes open under these medicines. So hard.

❧

You weren't there when the nurse intercepted her in the corridor.

"No!" she was screaming. She was a small lass, but that voice had power and her eyes could skewer a person.

*Another promise broken.*

"No, he couldn't be," she wailed louder.

*You weren't able to hear her anymore.*

"I just stepped out for his chocolate." Her voice broke. Tears streamed down her cheeks.

The sister nodded sadly, put her starched white arm around Mae.

"He didn't say good-bye."

Another nurse appeared and urged Mae to sit.

"Maybe he's just sleeping." Mae's face went red as she tried to fathom this last of your betrayals.

The women shook their heads, urged her to come back to the nurses' lounge with them, for a sit and a cup of tea.

"Let me see him," she demanded fiercely.

They tried to calm her, nudging her out of the bright corridor to the comfort and privacy of their lounge.

"You have to let me see him!" she screamed.

*Public display was so unlike her.*

In the small lounge, it took an hour to calm her down, to persuade her that you had gone.

Then she followed them quietly to a little office, gave them answers for their blue forms.

(Did you consider what you were doing, leaving these last tasks to a fourteen-year-old girl?)

Not thinking to be afraid, she walked numbly down the corridor toward the stairs.

"Are you all alone?" called one sister.

"Can you find your way by yourself?" asked another.

What did they think? That she was a child? Wordlessly Mae ignored their dull questions and opened the heavy door to the stairwell.

Dazed, she ran along the pavement, past the sheep ever-grazing in the meadows, envying the animals, who ate and slept whenever desire called. Violently, she wadded the chocolate in the newspaper and slammed them down on the kerb.

The tram stank of liquory breath and the stale sweat of February. Just 1 P.M., but when there was so much alcohol from so many different mouths, thought Mae, the world smelled like turpentine.

These revelers were laughing, at nothing, really. Laughing and talking too loudly.

There she sat, an uncomprehending refugee.

This had been her fault. If she had stayed by your bed, she could have called the sister when you started to fail. Maybe you choked to death. She hadn't thought to ask for details. Maybe she could have held you up, brought you water. Had you awakened, delirious, and seen that she had abandoned you? Tears streaked her face. "Come back," she whispered. "Come back, I didn't mean to leave you. Come back."

"Hey, there, lassie, brighten up. It canna be all that bad." The man occupied three-quarters of their seat, squeezing her slight frame against the window. He reeked of smoke and beer.

Two men behind her were singing. Too loudly and off key. "Rose of Picardy." "The Long, Long Trail." Folk liked the war songs more now than they had during the war.

How could they be so happy? How could these people be singing and joking and laughing when *her father had just died?*

"Come along, lass," her fat neighbor cajoled cheerfully, this lumbering ox, faced flushed with the color of his scarlet jumper. "Join us in a song."

Rage coursed through her, the likes of which she almost never would allow herself to feel again. Abruptly, she stretched up for the cord, calling the tram to a stop.

The tram had reached Register House. The walk home was long enough, particularly in winter, but she couldn't bear these laughing fools another second. Besides, she had a lot of thinking to do, about herself and Colin, and about how they would live the rest of their lives.

# CHAPTER THIRTY-SIX

# "The Last Page"

## *Mary and MQS, England, 1587*

THIS IS THE MEMORY. A SOLEMN BLACK DRESS, HER RED HAIR FLAMING. The dog hiding under her wide skirts. Handmaids weeping and trying not to, for her sake.

Ladies and gentlemen are seated, expectantly. All of them know, each a different truth, about how Rizzio was murdered in her chambers. Three hundred people fill the audience.

Beneath her somber robes—undressing is the ritual's first stage—is a brilliant red bodice and petticoat.

People gasp at her liturgical bravado. At this celebration of the Eucharist. At what they know will happen.

A blade drops, just slicing into the back of her skull. It is raised and dropped again, this time chopping through the neck.

Her head rolls forward, and when lifted for the crowd, a crimson wig drops off, to reveal grey hair attached to the skull of the finally dead Scots queen.

Her dog goes to sit by the body. So familiar, unfamiliar. Waiting patiently. Oblivious to the weeping women in the audience. The youngest handmaid is vomiting.

# CHAPTER THIRTY-SEVEN

# "White Lunch"

### *Valerie, Australia, 1988*

THE FEBRUARY SUMMER MORNING IS HOT AS I RIDE FROM MELBOURNE south to Grovesdale, a box of chocolate cherries grinning at me from the next seat. I feel like a hypocrite because I hate chocolate cherries—milk chocolate at that—but they are all I can find that look like gift candy in the hotel. By the time I arrive in Grovesdale, I know these aren't enough. Does *any*one like chocolate cherries? Perhaps this is the same box at which I turned up my nose in the Campus Rexall Drugs when I was searching for a get-well gift after my father's kidney stone operation. Perhaps they ship unbought chocolate cherries to Australia the way they send unsafe pharmaceuticals to Third World countries. If you think about it, chocolate cherries are a kind of pharmaceutical. Anyway, I decide to supplement the deadly orbs with flowers. When I stop in Grovesdale and the shopkeeper opens her mouth, I know I have made a serendipitous decision because she is from Aberdeen, like my Aunt Isobel.

Aunt Isobel rushes out of the white wooden house to greet me—I don't even have time to notice the house's shape and size because she propels herself forth as soon as the car is parked, her energy drawn directly from the sun on this zingy blue day. Like all my aunts, she is short and has curly grey hair. My mother seems to be the only one who remained auburn, and her hold on that is increasingly dubious as her follicles interpret pink into Clairol's Loving Care formula.

"Welcome, Valerie, Welcome." There's quite a bit of Australian in her Aberdeen. "Oh, this is a fine day. I just wish you could visit longer. It's a pity to come all this way and stay only for lunch."

I don't need any more proof of relation. Here she is missing me almost before we've met.

"Come in, come in. Uncle Colin's been waiting all morning, he has."

"I'm not late, am I?" My face falls. "It was ten o'clock that we said?" I can hear the Scottish creeping into my inflection. My mouth is filling with saliva to cope with rugged "r's."

"Not at all." She shakes those great grey curls. "Not at all. It's just that your uncle has been looking forward to seeing Mae's daughter, to meeting you. And Anita, too, she's come all the way down from the city to see her cousin."

᯼

I have trouble, now, separating Uncle Colin, old and feeble in Australia, from the bright, blond Colin of my mother's Edinburgh reminiscences. Colin Campbell, born with the Great War, grew into a sweet, loyal brother, and I planned to name my son after him. Colin—my husband and I had decided—Colin and Anna, in that order. Sweet, wee Colin, my mother often said. He was the youngest, nine when their father died, and sent to an orphanage in Aberdeen. Sometimes she talked about "Uncle Colin in Australia," who immigrated in the 1950s to work on a sheep ranch. I always pictured him shearing a large, white ewe on a windy plain. Uncle Alex had gone to New Zealand, and I imagined the two of them visiting while their wives made scones in the kitchen. That was before I understood the distance in time and miles between their journeys. That was before I tried to measure any of the profound distances in our family.

In recent years, Mom had developed a correspondence with Colin's wife, Isobel. "Your brother isn't much of a writer, but he sends his best love," she would say.

Suddenly one Sunday in the late 1970s, perhaps because the letter writing had been safe, Mom asked me to phone Uncle Colin for her. I suppose she thought that I, as a representative of the technological generation, would be better at dialing all those numbers. After the long-distance connection was made, Mom spent a long time talking with Aunt Isobel. My uncle spoke on the phone just a minute. Then Aunt Isobel returned. "He's crying, Mae, he was so moved to hear your voice."

Mom never did manage to make those calls herself. The next two times I dialed, he wouldn't talk at all. However, Mom had lively conversations with Aunt Isobel, who kept inviting us down for a visit. Finally, *I* managed to get to Australia, a year before Uncle Colin died.

❦

As we walk along the flagstones toward the modest wooden door, I wonder at how all my aunts and uncles in Victoria and Toronto and Cleveland and Burntisland have lived in tiny houses with white doors. Perhaps if you were brought up in an Edinburgh tenement, no place was small if there were a bath inside and grass around the perimeter.

A braided green rug paves the entryway into the brown, broadloomed living room. Uncle Colin sits in a stuffed green tweed chair, and at first I am surprised by his fairness—blond hair and blue eyes, in contrast to my mother's darkness. But then I remember stories about blond, wee Colin. I think of my own blue eyes—which didn't come from my dark father, either—and the eyes of my unborn son. Colin smiles stiffly as I bend to kiss him, stranger's lips on stranger's cheek, and I can feel the shaking of his Parkinson's. His wattled elbows hang over the fluting arms of the green chair.

"He's a sick man, your uncle." Aunt Isobel has told me this on the phone, and she says it again. I think of Aunt Jean and Aunt Chrissie tending their men. "He's suffered from the Parkinson's for four years now. On top of that he has emphysema and heart trouble, and last spring he had a stroke." Aunt Isobel has a lot to talk about. For many years, it's clear, she has done the talking in this family, the letter writing, the answering of phone calls.

"Sit, sit," Isobel ushers me now to the couch next to Colin. Between his chair and mine stands a small, beige fan, whirring heat out of the room. Still there is an almost suffocating closeness and I wonder at my hubris in drawing family back together. Above the noise, I can hear the heavy asthmatic breathing, which makes me think of Uncle Louie gasping for breath as he carves the Thanksgiving turkey, or Mom lately on the phone, the voice lost in soft lung shadows. Whatever they spewed into the city air was potent enough to make Edinburgh's children talk in sighs seventy years later.

"He hasn't seen your Mum in sixty years," Isobel is saying. "But he remembers as if it were yesterday. Now what am I thinking about—here's your cousin Anita. Yes, yes, I think there is a family resemblance."

Anita is a sturdy woman, ten years older than I, in a black cotton sheath and green silk scarf. She has a wide, handsome face and an Australian accent. I feel shy around her—because she is my generation, I can't hide in a niecely role. After we smile and nod hello, I find myself staring at the print of a Highland scene above her head. The walls are painted a pale beige, reflecting the trim on nylon curtains. Uncle Colin is fiddling with a TV remote control wand. I imagine him pressing a button and making us all disappear.

Aunt Isobel returns—she left the room?—with tea and biscuits. "We've made a reservation at the hotel for lunch. But that's not until 12:30."

Colin has Mom's wistful eyes, worried mouth, her whole facial structure. I can't stand it. And he is quiet, as she has been until recent years.

I pull out my photos. "From Christmas," I explain. "This shows the whole family. Mother, John, Larry, me, Mary Anne, Dee, my nieces."

Uncle Colin examines the picture for a long time. Silently, he passes the Christmas portrait to Anita, who gives it on to her Mum, who asks polite questions about my mother's health and my brothers' jobs.

"Amazing that your mum has done restaurant work for so long. She must be a strong woman."

"Yes," I smile, thinking about her will, although Anita was probably referring to her body.

"And your brothers, where do they live now?"

"California and Washington State."

Other snapshots make the rounds, and after a while I see Colin staring at the family portrait. "Which one is she?" he demands, jittery hands gripping the photo.

Clearly, she is the oldest, the one in the middle. But of course he remembers a twenty-year-old girl.

"There," I point gently. "There's Mom."

He nods and carefully studies the picture.

I want more than this: a cry of recognition, a memory, a ranting at the fates that separated them all these years. But obviously my mother's brother, he just nods and releases an almost inaudible sigh.

"I'll always remember one snap of Aunt Mae," Anita declares. "She's standing by a bridge and there are ducks in the background. She's wearing shorts and a white flower in her hair." A chill darts along my shoulders, because I know this photo well, a souvenir of my parents' honeymoon, of—as they say—happier times. Mother with the gardenia in her hair is a family classic. How sweet that she would have sent a copy to Colin, and that he would have carried it from Scotland to Australia.

Aunt Isobel ducks into the bedroom and returns with a shoe box of pictures. Anita brightens as she leaves through the old snapshots and triumphantly pulls out a photo with Mom grinning from ear to gardenia-crested ear on her impossibly happy honeymoon. The story of my parents' love-struck trip to Spring Lake is one of my perfect moments, the kind of indelible secondhand memory children cherish.

Still, my mother never liked the spotlight, and embarrassed for her, I change the topic. "Now when, exactly, did you come to Australia?"

Uncle Colin looks drained, staring out the window, perhaps to recover some privacy.

Aunt Isobel quickly swallows the last of her biscuit.

"He came out in 1950," she says, dabbing her lips with the napkin. "Assisted passage to work on a sheep farm. Then in 1952, he had saved enough to send for us. It was a long journey—three weeks."

"That must have been hard for you, the separation," I murmur.

"Oh, you do what you have to do. He was restless in Scotland after the war. Aberdeen was terribly depressed then. I knew I'd married an adventurer. Knew what I was getting into."

Anita smiles ruefully. "To my brother Rod and me, the voyage felt like three years."

"We lived for a while in New South Wales," Isobel continues. "Then your uncle had saved enough to start his own pig farm. Now, that was an experience, I tell you. We could have made a go of it if it hadn't been for the floods. But who could have predicted those—acts of God, they were."

So much for my fantasies of a broad-brimmed uncle riding horses through fertile, green meadows dotted with fluffy sheep. I sip the milky tea, thinking it sad that Mom had switched completely to coffee in recent years—too many jobs in American cafes. For the last two decades, she hadn't cooked for herself at all, but ate all her meals free at work. And, as everyone knows, Americans never bring the water to boil before serving the catastrophe they call tea. Even the coffee was never strong enough for her.

"So he returned to sheep shearing and worked hard. We saved a lot—enough to buy this house."

I look around appreciatively, thinking of Bella, Chrissie, and Jean. Colin and Anita sit placidly in their chairs, overstuffed figurines, listening as they have done for fifty years—to the gregarious Mother. They both call her Mother. She calls Colin Father.

I think of my own nieces. They are to me what I am to Colin— offspring of a sibling. Yet they seem so much more *like* me than I seem like Colin. Born in the same country; living in the same country. Well, maybe I'm *not* so different from this man who is hunkering down deeper into blankets of silence. I've lived many years as an expatriate, and my American identity is still reluctant, always temporary. I am a lesbian. Perhaps these personal choices are unconscious assertions of idiosyncracy and distance, the authentic blood marks of our family.

"Your house is lovely," I observe, mortified by how long this simple comment has taken.

"I'll show you around then," Aunt Isobel says with the kind of alacrity that lets me know she has been waiting for her cue. "What have I been thinking of?"

As she takes my hand, I notice hers is bigger. She reminds me of Aunt Jean, with her thick, competent limbs, and I consider the subtle ways in which these women have invisibly supported my uncles.

"This is the kitchen."

I smile at the gleam of sink and counters. She introduces me to the fully electric range. "We never had anything like this in Scotland. The life really is a better one here."

"So how did you and Colin meet?" I ask as she shows me into the hallway.

We stand in the doorframe of the master bedroom. I am discreet, but notice the olive green chenille bedspread, the pink roses painted on their porcelain lamp, the ceiling light shining down from the thickly cut rose glass shade. The bedside telephone is white. There is nothing of Edinburgh or Aberdeen in this room. Only newish, assembly-line, durable goods. Like my mother's San Francisco apartment. I'm sure Colin and Isobel are proud of these acquisitions. Besides, who would have wanted to cart heavy, broken-down goods from Scotland? Realism and practicality, Mom always tells me, are family traits I failed to inherit.

"And this is the guest room. We keep it for when Anita comes down from the city. Or the grandkids. That's why we have the crib. Rod's got two very wee ones. And another on the way." She grins.

I nod, knowing I'm expected to say, "Congratulations," and knowing that I cannot say this. Reproduction has never seemed an accomplishment in itself. Another sense in which I am a dysfunctional relation. What would it cost me? I can hear my mother ask. One word.

"Anyway, how Colin and I met." She is loquacious, less superstitious, now that we stand in a more public doorframe. "He worked at a farm near my father's pub."

"Your father owned a pub?"

"Aye, and I was the barmaid. Colin was a handsome man then—still is—just before the war. He'd been adopted by a local widow, more as a farmhand than as a son, really. She worked him outside without proper shoes." Her jaw tightens at this. "Of course, this was before I knew him." Embarrassed by such vehemence, she lowers her volume. "And all that outdoor work couldn't have done him much harm—for he was in a fine glow of health. We made plans to marry. Then the war came. And when he returned—thank God he came back, God has been good to me—he was too restless for Scotland. For the first few years he was absorbed in the children's births. Then he got this Australia bug and, well," her nervous voice rises like a high-pitched balloon releasing helium, trailing off.

"Mother," Anita calls gently. "Time is getting close."

"Oh, my, yes," Isobel frets. "We have a reservation at the hotel. And we don't have Valerie with us all that long today."

In the living room, Uncle Colin sits staring at the blank TV screen, as if identifying with another object in the room that can be switched off suddenly. Isobel finds her purse and Anita collects Colin's jacket from the cupboard. I surreptitiously study my uncle's stooped, defeated posture. Where has he gone? Did he make the decision to leave? I wonder if this old man's system broke down from overuse or despair or abuse. How much of him is here today? I imagine his childhood: the golden lad, apple of his sisters' eyes. He was too young—at two—when his mother died, to remember much. But he was nine when Grandfather passed on. Nine when he was sent to an orphanage, separated forever from his family. He must have considered Mom—five years his elder—as a little mother. And I'm sure that's how she behaved toward him: caring, tender, worried.

Are we together so that I can see him, the legendary baby brother, or so that he can see me, a living extension of his beloved sister Mae? Does my presence reassure or unnerve him? Do I represent safe landing in North America, an escape from that cold, dark country? A ring tossed at the future? Yes, I suspect that, like Mom, he was counting on my fortunate generation to make it better. For someone.

We have lunch at a slightly down-at-the-heels village hotel. The same place, magically transferred in space and time, where Johnny and Jean took us when Mom and I visited Burntisland twenty years ago. Anita has driven us here: where, how far, and in what direction, I don't know because my attention is so absorbed by Colin's wheezing. What expense—physically, financially—my visit has caused. Of course, I would have been happy with an egg salad in Isobel's kitchen. Of course, I don't need lunch at all after that substantial morning tea. But they are going to do this visit right. Mae's daughter—visiting from America, even if only for half a day—has to be taken out for a proper hotel lunch.

A proper hotel white lunch: biscuits and white fish and boiled, skinned potatoes and cauliflower. White table cloth. White waiters. White diners. With Uncle Colin's heavy breathing and Aunt Isobel's chattering, I lose focus, forget the questions I have stored, the basic information I need. What was his father like? Colin, charter member of some Calvinist veteran's brotherhood, might have a different impression of their parent than my adoring mother did. How much could a nine-year-old boy remember of a fading father? As little as Mom recalled of her mother? How has Grandfather's image metamorphosed over the years? Which versions of which stories has Colin passed on to Rod and Anita and Isobel?

But Anita beats me to it. She is adept at navigating this wheezing, white world. "Tell us about your Mum, Valerie. She's still working in the restaurant?"

I'm distracted by her accent, for although I'm used to my rels having Scots accents, it seems exotic to have a cousin who speaks 'stralian like this. Do I sound like Sally Field to her?

I feel Mom leaning into our conversation; I notice her eyes carefully watching my mouth for signs of betrayal. I cannot tell them that at seventy-seven my mother got laid off her job, that the restaurant was an all-night coffee shop closed down by the health department. "Retired," I hear myself lying, only a venial sin because I don't say she retired voluntarily. "Reluctantly, she's left all that behind."

What she also seems to have left behind is the better part of her brain. Huge discouragement can do that to a person. Since I came to Australia to teach for six months, I've found her phone conversations have become more and more diffuse. I shouldn't be surprised. If your job is your reason for living and it gets stolen, what's the point? I feel such urgency here—between Colin's failing body and Mom's fading brain, I want them to fill in the pieces before it's too late. I want to help them touch each other, to make a link before one or both of them is gone. But this romanticism is perhaps just another symptom of my generation. I can see by the weariness of Colin's eyes that he will have had quite enough of old memories when I drive away at 2 P.M.

Another voice, another question, my aunt's fully Aberdeen inflection now, for as we have talked about Mom and Edinburgh, she has recovered more of her lovely Scottish brogue. "One thing Colin has never understood," she begins delicately and looks to him for assent, permission, attention, "is the difference in their names. Why was Mae's name 'McKenzie' and Colin's 'Campbell'?"

I take a breath, remember how, aunt-by-aunt, I learned the hidden stories. Recalling how Mom has always said I ask too many questions.

Isobel continues, clarifying her query. "Their father's name was Campbell, Daniel Campbell."

Yes, I nod, thinking of all the McKenzie tams and blankets and kilts I bought over the years before I realized that this was no clan of mine. I assemble words to explain how Mother—who would always be a Campbell—was named after her mother's husband.

Colin's lids lower; the Calvinist veteran nods almost imperceptibly.

"And while we're on the subject," Isobel persists, although, or because, she is a wise old woman. "Do you know about their mother? Do you know how she died so young?"

"In childbirth," I'm tempted to repeat Mom's longtime understanding. But we've all traveled too far for those kinds of lies. So I tell the truth as far as I know it.

# XIII

---

*Family Reunion, 1860s–1990s*

# CHAPTER THIRTY-EIGHT

# Family Reunion

### *Edinburgh, 1860s–1990s*

THIS IS A STRANGELY FORMAL PLACE TO MEET YOUR GRANDPARENTS, BUT I have traveled a long way, and Register House will have to do. The imposing nineteenth-century grey-stone building stands near the top of Leith Walk, right on Princes Street, behind the statue of Wellington. My Aunt Nan was told that Wellington dismounted at 4 P.M. every afternoon and, one evening, little Nan was found on the pavement after dark, staring up at the figure, still waiting for the tardy duke to get off his horse. Perhaps my own expectations here have been equally naïve.

The national research facilities are located in a Victorian room under a beautiful blue skylight dome. Circling the august chamber on a spiral of caged floors are shelves of Scottish records. At night, in the empty room, ghosts rattle the wire cages, whispering secrets from the registers, from the census collections, from the files on birth, adoption, marriage, and death.

This family reunion is different from the ones with Uncle Johnny in Burntisland and Aunt Chrissie in Toronto and Uncle Colin in Australia. More public, colder. After paying the seventeen-pound access fee and promising to write only in pencil and to refrain from eating snacks, I am admitted to the dome room, assigned a desk and a microfiche viewer for the day. With Johnny and Chrissie and Colin, I ate cake and leafed through the blurry snapshots of their recollections. Here, meeting family is more like examining medical X-rays. No snacks; no cake.

First you look up a name on the computer, where you locate the number of the microfiche containing your record. The microfiches are stored in tiny, morguelike wooden drawers. Once you have selected and studied the proper microfiche, you can pay to have a copy made of your record. More often, the record isn't the right one and you return the microfiche and dig out another. It's all very orderly. In the red plastic tray, you return the marriage certificates. The death certificates are put in a black tray.

On my first trip to Register House, I am looking for Mom. Suddenly, I am seized with panic, watching the computer scroll through birth records. What if she wasn't born on 17 June 1910? She imagined so many other details of her life—why not that? Then, tears in my eyes, I see her on the screen—Mary Gill McKenzie, born 17 June 1910, at 9:30 P.M. at 8 Springfield Street, Leith.

That day I also spend hours searching for a record of my grandparents' marriage, to no avail. Then I look for the divorce certificates indicating the divorces of Mae from John McKenzie or Daniel from Maggie Campbell. After a few hours, I decide I must be doing something wrong.

Frustrated, I check with the supervising archivist. He kindly reviews my procedures, nodding approvingly at each turn. Suddenly his face blanches from concentration to condolence. The middle-aged archivist opens his brown eyes wide, as if in some primal defense. "Have you ever considered," he clears his throat, "that your grandparents never actually married one another?"

I am shocked.

"I mean," he says appeasingly, careful not to cause offense, "divorce was expensive in those days, especially for poor people. Possibly your grandparents couldn't afford it."

He thinks I am embarrassed. In fact, I'm just surprised by my own innocence. I want to make him feel better. I think of saying, "That's OK, I'm not offended. Helen and I aren't married either."

He waits, fiddling with his pencil.

I am my mother's almost proper daughter, so I simply nod to the man with dignity and thank him for his help.

During the next few years, I make more trips to Register House, which, since all our family tenements have been torn down, I think of as the family mansion. It is here that I learn details about the births of grandmother and her parents. Here that I find birth certificates for Aunt Bella and Uncle Colin and Uncle Matt.

It's very hard to locate any details about my grandfather. Since Mr. McKenzie graciously signed my mother's birth certificate, *he* is listed as her father. Daniel Campbell was dropped discreetly out of sight. Mom told me her parents had married by the time Uncle Colin was born. Maybe she was right and the archivist was wrong. Finally, after hours of dead ends looking for Uncle Colin, I find his birth certificate. And, yes, Daniel Campbell is listed as the father. I search for a wedding date (which will lead me to Grandfather's birth date), but no marriage is listed. Instead, the document identifies Colin's mother as "Mary Gill, wife of John McKenzie, Biscuit Machineman, who she declares is not the Father of the child and further that she has had no personal communication with him since they ceased to live together in November 1914."

The disappointment at not being able to trace more about Grandfather—how else will I learn his birth date?—is overtaken by my surprise at the candor of this document. Immediately, I request a paper copy of Colin's birth certificate, similar to the documents I have about my mother and grandmother.

The clerk takes my money. Briskly, she says that the process takes several days, that I'll receive a cleaned-up version of the document by mail.

"Cleaned up?" I ask.

"Well, this writing," she answers nervously, "we'll remove the writing."

"Oh, no, I need that. I mean, that's why I came. To find out."

Patiently she explains that since the document reveals a crime (adultery) less than one hundred years past, she cannot release the details to the public.

"I'm not the public," I explain reasonably, "I'm family. This is my uncle."

The clerk shakes her head at my futile protest. "But," she adds knowingly, "you can go back to the dome room and scribble down any of the details you like before we make the official copy."

One day, I do find a trace of Grandfather, on Aunt Bella's birth certificate. Bella was the oldest of his children with Maggie. Then I locate Grandfather and Bella in the census. The censuses are a treasure. These documents must be at least one hundred years old before they are released on public microfiche. Yet I have seem to have an ancient family. Here on the 1881 census, I learn the names of my grandmother's brothers and sisters. Here on the 1891 census, I discover how to spell the name of my mother's brother, Uncle Alex—not Alec, as I had always thought.

My days at Register House are suspenseful, tiring, rewarding. I feel as if I've paid a very expensive admission each day, to read a new chapter of the family mystery. Back in the death certificates for 1917, I find that when Grandmother dies, Daniel Campbell is listed as the witness, but the deceased is described as "wife of John McKenzie, Biscuit Machineman." And in 1925, my grandfather's death certificate is signed by Uncle Donald. Daniel Campbell is listed as the "Widower of Maggie Thompson Campbell." So now I know, for sure, that my grandparents never did marry one another.

This April I have returned to "finish" my research. Edinburgh is bursting with spring; the light lasts longer each night. At first, everything goes according to plan. I pick up the keys to my bedsit, go down to my research office at the university, have dinner with old friends. Each morning, I awake, thrilled to be here. Yet silence shrouds my desk. And each evening, for the first few weeks, I feel I have nothing to add to the book. During the day I read Scottish history, visit museums and libraries, take naps, fiddle with the language and structure of this book, walk around Mom's old neighborhoods. I realize that I have hoped that being in Scotland will make the final work go faster. Yet, if anything, it is slower here. I keep running into those troublesome ancestors, censorship and self-censorship.

The public censorship ranges from Mr. McKenzie's appearance as Mom's father to Uncle Colin's "cleaned-up" birth certificate to the medical details on my grandparents' death certificates. Since Aunt Jean had told me about the abortion, I am surprised to see the cause of my grandmother's death listed as "Miscarriage (due to premature death of foetus, six weeks)." And, although Mom always said her father had TB, his cause of death is noted as "Chronic Bronchitis (4 years) and Myocarditis (5 years)." I check these records with a historian and a doctor, who explain that I should continue to believe Aunt Jean and Mom about the causes of these deaths. Doctors didn't like to record illegal abortions or the spread of Tuberculosis. When documents and memories are reconstructed, where do you find the story?

The self-censorship comes in the form of an inner voice that sounds suspiciously like Mom, saying, "Don't make a scene." I worry about betrayal. I've learned more than Mom ever cared to know about her family. Is it her family or *our* family? Sometimes this silencing impulse feels protective. I do not want to reenter the old pain, to experience new separation and loss. Every discovery brings with it some understanding about the dreariness or tragedy of my family's lives.

Just as secrets muted the story for decades, now my obsession for facts keeps me from telling what I do know. I lose track of my uncles Matt, Alex, and Donald after they left Scotland. I never find a trace about Uncle Jack. Aunt Peggy, too, remains a ghost. Still, I tell myself, I have to start writing, stop researching somewhere.

April turns into May, and my optimism expands with the evening light. There's always one more place to go, and my old journalistic conscience drives me forward, backward. Returning to the 1891 census, I track details about Grandfather's first set of kids. I look up all my aunts' and uncles' birth certificates, locating only a few. I try to discover if Mom had any children before she emigrated from Scotland. This is a new preoccupation—perhaps *I* have more brothers, or a sister, out there. Should I take out an ad in the *Evening News* or the *Scotsman* to track down my missing aunts and uncles, the truth about my own half-siblings? Secrets and details are now equally paralyzing: Have I reached the point of madness?

As I shop at my local Tesco supermarket, I think about how this whole book is rooted in fantasy. I have spent thirty years coming back to Scotland. Yet this is, of course, such a different country than the one in which Mom was born and grew up. At the market, I buy Dutch tomatoes and Italian cheese and Spanish lettuce and discounted-by-bulk French muscadet. I find South African apples and Pennine water. (I don't know if Mom ever drank a glass of mineral water in her life). Tesco has no bin of chipped fruit. They sell Grandfather's *News of the World* near the counter for fast photo processing.

Scotland is now part of Europe. As the spring election campaign whines on from my radio, even the Tories are pledging to support the NHS, a health system that didn't exist until Mom was seventeen years gone. In the 1920s, Mom had to wait months for a letter from her brother in New Zealand or her sister in Canada. Now, I email across the oceans several times a week. Walking up and down these damn hills is the only exercise my mother ever got. Meanwhile, at the University Sports Centre, I take a regular aerobic class where we do knee lifts and hamstring curls to a mixture of Bruce Springsteen and bagpipe music. Forget the return of the prodigal daughter, late twentieth-century culture makes this experience more like *The Return of the Jedi.*

Any minute now, Arthur Wellesley Wellington will dismount from his horse.

# CHAPTER THIRTY-NINE

# "Thistles in California"

### *Valerie, Mendocino, 1980s–1990s*

AT 5:30 THIS WARM AFTERNOON, CROWS CIRCLE LOW FOR THE LAST BUGS. Golden waves of grass shimmer down hills to the pond. It's been a quiet day between the noises of our typing and an occasional plane flying overhead. If you listen closely, wind scratches through the dry grass, crickets twitter, the woodpecker taps in a straggle-limbed oak; you can also hear the call of roosters, the buzz of yellow jackets. Simmering at a maddening pitch, the pot never quite up to boiling, still threatening to spill any moment. As I watch the sun shredding magenta clouds, a single deer prances from a grove of trees.

I cherish these sunny winter evenings at the cabin Helen and I have built, remembering the brilliantly naïve possibility in today's blue sky. Overcast weather fills me with uneasy pressure. In that greyness, shapes and colors juxtapose, rather than flow through one another, creating an "or" day rather than an "and" day. It's hard to crank up imagination in such a cotton-padded world. No atmosphere for daydreaming, it seems easier to fantasize in sleep. But today has been bright, shaped by small successes and mistakes at home.

Home—I test the confines and options of that word. Always, I have been a traveler; curiosity about people and landscapes runs in the blood. I am happiest when I am moving. Like my mother, I flirt with notions of home. I think she finally found hers in that Tenderloin apartment. Perhaps for me, it will be these inland hills of Northern California, because of the very changeability of the environment and our space within it.

*Ro*

This morning, I am working on *The Low Road* at the cabin. No, truthfully, I am staring at the glimmering hills and beyond, the ugly patch of clear-cut across the valley. The writing even at this late stage is still painful and thrilling and humbling. My mother used her wit to imagine herself into a life. I use mine to imagine novels. So far, she is the superior fiction writer. Although Mom has been dead since 1991—is that possible?—this project has kept her close to me, more intimate, in some ways, than we were during her life. I don't want the book to end.

Enough mooning, I can hear her rousting me from idleness. I'll return to the desk later. Time to cut some of that high grass. You need a serious firebreak in this brittle country.

*Ro*

## 1980s

I often recall how Helen and I introduced Mom to these Anderson Valley hills, during the early days of cabin building. A trip to Mendocino? She is—as always—ready for a road journey on her days off. So Helen and I load the car with lumber and nails and tools and suitcases, settle Mom in the front passenger seat, and drive north for three hours. She will visit the land briefly, we'll leave Helen for a couple of days of construction work, and Mom and I will ride into Mendocino Village for a seaside holiday.

Our drive is particularly beautiful at the beginning and the end. First the green, green Marin hills. As we pass Sausalito, Mom gazes out at the boats and restaurants and remembers the times Helen and I have taken her to dinner there. Soon we are in Santa Rosa, always hot in August, reminiscing about a family holiday on the nearby Russian River, in a borrowed cabin. Then north, heading through Healdsburg, Cloverdale, around and over the dry hills. Mom asks politely how long this trip takes. Finally, we arrive in the beautiful Anderson Valley. "Anderson," my mother nods approvingly, "is an old Scottish name."

Doubt crosses her face again as we stop to unhook the padlock on the large wooden gate and then drive carefully, slowly up the bumpy gravel and dirt road to the parcel of land Helen owns collectively with twelve other women. Mom looks out the window in wonder, perhaps imagining how she might escape. Up, up the hill, past the buckeye trees and blackberry bushes, turning at the corral down another steep dirt hill. Eventually we reach the pond. "Lovely," Mom says as she glances at the cool water and ancient oaks. Standing uncomfortably in the hot afternoon, I can tell she thinks this place we've chosen is a little too picturesque to be civilized. Cordially she shakes hands with three or four of our friends, strange women, slouching in blue jeans and T-shirts. "Did you know?" she inquires brightly, ever ready to be hospitable, even to her hosts, "that Anderson is a Scottish name?"

Hot. August in the inland Mendocino hills. My mother, who never sweats, is drenched. She looks old. We wave farewell and head off to our seaside weekend.

As we drive through the cool Redwood forest northwest toward her beloved ocean, I rhapsodize about the exhilaration of building a cabin. The most exciting stage is after the frame is raised on our wall-less house. I like to stand in the middle of the skeleton, smelling the Douglas Fir, savoring the limitless space, gulping the view, wide-open frame from all four sides. Conversely, I hate the making of sides and ceilings, that transition from youth (where all views are possible) to middle-aged compromise. Then again, after we tack up the walls, we get to cut holes in them for windows. And each slice admits a new surprise.

She smiles, that content, curious smile. She doesn't say much except, "Middle-aged! Who's middle-aged? Certainly not you."

I tell her how the work varies from day to day. One morning I align plywood on the roof and pound in nails along the seams. That afternoon I hammer floorboards, a less rewarding task in one's vista and sense of daring. You discover a lot about character this way. I have zero confidence about obtaining new skills. When the nail doesn't penetrate the wood, I assume I have the wrong nail or that the wood has changed from last year.

"Patience was never your strongest suit," she says, her hands folded in her lap.

Maybe if I hit each nail several times, I'll win. I notice that if I aim carefully and proceed with measured strokes, I'm more successful. I add force behind each slam and learn to raise the hammer high enough for a maximum blow, so I know when the nail is going in and when I'm wasting my shots. Eventually I become competent. Instinct functions better than will. Invariably it's when I'm concentrating too much that I mess up. Usually hammering is a good break from writing. Yet tender, newly discovered muscles in my thumb make it painful to hold the pen.

"Then why do you do it?" she asks.

I remind her about Dad's endless paneling, about how my older brother became a carpenter.

She shrugs, "So long as you enjoy it and don't hurt yourself."

We continue, in companionable silence, along the tranquil Redwood Highway to the sea.

℞

### 1990s

Four years after her death and two days before what would have been her eighty-fifth birthday, I wake up from vivid dreams.

I am visiting Mom in the City.

"You look so well," I declare.

She is puzzled.

"Really, really well. How are you feeling?"

Now she becomes irritated. "Fine, why do you ask?"

Yes, of course, she wouldn't want me to know she had been so ill. (Wouldn't want me to tell her I thought she was dead.) We agree to go shopping.

Walking along Taylor Street, I start to take a bridge up, over the road. She points to a walkway that goes under the road, shows me that it involves less climbing, is easier on the lungs. Easier for everyone, really, if they only knew. There *is* so much she hasn't taught me yet.

I tell her she should retire. She should take care of herself when she gets a cold.

She rolls her eyes, as she does when I'm acting odd.

Mom buys me a beautiful short-sleeved, muted green sweater with a little collar and three buttons down the chest. I love its soft blend of merino wool with just a touch of angora.

Abruptly, the dream flashes forward and I am at home, at somebody's home. I hang the sweater in a large closet that is neatly crowded with Mom's clothes and mine. I am distracted by the sound of ticking and move aside some sweaters. The ticking of an old clock. My mother's clock. My mother.

Now, shifting back to the same shopping trip—we're at a cosmetics counter, where I ask for a makeover. Mom is watching closely. She is bigger, sloppier, spilling over the edges. Is this simple ageing? Or is she letting go, relinquishing some of that damned dignity that defined and confined her? As much as I've always wanted her to loosen up, I am alarmed.

At the end of the session, I stare into the makeup mirror. Mom looks over my shoulder, I see the two of us together, notice how lucid and healthy she looks.

Oh, I am so relieved to have my mother back. Grateful for one more chance.

℞

Back at the desk again, I wonder how I can write, after those dreams.

It is hard to discuss social class and immigration and poverty and early death without people speaking platitudes or sociology to you. They say things like, "She had a better life than if she had stayed behind in Scotland." Or, "Immigrant women are always more resilient than men."

Then there are those empathetic people who say they've had the same experience. They compare having immigrant grandparents or great-grandparents to being an immigrant's only daughter.

What a life Mom had—struggling with the stigma of illegitimacy, trials of tenement life, orphanhood, surrendering her scholarly dreams to work in a dance hall, bravely leaving Scotland alone at age twenty, marrying a man with an invalid mother and nursing her until she died, losing a child, raising three other kids, being abandoned to work in an all-night coffee shop, getting laid off her job at the Yum Yum Room when she was seventy-seven. And continuing through all this, as she would put it, to keep her pecker up. The echoes grow louder and louder and I am going deaf after so many stereophonic acts of the Scottish Opera.

One day my Scottish boyfriend met Mom after years of hearing her saga. Andrew, laughing at my melodramatic nature, said he had a hard time reconciling the sad character I had described as my mother with the cheerful, charming woman, Mary Miner. Was he right? Was she more happy than I imagined? Happier than I?

Sometimes it is hard to see or maintain the lines between us. This is one of the scariest things Mom ever told me (scary because I felt so responsible for her, so guilty when I couldn't oblige her): On her days off, she confided, she would take the bus or train over to my Berkeley neighborhood and sit in the deli across from my apartment and watch my window. She knew I was busy writing, grading papers from jobs at three colleges, and she didn't want to disturb me. But, she said, she liked being even that close to me.

Since we often did spend time together—attending movies, going shopping, having dinner—I asked her to stop these ghostly trips. Terrifying suffocation descended as I feared that I could never do enough, never be enough for her. Then I felt remorseful: Did I have a right to ask? It was her day off, she could go anywhere, do anything, she liked.

. Perplexed, but considerate, she said she would stop hanging out at the deli if it really bothered me.

Another morning at the cabin, another blank page. I decide to go for a walk. Every day I make this three-mile walk, up and down a few steep hills to the wooden highway gate and back to the cabin. This morning the valley between our ridge and the next is filled with oceans of grey fog. With the neighbor's wacky dog, Yuma, I head down from the sunny heights to the cool, moist atmosphere by the pond. The brown cattails stand upright, almost metallic in attention, stalwartly guarding the water. The oak trees look even more enveloped in moss than usual. Ah, this yellowish green is a color we don't see in Minnesota. I love the way light hits that moss, rippling in shades of olive velvet.

The land is crowded with voluble birds in morning and evening. Afternoon is insect time as the high, yellow grass resonates with crickets, bees, flies. Bats appear at dusk, dropping from eaves outside the house, swooping across the grass, then speeding back and forth to gain their bearings. When Helen and her friends bought these secluded acres in 1977, the Anderson Valley seemed remote. Now the main road is lined with vineyards and wine-tasting chateaux. Worse, interlopers like us have begun to colonize in the nearby hills. Yesterday morning the buzz saws from several miles away were a faint but persistent reminder of neighbors.

You're never a full step ahead; you have to make some beleaguered peace with change. I watch the turkey vultures glide over the pond and I grow more aware of the vanities, liabilities of my own material claims.

As Yuma and I proceed up the hill toward the corral, the golden grass sighs in waves. We are surrounded by perfect morning stillness. Until Yuma catches a high-pitched noise. She stands rigid, listening. A wounded doe or a baby bobcat? No, suddenly, a flurry, then a parade of wild turkeys bustle along the far road. We proceed briskly, Yuma discovering other amusements rustling in a ravine of poison oak. By the time we reach the gate, the foggy sea has evaporated, our day has turned to sun.

I guess this is when the following conversation begins. I am thinking about Mom's favorite way of expressing an opinion, "according to me, myself, and I."

℞

I wonder, in the earnest moralism that has haunted me from girlhood, if it's OK to own my college education, my books, my tenured job, my comfortable house in Minneapolis, my funky California cabin? Do I have a right to them? Did I, in any sense, earn them? Did she earn them for me?

"So what's the problem? She wanted you to be happy, didn't she?"

"But not this way. She wanted me married, with kids. Maybe with a good job, first, at the Telephone Company."

"There *is* no Telephone Company anymore. Anyway, that's really what she wanted for herself."

"Since she didn't get it, it became my job."

"So?"

"When I rejected her dreams of a safe, settled life, I rejected the most sacred part of her."

"But her dream was success, happiness—not necessarily in telecommunications—and she must have been proud of you professionally, glad for you."

"More baffled, I think."

"But look, after the divorce, she dreamed of marrying a professor and you became a professor!"

"Talk about betrayal."

"What?"

"Anyway, I'm not really a professor. Not a scholar, just a writer."

"She was proud of your books. She told people. She read them, unlike your father."

"Yes, a little proud."

"She once told you—remember in your Russell Street apartment, when she stayed overnight to have dinner and watch *Golden Girls?*"

"Told me what?"

"Don't you remember that she said she admired you, that she sighed happily, 'Who could have imagined . . .'"

"But she also said—and much more recently—'I pray that you'll meet a nice young man.'"

"Young!"

"She was a romantic soul."

"Right, then, what would have happened if you had married the nice young man—after your apprenticeship at the Telephone Company—and had four kids and made a cosy room at the back of the house for her to nest in as your kids grew up?"

"I would have died."

"That was quick."

"I couldn't have survived."

"So, to survive, you immigrated beyond your parents' imaginations. You just followed her lead."

"That's far too simple."

"No, not simple."

*꩜*

On the way back up to the ridge, I spot a red-tailed hawk. Then a ruby-throated hummingbird. And suddenly, in that exhausting stretch of road which seems insurmountably steep, I glance over at a tiny patch of glowing goldenrod.

I consider how, over time, Mom accepted Helen. Helen, who was often more patient, more generous, than I. A charming flirtation developed between them. Nothing was simple, of course: in one phone conversation, Mom asked about eligible men in my life and then a few minutes later inquired warmly about Helen's health or her job or her sisters. I know she came to love Helen, hugging her tightly in greeting, taking her arm as they walked. And ever conscious of being socially appropriate, Mom introduced us at her cafe or out on Taylor Street or later at the retirement home as "my daughter Valerie and Helen, a friend of the family."

I can't go back to the desk just yet. Yuma and I continue up past the cabin, through the high grasses (me alert for rattlers), to the highest hill. Just a little further back is the Apple Forty, where people claim to have sighted bear. Someone saw a mountain lion last year. I think the stories are apocryphal. Still, whenever we hear the coyotes, they come from that direction. Today there are no lions or coyotes or rattlers as Yuma and I enjoy our peaceful view about the tree line.

❧

## 1980s

When I think back, I know now that for my mother, daughter of the Scottish *haar*, these inland hills were always far too dry. "A lovely landscape," she muses once we are safely en route to the misty coast. "Lovely," but I know she is thinking "Dustbowl," worrying that this construction project is crazier than my schemes to settle in Canada and England. Her daughter the writer, the socialist, the lesbian, is now a Wild West pioneer. Mendocino Village is as sweet and foggy as she has hoped. While Mom and I settle at our small hotel, shop around town, eat dinner at a place that's too dark and too French for her taste, Helen is sawing and hammering and barbequing a salmon with our friends on the land. We spend a quiet weekend, sleeping late, walking slowly, buying a few gifts.

That Sunday, before we ride back through the Giant Redwoods to collect Helen, I drive Mom to the coastal headlands. Thoughtlessly, I have imagined us hiking a bit along the cliffs that remind me so much of Western Scotland, of the trips Mom and I took to Skye and Oban. I have forgotten how breathless the emphysema makes her, especially in the wind. Instead we sit in the car, watching the huge waves rise and crash and swing back into the ocean. She takes my hand, something she likes to do in movie theatres, in church. And I do not notice anything until she squeezes hard. Tears stream down her face. Then down mine. She tells me she is afraid to die, afraid the end is near. Oh, no, I protest, you've got years ahead, you're a warhorse, you'll last forever. (So often since then, I wish I had had the courage to enter this rare intimacy. I should have held her, safe for the moment, against these fears. I should have ignored my own grief and the old terrors of suffocating in her suffering. I wish I could simply have, in my silent listening, given her comfort.) Instead of replying to her cheerful earful daughter, she squeezes my hand again and we both pretend to lose ourselves in the waves.

ℛℯ

## 1990s

The day after she dies in 1991, it is to this same piece of Scottish Coast I drive, to breathe in the moist Mendocino *haar*, to walk and cry and pray and say good-bye.

ℛℯ

It seems right to finish our book at the cabin in this "Scottish" valley. I think of her whenever I see a patch of brilliant purple thistles. I see her huddling from the San Francisco fog when North Coast mist thickens between our high ridges. Yet I also remember how foreign, slightly frightening, she found this countryside, and that understanding makes me feel both sad and free.

So much has changed in the nineteen years Helen and I have been coming to the land. We no longer have to climb to our loft bed, because we've built a staircase. The water barrel has been taken from the roof since we've plugged into the well. We've replaced the rusty gas rings with a small stove. What comfort will we next introduce? Will our accommodations insulate us from the rhythms of the land we sometimes call home? It's dark now, as I lie in bed. Helen is sound asleep. I close my eyes and find three red-winged blackbirds, then a kite, treading air by the Western hills. Too awake yet for dreaming, I creep to a window and watch the Milky Way, sprayed generously though the center of a blue-black sky.

# CHAPTER FORTY

# "A Spare Umbrella"

## *Valerie, San Francisco, 1990s*

COLD. WET. SLOPPY. TRAFFIC ON THE BRIDGE IS HEAVY EVEN THOUGH I waited for morning rush hour to end. Perhaps there is no end to rush hour. Fax. E-mail. Supersonic jets. We're all racing at greater and greater speeds, going around and around, stuck behind each other on the bridge. Except Mom, who in characteristically subtle wisdom has maintained her own pace at the retirement home, moving slowly in reverse, faded to her adolescence now, recognizing me occasionally as daughter, sister, mother.

Mom used to love this ride from my place in Oakland to her apartment in San Francisco, particularly once we got past Treasure Island. She would point at Alcatraz and Coit Tower, as if I had never seen them, as if I were twelve years old, as if she were behind the wheel. The truth was, she never learned to drive. Rather, she became an expert rider of buses.

"How can you let your mother visit you on the bus from San Francisco?" friends would ask. "How can you let her live in the Tenderloin?" I never let my mother do anything. Some people need food; my mother sustained herself on will. Born in a city, she was going to die in a city. And she almost did.

I have taken a day off work to clear out Mom's studio apartment. The backseat is cluttered with a dolly, boxes and twine and large, green plastic sacks, body bags for memories. I reach her neighborhood and immediately prepare the vulture swoop for a parking space. You have to be quick in San Francisco. People swerve in front of you from nowhere, from the next block, from the sky. All that City of Light nonsense evaporates in the parking duel. Ten minutes. Fifteen minutes, circling, a buzzard on wheels. Suddenly, stunningly, there is a space right in front of her apartment building. The meter eats seventy-five cents an hour, but I have come laden with quarters. Rain pours heavier now, soaking me before I duck under the front awning.

Damn keys don't work. It's a dangerous building, and they change the locks every few months. How can I let my mother live in the Tenderloin? Drenched, cold, I summon her common sense and ring the manager's bell.

Nell, a stocky woman in her mid-sixties, waves to me as she approaches with a ring of keys. Sister Matthew used to wear the large brass ring of school keys on her wrist and tell us it was a charm bracelet; wearing it, she could charm her way through any door. Charm has never been one of my talents. Nell nods at my discouraged, shivering body. She is followed by two of the ugliest cats I have ever seen. Short, squat Winston Churchills. Somebody's sons, Mom used to joke. I miss my mother's ironic laughter.

"How is Mary? We talk about her all the time. Please give her my best." She says all this in rapid succession as if she forgets Mom's Alzheimer's. Maybe Nell is developing dementia; lately I have begun to wonder seriously about my own memory. Nell has been kind to Mom. Took her to the movies. Phoned immediately when she broke her arm. Let us keep the apartment for months after Mom moved, just in case. Just in case there was a miracle. A Presbyterian, my mother never had a taste for miracles.

The building has been only modestly maintained over the last fifteen years, and the red flowered carpet suffers into a painful pink. They have started to take more monthly and weekly tenants. The downstairs lobby is lined with menacing plastic trees; two large chairs are chained to the floor; thick iron grillwork grips the window and door. I check the mailbox, saddened that, unlike the others, it bears no name, just an apartment number. Briefly I am indignant for Mom; after all, her rent is still being paid.

The box is empty.

Waiting for the familiar elevator, I think about my mother being held up here by some thug between the second and third floors. "Well," she had shrugged after a couple of margaritas, "it happens. I don't carry much cash." On the third floor, I safely disembark from the creepy elevator and walk down to the end of the corridor, where she used to stand with the door open, welcoming me with a cup of afternoon tea or a drink before I took her out to dinner. Never did she cook a meal for me in that place. Didn't cook for herself, either, preferring to eat between her work shifts at the cafe, saving money, evading loneliness. The fridge was always stocked with Coke and cheddar cheese. Today she is not waiting for me. Stupid, clichéd to feel abandoned, yet I do. Lost about how to begin this task, this life, ahead without her. The door to apartment #310 is closed.

We walked along the shore at Long Beach, a balmy evening, the final night of the last family holiday. That night Dad took my brother to a baseball game. Mom and I had a blast shopping, seeing Elvis Presley in *Blue Hawaii,* ambling barefoot along the beach. It seemed a perfect time to confess that I wanted to go to college. A quiet, peaceful, private moment. Both of us feeling optimistic. And although her cautious response was entirely predictable, I had hoped for more. OK, if college was what I wanted, she said. "Remember to take typing. It's something to fall back on." That was the difference between us: I was conscious of climbing; Mom, of falling. As we strolled, I swung the bag containing the "drastically reduced" sale blouse, a secret audition for my Ivy League wardrobe. Oh, yes, I insisted, talking hectically to cover my panic, I had to go to college if I was going to become a teacher. She smiled and turned toward the ocean, her eyes even with the horizon.

Now, in the grim corridor light, I notice that the beige and brown art nouveau design on her door is peeling. Tentatively I approach the locks. The keys work, and soon I am inside the studio apartment, smelling a familiar stuffy sweetness: the room is redolent with the aromas of her foot sweat, Ivory soap and whatever shampoo has been on sale at Walgreens. She didn't wear deodorant or perfume. I am enveloped by her, as if she were really here and whole and not fragmented into ten thousand detached synapses in a room across San Francisco Bay.

We cannot say good-bye in person. She slipped away before either of us understood what was happening. But I can say good-bye to her here. With this understanding, I am immobilized, recalling times we sat in this living room—the Murphy bed invisible behind the wall—gossiping and recollecting and laughing. I think about our dinners at cafes like Nathan's and Mama's and, for special occasions, some of the fancy downtown hotels. I remember our excursions to Macy's. Shopping was in her blood; she could sniff out a sale weeks ahead of time, hide her item in the size 16s, and then snap it up on the right day. This frugality—this poverty— drove me nuts, and I promised myself that once I got a full-time job, I would buy something straight off the new arrival rack. When I showed this fashionable suit to my mother, she looked vaguely betrayed. In fact, I wound up giving away the outfit. I came to understand that in our family shopping was more than bargain hunting. It was a social event, an outing, an entertainment. While my college friends told me about childhood excursions to museums and galleries, I thought about those shopping trips, but was too embarrassed to mention them.

As I move through the apartment for the last time, I remember flying home from my new job and surprising her at this door. Her face revealed utter disbelief. Then doubt. Then pleasure. Nothing has ever been more gratifying to me than the look of pleasure in my mother's eyes.

First I will pack the clothes. Three small closets. One behind the Murphy bed, next to the bathroom. The dresses are hung neatly, ready to wear to work. The shoes, carefully selected compromises between style and comfort for her corn-encrusted feet, are evenly lined on the floor. I don't have my mother's talent for tidiness, but whenever I do manage to straighten a shelf or a drawer I feel an enormous sense of accomplishment, approval, serenity.

The noise of the traffic outside is deafening. In futile response, I keep turning on more and more lights. It's only 11 A.M., but I am fading. The rainy grey weather seems to have oozed right into this room. During the first few years after I moved back to California, I would often spend the night here with her, lying together in the lumpy double Murphy bed or, when her snoring grew serious, dozing on the couch. I never slept through the night, because of the street noise. Drunks shouting at the creator. Horns honking. Buses wheezing. Sirens whizzing down the street. And so it became more common for her to spend the night in Oakland, where she complained about the morning racket of jays and doves, but always managed to fall back into a sound, long slumber. I wonder now about her capacity to shut out this inner-city cacophony; perhaps it explains her ability to dismiss my father's static for so long. Perhaps she found the noises reassuring, and that says something else about their marriage.

Next I approach the dishes, chipped Noritake that Dad proudly brought home from Japan. Smudged jam jars and dusty cocktail glasses. My heart catches at the orderly line of dirty glassware and I consider how her eyesight has gone in recent years. As well as her sense of smell. How many late nights did I stay awake worrying whether she had left one of the unlit burners on? Perhaps it would have been better if she had died that way; her pride would have preferred asphyxiation to Alzheimer's. And I admit this: There have been times in the last year of forgetfulness and high anxiety that I have prayed for her death.

In the cutlery drawer, behind the mismatched stainless, is the Norwegian cheese slicer I bought her. Still in the box. I should have remembered she liked to use that wobbly serrated knife with the wooden handle to cut her cheese. I thought I had ceased trying to improve her when I was in college. Apparently not.

Everywhere in the flat—around her desk, by her bed, on the bath-mat—lies evidence of how bad her psoriasis had gotten. Once meticulous about cleaning her apartment, eventually she gave up trying. On the floor by her desk and on the rug beneath her bed are beaches of white flakes that had once been skin covering her muscles and bones.

We did become friends in the last ten years—a break between her mothering me and me mothering her—we did go to movies, have passionate arguments, take road trips. Sometimes we attended Saturday matinees when her friend, the prop man at the Geary Theatre, could get free tickets. Sometimes concerts—she liked modern dance; hated atonal music—when she was feeling daring. But what she liked best was to take the bus to Oakland for the weekend, go out to dinner with me, and then watch TV, laughing and interrupting the show with her barbed comments. I've never understood people who thought my mother was a saint. She was a bawdy, critical, tough old bird. We had roaring fights, fuming silences, hilarious reconciliations. She was a hero, perhaps, but no saint.

All over the apartment now, I find what she would have called, in her better days, j-u-n-k. Boxes within boxes. Assiduously folded paper and plastic bags. Used casings from her casts. Crutches. A three-year-old Christmas card from her boss. Some of the clutter makes sense. Hairpins and pennies lie everywhere. Gelusil. Matchbooks from the restaurants where I took her to dinner. Bureau drawers are littered with scraps of paper to combat dimming memory. "Annie, 7 P.M., Saturday." "Larry will call Friday." But she would forget where she had put these notes and phone repeatedly to check on a date or a plan.

The afternoon Mom entered the retirement home was a turmoil of relief, guilt, and terrible sadness. Yet nothing compared to my sheer panic two hours later when the manager called to say she had disappeared. Disappeared? How can you lose a slow, old woman? After missing persons' reports and hours of searching by family members, I found her, back in the apartment, of course, a specter at the end of her couch. "Don't scold me," was the first thing she said. Both of us weeping, I held her tightly as she pleaded, instructed, "I just need one more night here. One more night alone."

The bathroom is the sparest part of the flat. Just aspirin and Merthiolate in the cabinet. Do they still sell Merthiolate or should I donate the vial to a museum? Even the half-full aspirin bottle looks ancient. She has never believed in mind-altering drugs, with the exception of that margarita now and then. When Dr. Hanson gave her valium, Mom asked me what it did and then flushed the whole bottle down the toilet. The peppermint bubble bath I brought her every three months has turned color, from green to purple. So much for Berkeley natural products.

At her desk, I lift the disintegrating drapes, peering out the window at the boarded-up hotel and the coffee shop where she worked for many years. How depressing it must have been for her at times, with such a view, in this shadowy, loud apartment. The furniture is sunken, sooty. The plastic ficus tree thrives in the corner. Turning back to the desk, I pack the Learn-to-Type book. Goodwill can use the typewriter. Her adding machine—she was always proud of her ability to balance her checkbook, another talent I didn't develop—is missing its cord. The calculator remains on the desk as a kind of testimonial.

Almost finished, I look around. My eyes fill again, with anger, grief. I don't mind picking up the pieces; I wish there were more to pick up. Just this after eighty years? It could have been worse, is my mother's reply. Whenever I would ask if she regretted immigrating, she shook her head vehemently and said here she found work, for a time the love of a man, and she would always have her children. It is hard not to feel guilty in my spacious place across the Bay, where I have lots of light and an answering machine to screen calls from a mother who rings ten times each morning to ask the same question. Yet pointless guilt was never something she courted (she used shame only occasionally, to win an argument) and I feel myself encompassed by a genetically linked trait of practical cheer. Get on with it, I tell myself, she tells me. You've run out of quarters for the damn parking meter.

Left for last are the nightgowns and underwear. Perhaps I'm still terrified of the adolescent taboo hovering over my mother's "confidential drawers." Sorting through the slips, I am struck by how tiny she is. It's hard to think of your mother as small. I have her slightness, and if I had a daughter, she would be a short woman, too. I have also inherited a penchant for saving things. I pack the three umbrellas from the bottom drawer, even the one with the broken handle—you never know when you might need a spare umbrella.

Shifting the remaining boxes onto the dolly, I lock Mom's door for the final time. She wouldn't want me to cry out here in the corridor, in public. I compose myself, breathing deeply, thinking there is plenty of time for weeping and raging. There are months, perhaps years, ahead of visiting and listening to and nodding at a person who sometimes reminds me of my mother. Although this feels sentimental and faintly sacrilegious, I am seized by a desire to go shopping at the winter sales. As I press the elevator button, I imagine the two of us together again.